EMPLOYEE RELATIONS

Second Edition

Roger Bennett

BA, MSc (Econ), DPhil
London Guildhall University

M&E
PITMAN
PUBLISHING

··· Hong Kong · Johannesburg · Melbourne · Singapore · Washington DC

PITMAN PUBLISHING
128 Long Acre, London WC2E 9AN
Tel: 0171 447 2000   Fax: 0171 240 5771

A Division of Pearson Professional Limited

First published in Great Britain 1994
Second edition 1997

© Pearson Professional Limited 1997

The right of Roger Bennett to be identified as author
of this work has been asserted by him in accordance with the Copyright,
Designs and Patents Act 1988.

A CIP catalogue record for this book can be obtained from the British Library

ISBN 0 7121 1071 2

10 9 8 7 6 5 4 3 2 1

Typeset by WestKey Limited, Falmouth, Cornwall
Printed and bound in Great Britain by Bell and Bain Ltd. Glasgow

The Publishers' policy is to use paper manufactured from sustainable forests.

CONTENTS

Part Three
THE FUTURE OF EMPLOYEE RELATIONS

Part Four
INTERNATIONAL COMPARISONS

1

THE NATURE OF EMPLOYEE RELATIONS

FUNDAMENTALS

1. Definition of employee relations

The subject 'employee relations' deals with all the formal and informal relationships of an interpersonal nature that arise from management/employee interactions in working situations. Hence, it encompasses *inter alia*:

- Industrial relations, i.e. the systems of rules, practices and conventions associated with collective bargaining and the avoidance and resolution of industrial disputes.
- Procedures for securing employee participation in the management of enterprises (via works councils (*see* 6: **14**) and/or worker directors on company boards (*see* 6: **17**), for example).
- Policies for improving co-operation between management and workers, the control of employee grievances and the minimisation of conflict.
- Systems for involving employees in total quality management (TQM) programmes and in the improvement of customer care.
- Communication between management and workers in order to inform the latter about company policy.
- Strategies for managing relations between a company and its employees.

Clearly, employee relations is a far wider subject than conventional 'industrial relations' *per se*. Indeed, the managements of many businesses today greatly prefer to use the term 'employee relations' rather than 'industrial relations' as it avoids many of the mental images of conflict, strikes, social disharmony and disagreement that the latter term sometimes invokes. Also, employee relations as a subject is better able to accommodate the new realities of working life: computerisation, information technology and the widespread use of robotics and advanced manufacturing methods; new work patterns and working practices (teams, lean production, quality circles, flexible manufacturing, just-in-time systems, and so on) than can orthodox 'industrial relations'.

As a field of study, employee relations impinges upon human resources management, organisational behaviour, management principles and practice, operations management, and several other important business subjects. It is especially concerned with the influences of culture, change and employee motivation on management/worker interactions within firms. Employee relations, moreover, is internationalist in orientation, seeking to identify and explain common and disparate elements in the employee relations systems of various states. The situations prevailing in Japan and the Pacific Rim, the United States and the European Community are discussed in Chapters 15–18.

2. Employee relations and human resources management

Human resources management (HRM) is concerned with the human side of the enterprise and the factors that determine workers' relationships with their employing firms. It covers, among other things, elements of industrial psychology, personnel management, training and employee relations. In contrast with 'personnel management' which deals with the practical aspects of recruitment, staff appraisal, training, job evaluation, etc., HRM has a *strategic* dimension and involves the total deployment of all the human resources available to the firm. Accordingly, HRM affects employee relations in (at least) the following respects:

(a) HRM policies determine the aggregate size of a company's labour force, how the firm is organised and structured, and so on. This has implications for the terms under which workers are employed (part time or full time, permanent or casual), for the continuity of workers' employment, the incidence of redundancies, and hence the morale of the workforce.

(b) The firm's HRM strategies establish the basis of its relations with trade unions, including whether to recognise trade unions and if so for what purposes.

(c) HRM policies are needed to cope with the human implications of the introduction of new technology, especially with regard to the encouragement of flexible attitudes and the acceptance of new working practices.

(d) It is desirable to create within an organisation a *culture* that is conducive to employee commitment and co-operation. Note how conventional approaches to industrial relations have been criticised for being overly concerned with *imposing* rules and procedures on employees rather than encouraging their loyalty and commitment to the firm.

The HRM approach seeks to integrate all the employee relations that occur within an enterprise into a coherent and (hopefully) harmonious whole. More contentiously, it is often associated with the 'unitarist' philosophy of employee relations.

3. Unitarism

Unitarism is the belief that management and labour have identical interests and hence may be expected to pull together towards the same objectives. Willingness to co-operate is taken for granted; dissent cannot be understood. Hence management expects workers to act as a team and to assist the firm achieve its aims. Strikes and other disruptive behaviour are, in the unitarist view, malevolent and just as destructive to those who participate in them as to employing organisations. Industrial action simply does not make sense since *everyone* should be working together for the common good. Conflicts, where they occur, are due to the emergence of factional interests (which a good management would not allow to arise in the first place), to faulty communications and misunderstandings, or to the efforts of troublemakers. The unitarist approach might be said to have the following implications:

(a) *For workers:*

(*i*) Working practices should be flexible, with individuals prepared to undertake whatever tasks are required in whichever way is the most efficient.

(*ii*) The main role of a trade union is to act as a means of communication between the individual and his or her employing company.

(*iii*) Employees should be willing to negotiate their pay and other terms and conditions of work on an individual basis (rather than through collective bargaining).

(*iv*) Worker participation in workplace management decision-making must be accepted as a normal part of working life, with individuals actively supporting quality circles, productivity improvement programmes, etc.

(*v*) Employees should recognise and accept the right of management to manage (*see* 8: **25**).

(*vi*) Workers need to accept personal responsibility for the quality of the firm's output and for achieving total customer satisfaction.

(b) *For companies:*

(*i*) Management policies should seek to unify effort and inspire and motivate the workforce.

(*ii*) Employees should constantly be made aware of the organisation's wider objectives.

(*iii*) Pay systems need to be designed to secure workers' loyalty and commitment to the enterprise.

(*iv*) Wherever possible, heads of department and other line executives (marketing or production managers, for example) should be responsible for personnel management. If the firm has a personnel department then its functions ought to focus on supporting line managers and providing advice on technical/legal matters.

(*v*) Since conflict is regarded as the result of ignorance or the activities of troublemakers, great care is needed when recruiting workers in order to ensure they have appropriate outlooks, will fit in with the culture of the organisation, and will quickly learn the company's conventions and norms.

(*vi*) Management should discuss and agree personal objectives with everyone in the business and supply individuals with the training, support and resources necessary for them to attain their goals.

The *advantages* of unitarism are that:

- It encourages consensus and harmonious employee relations.
- Individuals become part of a team.

- Managements are obliged to treat their employees with respect and dignity.
- It facilitates the integration of functions and activities within the enterprise.

Problems with the unitarist approach include:

(a) It cannot comprehend the motives of individuals who do not regard everyone in the organisation as 'being in the same boat'.

(b) Arguably, it fails to recognise the *inevitability* of conflicts of interest in certain management/employee situations.

(c) It can impair the efficient resolution of disputes.

4. Pluralism

This has been recommended as a more pragmatic and effective alternative to the unitarist philosophy (Fox 1966). The pluralistic approach sees conflicts of interest and disagreements between managers and workers over the distribution of the firm's profits as the normal and inescapable state of affairs. Realistically, therefore, management should accept that conflict will *necessarily* occur, and thus should seek to resolve conflicts by establishing sound procedures for settling disputes.

Pluralism assumes that the best way to achieve consensus and long-term stability in management/worker relations is for management to recognise conflicting interests, to negotiate compromises, and to balance the demands of various groups. This implies the need for grievance procedures, joint-negotiation committees, union-recognition agreements, arbitration arrangements and so on. Trade unions are seen as occupying a key role in the process of resolving conflicts, which are viewed as normal and sometimes healthy in that they release emotions which otherwise would be (harmfully) repressed. Collective bargaining is regarded as a particularly efficient means whereby management and labour can distribute the profits of enterprises in an orderly fashion. Implications of pluralism include:

(a) The firm should have a personnel manager to act as a sort of intermediary between management and labour.

(b) There should be widespread use of independent external arbitrators to resolve industrial disputes.

(c) Negotiating skills have great importance for both employee and management representatives.

Advantages of pluralism include its emphasis on forward planning, orderly and consistent procedures, realistic approaches to dealing with unions, less uncertainty in employee relations processes, and the development of effective arrangements for resolving disputes. Further benefits (to management) are that:

- It encourages management and labour to discuss issues frankly and to perceive them from contrasting points of view.
- Through institutionalising conflict, it can enhance management's power.

- It increases the flow of information from the workforce.
- It adopts a hard-headed approach to employee (and management) motivation.
- Stability is sought through *compromises* that are acceptable to all the parties to a dispute.
- It balances the interests of the various stakeholders (owners, management, workers, etc.) involved in the creation of the firm's wealth.

Criticisms of pluralism

Despite its essential pragmatism, pluralism has a number of disadvantages. Arguably it encourages destructive 'them and us' attitudes and creates bureaucratic and inefficient procedures which stifle initiative and are highly resistant to change. Further problems include:

(a) It has little to offer the small business where there is extensive face-to-face contact between owners and employees.

(b) The establishment of procedures for settling conflicts and grievances could *itself* encourage 'them and us' attitudes which lead to disputes.

(c) It may cause friction between a worker's loyalty to his or her trade union and loyalty to the employing firm. Employees' long-term commitment to attaining the goals of the organisation may be jeopardised.

(d) The committees and other procedural machinery that emerge from pluralistic approaches could eventually become part and parcel of the firm's management system and be used to legitimise existing (and perhaps inappropriate) employee relations practices.

(e) Pluralism assumes a roughly even balance of power between various interest groups. This fails to recognise that in many employee relations situations there is a dominant participant possessing the power to *impose* its will on the other side.

(f) It could undermine management's authority and create an atmosphere conducive to trade union activity, even within environments where this (from management's point of view) might be counter-productive.

(g) It may be naive to expect management not to wish to exercise managerial prerogative (*see* 8: **25**) to the maximum extent.

(h) Management might pretend to hold pluralistic attitudes so long as this is convenient, but quickly adopt a unitary approach as soon as circumstances change.

PERSPECTIVES ON EMPLOYEE RELATIONS

5. Frames of reference

A frame of reference comprises all the attitudes, preassumptions and psychological influences that determine how a person perceives issues and events. It is

7

a sort of filtering mechanism that blocks out psychologically unacceptable facts and opinions, reinforces and embellishes data that is more to the individual's liking, and generally structures information. Pluralism and unitarism themselves represent frames of reference. The unitary frame (*see* **3**) stresses the importance of common goals and team effort; the pluralistic frame emphasises differences in interests. In a sense, unitary and pluralistic frames of reference represent complete and self-contained theories of employee relations: of what represents correct thinking and behaviour, how managements should administer firms, the proper role of trade unions, etc. The frame of reference that management adopts affects **(a)** its attitudes towards and willingness to accept collective employee representation, **(b)** the extent of its insistence on being able to exercise managerial prerogative (*see* 8: **14**), and **(c)** approaches to the resolution of conflicts and disputes.

Other important perspectives on employee relations include:

- systems theory
- social action theory
- class conflict theory.

6. Systems theory

The systems approach views employee relations as an 'open' system (i.e. one that constantly interacts with the wider social environment and which has boundaries with the social environment that cannot be precisely defined). This system is said to comprise 'actors', 'contexts' and ideologies. The approach is based on the work of J.T. Dunlop, who developed and advocated systems theory in the 1950s and 1960s, drawing heavily on the ideas of the eminent American sociologist, Talcott Parsons.

According to Dunlop the actors in an industrial (rather than employee) relations system are the various hierarchies of management and employee representatives plus government agencies. Actors determine the rules and procedures of the system, plus its outcomes (agreements on pay, working hours, etc.). 'Contexts' consist of the technological environment (which influences skills requirements, the demand for labour by enterprises, etc.); the market environment (size, structure and buoyancy of the market for the firm's product, economic and monetary factors); and the relative power of various social groups, e.g. whether there is high union density (*see* 2: **23**) and/or restrictions on workers' abilities to take collective action. The ideology of the system is the totality of all the ideas, perspectives and opinions that bind the actors together and enable them jointly to make rules. There has to be some form of ideological consensus or the system cannot survive.

Systems theory provides interesting and useful categories for the description of industrial relations situations. Dunlop claimed, moreover, that the systems approach had universal application, could be used to draw international comparisons, and was equally valid in all contexts and situations. The rules of the industrial relations systems of many countries and industrial settings, Dunlop argued, could be explained in terms of technology, market conditions, etc., regardless of national boundaries. This claim to have discovered a universally applicable mode of analysis has been contested, notably by 'social action theory' (*see* **7**).

Advantages and criticisms of the systems approach

The systems approach enables changes in the key elements of an industrial relations system to be analysed methodically and the effects of an alteration in one variable to be traced through to its consequences for the system as a whole. Systems theory is holistic: models for depicting connections between cause and effect can be constructed. The main problem with systems theory is that it suggests few tangible propositions about how exactly managers should behave. It is one thing to think about businesses in systems terms, but quite another to translate these thoughts into concrete action. Systems theory is abstract, and lacks immediately discernible applications. Further criticisms of the approach are that:

- It applies *static* analysis to essentially *dynamic* and fast-changing situations.
- It presupposes (perhaps wrongly) that social structures and systems determine human behaviour. Different members of the same system may have entirely different interpretations of its structure and aims (*see* **7** below).
- It considers only a few of the potentially vast number of behavioural and other variables that might be relevant to a particular employee relations situation.
- It has little to say about psycho-social factors, particularly those concerning employee motivation.
- It cannot of itself *explain* employee relations without taking other considerations into account.

7. Social action theory

This asserts that an individual's own perception of the nature of the situation in which he or she is involved best explains that person's social behaviour. It rejects the view that there exist general principles capable of explaining all employee relations events. Thus, for example, highly paid workers with secure jobs might have entirely different attitudes to work, unions, etc., than other employees and, in consequence, a completely disparate view of how management/worker relations should proceed. According to social action theory it is *individual attitudes* that matter, not structural factors. Advocates of the theory assert that situations are evaluated subjectively: what constitutes 'reality' for one person might not for someone else. Note that social action theory simply recommends an approach to how issues should be investigated. It does not, of itself, offer solutions to problems or explanations of observed events.

8. Class conflict theory

This derives from the work of the nineteenth-century political, social and economic theorist Karl Marx who posited that inherent contradictions in the capitalist system would inevitably lead to revolution and the replacement of capitalism by socialism. Prior to the revolution, great monopolies would arise and the wages of working people would be driven down to bare subsistence level. Capitalists demand labour; workers supply it. Each side would naturally seek to maximise its own position, leading to incessant struggle and strife.

This Marxist theory is not the same as pluralism (despite the common concern with the inevitability of conflict and industrial disputes), for a number of reasons:

(a) Pluralism is concerned with the institutions for resolving conflict. The Marxist approach examines (*i*) the social structures that give rise to these institutions in the first place, and (*ii*) the *causes* of conflicts rather than measures for containing them.

(b) In the class conflict approach the role of trade unions is to assist in the overthrow of capitalism.

(c) Marxism is a far-reaching and self-contained philosophy that attempts to explain all aspects of work and society.

(d) The Marxist approach condemns pluralism for 'incorporating' trade unions into the capitalist system (through involving them in the process of resolving disputes) and hence encouraging union leaders to 'sell out' to the capitalist system.

Marx's theories are discussed further in 2: **35**.

CONFLICT IN EMPLOYEE RELATIONS

Conflict occurs in employment situations because of frictions between individuals, between groups of workers (sections, departments, divisions, grades of employee, full-time or part-time workers, casual or permanent staff, etc.) and between various levels of authority within the firm. However, the mere existence of conflict does not *necessarily* damage interpersonal relations or relations between management and employees. Indeed, conflict has positive aspects: it can spur initiative, create energy and stimulate new ideas. Often, it is better for a conflict situation to be brought into the open rather than suppressed, since the disputants may then explain their feelings and perhaps cause an unsatisfactory situation to be improved. Unreasonable rules or targets may be amended: disputants can be made to see issues from alternative points of view. On the other hand, conflict can be disagreeable, misdirect employees' efforts, waste time, involve large amounts of stress, and lead ultimately to major disruption.

9. Types of conflict

Conflict arises from employee opposition to management policies, feelings of discontent, and attitudes that interfere with the attainment of organisational goals. There are two general categories of conflict: conflicts of interest and conflicts of right.

Conflicts of interest

These occur when various interest groups compete for the largest shares in a fixed amount of resources, e.g. in wage bargaining, making new arrangements on terms and conditions of work, renewing collective agreements, etc. Such conflicts are best resolved through negotiation rather than adjudication.

Conflicts of right

Conflicts of right arise from alleged violations of (for example) agreed terms in workers' contracts of employment, a statute, or a collective agreement. The remedy is to obtain, via independent adjudication, a statement of the correct legal position.

10. Causes of conflict

Specific causes of conflict commonly include:

- arguments concerning 'who should do what'
- poor co-ordination of activities
- differences in the perception of group and organisational objectives
- unclear authority structures
- inflexible and insensitive attitudes and excessively formal personal relationships among employees
- differences in individual values and opinions about how people should behave
- petty status and wage differentials that could encourage aggressive and unhealthy competition among individuals and groups.

Poor communication

Communication problems frequently lie at the heart of conflict situations. These can arise from the following:

(a) Managers hearing only what they want to hear and disregarding all critical comment.

(b) Employees feeling embarrassed about approaching their bosses with important information.

(c) Managers assuming that colleagues have been informed of issues when in fact they have not.

(d) Information being sent to the wrong people, or incorrect and/or inadequate messages being transmitted.

(e) Failure to pass on important messages.

(f) Distortion of messages as they pass through the system. The meaning of a message might be slightly (or substantially) altered at each stage in the process.

(g) Communications overload, i.e. managers receiving so many messages that most are disregarded.

11. Co-operation and the resolution of conflicts

Even for disputes involving a conflict of right, the parties to the dispute should *agree* on the justice of the adjudicated solution. A conflict could, of course, be resolved merely through management imposing its will, but this might encourage resentment and retaliation and inhibit the free flow of information. Thus the effective resolution of any form of conflict requires mutual acceptance of outcomes. Amicable settlement of conflicts is most likely where there is:

- open and extensive communication between management and the workforce and between individuals, sections and departments
- joint problem-solving
- willingness to compromise (though note how compromises rarely satisfy all the conflicting parties).

Conflict within an organisation might be minimised through arranging work to ensure that it cuts across departmental and occupational boundaries, designing jobs to make them more interesting (thus overcoming problems created by boredom and frustration), the provision of group bonuses, and through teamwork and employee counselling (*see* below).

Teamwork

The characteristic of a *team* (as opposed to other types of working group) is that its members co-operate and *voluntarily* co-ordinate their work in order to achieve group objectives. In a team, each person feels inwardly responsible for promoting the interests of the working group and personally accountable for its actions. There is a high level of group cohesion, much interaction, mutual support and shared perceptions of issues. Team members will be willing to interchange roles, share workloads and generally help each other out.

Team spirit

This can be encouraged through group leaders encouraging members' suggestions for altering working methods, inviting discussions on issues affecting the group, explaining to members their precise duties and responsibilities, and vigorously defending the group in the outside world. The leader should welcome initiative, new ideas and independent attempts to solve problems, consult regularly with individual members and be ready to alter working structures and arrangements following consultations. The distribution of tasks within the team must be equitable, and members need to have reasonable job security.

Employee counselling

Counselling is the process of helping people to recognise their feelings about problems, to define those problems accurately, and to find solutions or learn to live with a situation. A counselling session could involve giving advice, encouraging a change in behaviour, helping an employee accept an inevitable situation, or assisting someone in taking a difficult decision. The need for counselling arises in many employee relations situations: handling employee grievances, disciplinary procedures, appraisal and objective setting, etc.

12. Organisational techniques

Conflicts can easily develop into industrial disputes, especially if they involve dissatisfaction with wages, physical working environments, absence of job satisfaction, denial of promotion or training opportunities, 'speed-ups' of work flows, and so on. To resolve grievances, impartial – preferably independent – procedures are required, which might include the following:

(a) *Joint negotiating committees*. These meet at predetermined intervals to discuss problems that have arisen since the last meeting. Members agree not to take any action that might aggravate a situation before the contentious issue is raised at the JNC.

(b) *Arbitration agreements* which provide for the appointment of an independent referee to hear and adjudicate cases. Parties agree in advance that the arbitrator's decision must be final. Each side nominates potential arbitrators and a mutually acceptable name is chosen. ACAS (*see* 3: **4**) will provide an arbitrator if requested.

(c) *Formal plant level or national agreements* specifying how grievances should be resolved. The commonest procedure is for the aggrieved employee first to approach an immediate supervisor and then, if the grievance is not settled, to put the case to a local union official who will also approach the supervisor concerned. Thereafter, the matter is passed upwards to higher levels in both management and the union.

MANAGEMENT OF EMPLOYEE RELATIONS

The modern approach to the management of employee relations is to emphasise co-operation rather than conflict and to integrate employee relations (ER) policies into the overall corporate strategy of the firm. This requires that management **(a)** recognise the critical importance of harmonious relations with the workforce, and **(b)** relate its ER activities to the achievement of increased competitiveness, improved quality and better customer care.

13. Employee relations strategies

Key decisions in employee relations strategy include:

- whether to recognise trade unions (*see* 2: **21**)
- the organisation, structure and scope of collective bargaining (*see* Chapter 9)
- whether to have a personnel department (as opposed to leaving human relations matters predominantly in the hands of line managers) and, if so, the extent of its power to initiate activity in the employee relations field
- the degree to which employee representatives are to be involved in management decision-making (through works councils for example – *see* 6: **14**)
- the roles and functions of workplace representatives (*see* 2: **6**)
- the contents of procedural agreements (*see* 7: **2**) and how these are to be determined

- managerial approaches to personnel policies and procedures that affect employee relations (recruitment and promotion; appraisal; selection of workers for training, redundancy, etc.)
- whether management is prepared to use external bodies to arbitrate and help resolve disputes
- the levels of expenditures to be devoted to employee training and development
- the basic formulae to be applied to the division of the firm's profit between the owners of the business and workers
- the methods to be used for communicating with employees.

Effective employee relations management requires *top-level involvement* of the firm's most senior executives, since only they have the ultimate power to take important decisions and implement strategic change. Also, top management needs to be kept fully informed of attitudes among employees and current developments in the workplace situation. Policies should be clear and explicit, and management must be *committed* to their implementation. They must be communicated to middle and junior executives and their effectiveness periodically assessed.

14. Advantages to having an ER strategy

The advantages to management of having a systematic employee relations strategy include:

(a) *Consistent* policies will be applied within all the firm's sections, divisions and establishments.

(b) Individual line managers will know precisely where they stand in respect of employee relations matters.

(c) Procedures for controlling grievances and conflict are rationalised (*see* Chapter 10).

(d) The emergence of informal *ad hoc* systems that operate in parallel with yet tend to undermine official lines of authority can be avoided.

(e) Employees will receive much more information about the company's structure, operations and level of performance than otherwise might be the case. This can greatly contribute to the establishment of common perspectives throughout the organisation.

(f) Management becomes proactive rather than reactive, may plan ahead and will not have to take critically important decisions during crisis situations when accurate information cannot be obtained

(g) Policies affecting employees can be dovetailed into an overall corporate plan.

The nature and scope of employee relations are changing rapidly throughout the world. Current and likely future developments are examined in subsequent chapters, particularly Chapters 13 and 14.

References

Dunlop, J.T. (Ed.) (1978), *Labour in the Twentieth Century*, Academic Press.

Fox, A. (1966), Industrial Sociology and Industrial Relations, *Royal Commission on Trade Unions and Employers' Associations Research Paper No. 3*, HMSO.

Progress test 1

1. How does the subject of 'employee relations' differ from that of 'industrial relations'?

2. What is meant by (*i*) unitarism and (*ii*) pluralism?

3. What are the functions of a frame of reference?

4. According to J.T. Dunlop, what are the three main elements of an industrial relations system?

5. Explain the difference between a conflict of interest and a conflict of right.

6. Give four examples of how communication breakdowns can lead to conflict at work.

7. Define 'employee counselling'.

8. List the key elements of a strategy for managing employee relations.

2

INDIVIDUALISM AND COLLECTIVISM

1. Individualism

The philosophy of individualism is based on the idea that society functions most efficiently if each person takes decisions independently from others and according to his or her own self-interest. In the employee relations context this implies that workers should personally negotiate their individual terms and conditions of employment and do this without considering the implications for other employees. Then, the market forces of supply and demand for labour will (so advocates of this position believe) equitably determine each worker's wage. Arguments in favour of individualism are that it upholds the liberty of the individual, should result in the most efficient allocation of resources, enables individuals to seek reward and recognition for their own contributions, and compels management to accept that each of its employees possesses unique personal attributes. Critics of the philosophy allege, however, that it is naive and simplistic, that it ignores the reality that an employing organisation is far more powerful than a single worker, and that it enables firms to exploit their employees.

'Collectivism', conversely, requires individuals to surrender some of their rights and abilities to take decisions, leaving these decisions to joint determination by a group of workers or (subject to democratic approval) by the elected representatives of the group.

2. Power and authority

Management possesses *authority* (i.e. the right to control) by virtue of its position and command over resources. The exercise of authority will involve the determination of employees' workloads, deciding terms and conditions of employment, introducing new technologies and working methods, and so on. Formal authority is often accompanied by outward displays of status – different clothing (such as managers wearing suits while operatives wear overalls), separate canteens, different modes of speech and behaviour, etc. These may even differ for each of several levels of authority within the managerial hierarchy.

Authority is not the same as power, which is a quality that other people *perceive* an individual to possess, giving that person the ability to influence the actions of others. An employee might have low occupational status and occupy no formal leadership role yet still exert enormous power within the organisation. This is often true of workplace employee representatives.

Determinants of power

Individuals can be powerful in consequence of their charisma, ability to satisfy other group members' needs, or their control over information or resources. Other determinants of power include:

- the extent to which a person is known, liked, trusted and respected by the group
- whether group members identify with that individual
- group members' perceptions that the person has expert knowledge of the activities on which the group is engaged, and/or their feelings that the person's position is legitimate – say, because of seniority within the group.

The question of union power and what determines it is discussed in **13**.

3. Official and unofficial leaders

Formal group leaders are appointed by management. They are permanent and hence offer stability of leadership and a focus for group identity. Also they can impose formal rules on individual members. Supervisors, for example, might be empowered to select individuals for better paid tasks, recommend workers for promotion, and might be authorised to suspend or dismiss subordinates who perform inadequately. However, within a formal group, an unofficial leader might arise and function in parallel with the appointed leader. Official leaders are responsible for communicating with other groups and for expressing the collective opinions of the group. In practice, however, unofficial leaders are frequently the people who actually direct and motivate group members and, in effect, exercise the most power. Such individuals are fortunate in that they do not have to take the blame when things go wrong.

EMPLOYEE ORGANISATIONS

Workers may group together for collective employee relations purposes on a temporary basis (e.g. to place a collective complaint before management) or in a more permanent form via trade unions or staff associations.

4. Trade unions

A trade union is an association of workers formed to protect their interests in employment situations. In order to enjoy immunity from legal action during a trade dispute (*see* 3: 7) a union must be registered as such with the national authorities of the country concerned (in Britain a government 'certification officer' undertakes this function) and be independent, i.e. not controlled or dominated by an employer and not liable to interference by an employer through the provision or withholding of financial support.

Types of union

The oldest type of trade union is the *craft union*, which requires individuals to have undergone extensive training (usually via an apprenticeship) prior to becoming full union members. Other categories of union are the *industrial union*, which recruits only within a single industry, the *general union* which caters for any kind of worker regardless of occupation or level of skill (though normally recruiting the unskilled), and the *white collar union* which draws its members from clerical and administrative employees.

Objectives of trade unions

Trade unions have very specific objectives: higher living standards for their members, provision of welfare services such as sickness benefits, insurance and pensions, and security of tenure for the people they represent. Additionally, unions in some countries have wider ranging social and political aims which they seek to attain by supporting certain political parties and/or through involvement with the machinery of government.

The main device whereby unions pursue their objectives at workplace level is collective bargaining (*see* Chapter 9), i.e. by substituting collective action for individual action and hence removing some of the bargaining advantage enjoyed by employers during negotiations. Increasingly the range of issues covered by union/management collective bargaining is being broadened to cover matters such as equal opportunities, employee participation in workplace decision-making, and the status of employees. These are discussed in Chapters 9 and 13.

5. Trade union structure

Typically, a trade union will organise its members into branches, which are the primary units upon which union hierarchies are built. Usually, a branch will cover a particular geographical area, and all members who work for firms in that area will be attached to the branch. However, very large firms with many union members may have union branches allocated to them so that members belong to a branch based in a firm. The branch acts as a medium for upward and downward communication, acts as a forum for debate, and elects representatives onto higher union bodies.

In practice the majority of union members do not bother to attend branch meetings. Control then falls into the hands of a few people, though of course every member has the opportunity to exercise his or her right to attend and vote.

Commonly, elected branch officers form a branch committee to deal with routine administrative matters without having to put such matters before the branch. It is vital of course that only relatively trivial matters be dealt with in this way. The branch committee must not be allowed to decide issues of major concern without the entire branch being informed. Branches send representatives to sit on district committees which exercise overall supervision over several branches in an area according to the particular industries to which branch members belong. The highest level of authority in a union is normally its National Executive Committee (NEC), which comprises members elected directly by the entire union membership.

6. Workplace representatives

In each place of work a union will have lay workplace representatives, who are themselves employees of the firm. Their role is 'unofficial' in that they are not entitled to take decisions on behalf of the union without prior approval. Nevertheless, workplace representatives (referred to as 'shop stewards' in some industries) are extremely important in employee relations because they are often the only point of contact between the worker and the union, and frequently are the only union representatives that managers ever see.

Workplace representatives recruit new members for the union, stimulate and maintain members' interest in union affairs, ensure that union dues are paid, distribute information about current union activities, and act as a channel for grievances made by workers against management.

7. Role of the workplace representative

Although the role of the union workplace representative is 'unofficial' as far as the union is concerned (*see* **6**) workplace representatives are critically important participants in plant level collective bargaining. They know the background of the company thoroughly (especially its payment system), and are immediately available, unlike the full-time officer who is generally overworked. Also they are in day-to-day contact with the workforce and should be fully aware of attitudes and sentiment on the shop floor. Any agreement concluded with a steward will probably be accepted by union members and not repudiated.

Workplace representatives may or may not be involved with management/union negotiations on pay and conditions, but will almost certainly play a role in:

- processing workers' grievances
- representing workers accused of disciplinary offences
- discussing with management planned changes in working arrangements, introduction of new techniques, staffing levels, etc.
- passing on management information concerning the overall state of the business
- *interpreting* and implementing collective agreements at the workplace level.

Regular discussions with management could, of course, cause a workplace union representative eventually to identify as much with the aims of the management as with his or her union, leading to accusations that the representative has 'sold out' to management rather than protecting the interests of the rank and file. Some managements realise this and incorporate it into their strategy for dealing with trade unions.

Note conversely that union workplace representatives are sometimes blamed for all manner of employee relations difficulties. The fact is, however, that while employee representatives *articulate* workers' problems and grievances to management, they are not necessarily the *source* of conflict and disputes. Unfortunately, managements do not always realise this and may wrongly assume that the representative is a troublemaker constantly looking for matters about which to complain. The situation is worsened if the representative has not been trained in the techniques of effective representation, and simply regurgitates members' grumbles without attempting to put them into a context or to suggest solutions. Representatives need to establish, moreover, which members' complaints are likely to be genuine and which will probably be frivolous.

8. Advantages to management of dealing with workplace representatives

Substantial advantages accrue to a management dealing with workplace representatives rather than full-time union officials, notably that a representative will:

- be instantly available for consultation
- possess detailed knowledge of the department's work and must live with negotiated settlements
- have been elected by his or her workmates and is accountable to them for agreements, so that a settlement with a representative is perhaps more likely to stick than are agreements with other union officers
- provide an informal face-to-face means for quickly communicating with the workforce
- come to know and (hopefully) trust the managers with whom he or she comes into contact
- offer a useful means for sounding out workplace opinion on intended managerial initiatives.

9. Motivation to become an employee representative

A variety of influences affect a person's decision to become a workplace employee representative. Often there are few volunteers for the position so that union members in a particular work unit have to be cajoled by the union hierarchy into electing a representative, with only a couple of workers being prepared to undertake the work. Such individuals might accept the role because they:

- feel a sense of duty to fellow workers and the union
- have personal values which correspond closely with those of the trade union movement
- are alienated from their work and see union activity as a means for improving the situation
- believe that *someone* should do this work and experience a sense of unease at the prospect of a certain workplace being unrepresented
- are looking for job satisfaction through involvement with union work and have self-confidence in their ability to complete relevant tasks

- wish to become involved in communications with management and with workplace management decision-making (being a union representative is sometimes a precursor to becoming a supervisor)
- are seeking power and status in the eyes of fellow employees
- have a political commitment
- fear the consequences of changes in technology and / or working methods being imposed without employees' interests being represented
- have personal ambition and feel an urge to lead
- have a caring outlook and sense of injustice at how employees are being treated.

Clearly, a wide range of motives cause particular individuals to become workplace union representatives. It is well-established, however, that strong ideological and / or political commitment is, on the average, among the less important. Rather, research has revealed that the majority of workplace representatives 'emerge' from the ranks, often because no one else is prepared to accept the post. Indeed, representatives themselves might have very little interest in the broad principles of trade unionism. It is interesting to note, moreover, that a significant number of union representatives move on to assume supervisory or junior management positions. This is not especially surprising considering that union work brings an individual to the attention of the firm's middle or senior management, who might be impressed by the efficient manner in which the representative completes his or her union duties.

Workplace union representatives receive no payment from their trade unions, except perhaps for *ad hoc* expenses. Note how a workplace representative has no formal authority within an organisation, but could exercise a large amount of power (*see* **2**). Unlike the full-time union officer the workplace representative is an employee of the firm and has expert knowledge of the workplace situation, of how union members are likely to react to various proposals, management attitudes, interpersonal relations in the work unit, etc.

10. Benefits to employees of belonging to a trade union

Employees join trade unions in order to try to improve their pay and conditions and to gain some control over their general working environments. Also, union members have access to extensive support and advice (including legal assistance) if they are unfairly dismissed (*see* Chapter 11), wish to express grievances, or become involved in disciplinary action. This is particularly valuable for employees who are inarticulate and feel uncomfortable when speaking to managers, especially about complaints and grievances. Such employees benefit from having a skilled union representative able to present a case to management in a lucid, ordered and powerful way. Further benefits of union membership are that:

- Unions can and do successfully challenge management's right to behave selfishly and without regard for workers' interests.
- A union may be able to help an employee who is unfairly discriminated against.

- Recognised unions (*see* **21**) have statutory rights to appoint safety repre-sentatives at members' places of work, to be consulted on proposed redun-dancies, and to receive management information for use in collective bargaining (*see* Chapter 9).

11. Benefits to management of dealing with trade unions

It is not necessarily the case that managements can control unorganised workers more easily than union members. Specific benefits arising from dealing with a union rather than with individual employees include:

(a) Negotiation with unions is an effective way of determining pay and working conditions and for settling disputes. If each employee were to negotiate his or her own pay individually, the firm's personnel authorities would need to spend enormous amounts of time in individual negotiations. Since every worker could earn a wage different to those of other employees, numerous petty differentials would arise causing frictions and resentments among staff. Agreements negoti-ated with recognised, official, trade unions will normally be accepted by union members, and can be expected to stick until the next round of negotiation.

(b) Meetings between management and unions provide a useful forum for discussion of wider issues concerning the progress of the firm, and for presenting workers' views to management.

(c) If unions are not recognised, labour will still make its opinions known in some way, possibly with disruptive consequences – such as absenteeism, lack of effort, non-co-operation, perhaps even industrial sabotage.

(d) Unionised workforces might feel more secure and hence be willing to co-operate with redeployment and alterations in working practices.

(e) Management decision-making may become more centralised so that a uni-fied company employee policy can be formulated.

(f) Co-operation with unions facilitates communication with the workforce.

12. Drawbacks to management of dealing with trade unions

Against the benefits outlined in **11** are the facts that managerial prerogative is reduced, decision-taking is delayed by consultation, and labour costs will prob-ably increase. Simultaneous negotiations with several different unions can be tedious and difficult, and the unions might not agree among themselves. Further objections are that unionisation might disrupt (harmonious) existing staff–management relations, will 'formalise' disputes procedures, create unnecessary divisions between management and labour, and could encourage conflict. Note how the existence of complex piecework and bonus systems create numerous opportunities for vexatious union representatives to raise problems over which they can demand negotiations, e.g. work speeds, manning levels, training re-quirements, redeployment of workers, shift rotas, and so on.

Unions, moreover, can provide alternative sources of leadership within organisations, hence increasing the potential for conflict and disputes. Employees may come to feel more loyalty towards their union than to their employing firm.

13. Union power

Trade unions become powerful (*see* **2**) through:

- the solidarity of their members and their willingness and ability to take industrial action
- their organisational ability, especially in relation to strikes
- union members occupying key positions within a firm (or indeed within a national economy – as with electricity workers for example)
- the negotiating skills of union officials
- support from and contacts with the government of the day
- their capacity to arouse favourable public sentiment, as is sometimes the case with disputes involving nurses and other workers in the caring professions.

Thus, union power may derive from union members' abilities to disrupt *or* to persuade. The capacity to disrupt might cause management to treat certain groups of employee more favourably than other (less strategically important) categories; the persuasive aspect requires union members to be able to influence people in different sections of the firm, possibly in other organisations, and perhaps in the community at large. Note, however, how a group of workers could be *potentially* powerful, but fail to realise that this is the case, e.g. through ignorance of how badly a strike will hurt a firm, or through lack of experience.

The power to disrupt

This depends on how quickly a group of workers can implement harmful industrial action, and on:

- the financial cost of the disruption
- whether and how soon other sections will be affected
- the extent to which the work done by employees involved in an action can be transferred to alternative units.

The power to persuade

Among the main factors affecting union members' persuasive capacities are:

- the justice of the union's case
- the *visibility* of group cohesion among the workers taking the action (employees must be *seen* to be united and determined in their resolve)
- whether outsiders identify with the issue and the individuals connected with the dispute
- the training in negotiating skills received by employee representatives and their experience of collective bargaining.

As industrial action escalates it becomes increasingly difficult for group solidarity to be maintained. Individual workers might feel that further sacrifice is not economically justified, or that it is not morally sound. Note, however, the tendency of particular groups of employee to become more militant once the initial hurdle of challenging management decisions has been surmounted. Examples of such employee categories include nurses, teachers, senior civil servants, medical doctors and other professionally qualified staff who, having tested out management reactions to their opposition on a limited range of issues, have then progressed to make further and more substantial demands. As these groups achieve early successes their confidence increases and (importantly) the outcomes to their taking industrial action become less uncertain, hence strengthening their common perception of being able to exercise union power.

Reducing union power

Management strategies for reducing union power could include preventing (if possible) certain categories of worker from occupying critical positions wherein they possess the capacity to disrupt the flow of work; regular communication with employees so as to present management's views on issues; and seeking to ensure that (whatever short-run concessions are given) industrial action is *never* seen to pay off in the longer term. Specific measures include:

- building up stocks in anticipation of industrial action
- having strategically important duties performed in several different units, so that no one becomes indispensable
- ensuring that the work of people in one group can be quickly substituted by individuals from other departments
- laying off employees in many sections immediately following a withdrawal of labour in any one section (in order to induce workers not directly involved in the dispute to exert moral pressure on striking employees to return to work).

WHITE COLLAR UNIONISM

An important long-term development in twentieth-century trade unionism has been the increased propensity of 'white collar' workers (clerical and administrative staff, junior and middle managers, shop assistants, scientists and technicians, professionally qualified employees, etc.) to join trade unions.

14. Background to white collar unionism

Prior to the second half of the present century, union density was low among white collar workers because of their close personal contacts with employers, job security and generally favourable employment conditions compared to manual ('blue collar') employees. Many clerks had middle-class status in consequence of their superior education in comparison to blue collar workers, their housing and lifestyle, higher pay, and prospects for promotion. Other factors inhibiting the spread of unionisation among white collar workers were:

(a) Physical separation from large numbers of fellow workers. Clerks completed their jobs in small groups in offices in close proximity to management.

(b) The absence of a 'factory' atmosphere in offices and no feelings of belonging to a homogeneous group.

(c) Lack of economic inducement to band together to take collective action.

(d) Identification with management, conservative attitudes, and a dislike of 'collectivist' goals.

15. Reasons for change

A number of developments caused a fundamental shift in the conditions of employment of white collar workers, including:

(a) Application of work study, work measurement, job evaluation and the division of labour to clerical duties. New working methods had the effect of distancing white collar workers from the management of the firm.

(b) Standardisation of office procedures, so that office work in one firm became basically the same as work in any other company. This created a clerical labour force with similar work experience, terms and conditions of employment and attitudes towards work. The amount of discretion allowed to clerical workers when completing tasks was reduced, causing them to identify more with manual workers doing repetitive work than with other categories of administrative employee.

(c) Huge increases in the number of white collar workers resulting from changes in technology and patterns of work, thus creating fresh opportunities for unions to organise in the while collar field.

(d) Erosion of differentials in fringe benefits afforded to white collar employees (longer holidays, a shorter working week, superannuation, etc.), especially during periods of statutory pay restraint (*see* 4: **14**) when managements offered some of these benefits to manual workers in order to circumvent incomes policies.

(e) The use by firms of large numbers of women to undertake clerical work, accompanied by lower wages for female clerks and hence general downward pressure on wage levels for white collar work.

(f) Automation of paperwork, which caused widespread redundancies among clerical staff as fewer people were required. Fears of change led to many white collar workers joining trade unions.

All these factors contributed to an increased willingness of clerical workers to join unions and, ultimately, to take industrial action in attempts to secure economic ends. As the number of white collar employees expanded, moreover, employing firms recognised the advantages of handling employee relations with clerical workers via trade unions rather than through individual negotiations.

16. Recruitment of white collar workers to trade unions

Unions today emphasise in their recruitment campaigns the problems created by change. A trade union can help its white collar members through:

- securing joint consultation with employers prior to the implementation of change
- encouraging employers to take measures that will avoid or minimise the extent of redundancies caused by new methods, and insisting that all legislation on redundancy procedures is followed to the letter
- relating salaries paid to white collar workers in one firm to salaries paid for similar work in other businesses (via salary surveys, feedback from members in various enterprises, etc.)
- encouraging employers to train clerical employees in skills they can easily transfer between different types of white collar work.

The problems involved

Arguably, white collar trade unions have different *perspectives* than do 'traditional' unions representing manual employees. Specifically they might be:

- less political
- less inclined to take industrial action
- more concerned with maintaining members' occupational status than with ideological questions of social class
- more willing to co-operate with management, albeit within a collectivist framework.

Some of the problems created by such perspectives for contemporary unions trying to recruit new white collar members include:

(a) Unions are still not regarded as socially acceptable by many clerical and administrative employees, especially unions which engage in strikes, picketing, etc.

(b) Many white collar workers are interested in gaining promotion and might believe that becoming involved with a trade union might jeopardise their chances.

(c) It remains the case in a large number of enterprises that white collar staff regularly communicate with management and hence will be quickly identified if they become union activists.

(d) Unions continue to experience difficulty in inducing white collar workers to perceive a common interest shared by all who undertake clerical and administrative tasks.

UNION RECOGNITION PROCEDURES

Claims for recognition of a trade union in a previously non-unionised firm can emanate either from the firm's employees or from external full-time union officials. The latter situation is especially likely in cases where individual employees do not wish to be identified as the people wanting to start the union.

17. The process of recognition

If management is not totally opposed to the idea of having a union it will normally want to assess the extent of support for the claim among the workforce and the implications of unionisation for the well-being (as management sees it) of the firm. Note how the actual estimation of the level of support might not be easy, since not only should the *present* number of union members be counted, but also the number of employees likely to join the union if it is recognised. Next, management must determine the threshold membership at which recognition will be granted (e.g. 51 per cent, two-thirds, etc.).

18. Partial recognition

It may be that management is only prepared to grant partial recognition in the first instance, e.g. for the purposes of representing workers in grievance or disciplinary interviews, but not for collective bargaining over pay and conditions. At this stage, unions are consulted but may not negotiate. Nevertheless, the establishment of formal procedures for discussing grievances does pave the way for collective bargaining over more substantial industrial relations issues and the decision to allow partial representation is often the first of several in a conscious policy for union recognition.

19. Recognition strategy

Management needs to have a well-planned strategy for introducing union recognition in an orderly manner. The objectives of this strategy should include:

- the efficient dovetailing of management/union negotiating procedures into the administrative structure of the firm
- establishment of mechanisms for defusing potentially dangerous conflict situations and for ensuring that appropriate unions represent the workers
- the systematic extension of collective bargaining to encompass issues of greater substance as both it and newly elected union representatives gain experience of formal negotiation. Initial management/union meetings consider grievance and disciplinary matters only. Thereafter, working conditions, pension schemes, sick pay and holiday arrangements, overtime and shift work systems and (eventually) wages and conditions of service will be gradually incorporated into the negotiating agenda.

A critical aspect of the strategy is to determine appropriate bargaining units (*see* 7: **7**), i.e. to establish whether negotiations should occur at departmental, divisional or company-wide levels. Clearly, disputes regarding working practices specific to a particular section of the firm should be dealt with initially by the workplace representative and supervisor of the section concerned, whereas workplace representatives and supervisors are not normally allowed to negotiate fundamental changes in wages or contractual conditions of work. Also, management and employees must jointly agree which unions should represent various categories of workers.

The case for having an orderly union recognition procedure is reinforced by the fact that if, following a protracted and unpleasant recognition dispute, management is then forced to accept a union, it will not enjoy as satisfactory a relationship with the union as it would have if recognition had been granted in the first place.

20. Form of the recognition agreement

The recognition agreement should be in writing and specify the procedures to be followed (e.g. which agreements shall be recorded formally and which may be negotiated informally without being written down), the matters that shall be subject to negotiation, and rules relating to the channelling of grievances and to the settlement of industrial disputes. Some firms issue written credentials to elected union representatives explicitly acknowledging their status, their entitlements to time off work for union duties, and their right to be consulted on various matters. Credentials will specify the people to whom representations may be made, the extent of the representative's constituency, and usually will include a clause insisting that the representative abides by the rules of the union.

Very occasionally a recognition agreement will impose restrictions on eligibility to hold union office, say to those employees who have completed some minimum period of service, or on the total number of workplace representatives the union is allowed to put forward. The agreement may further stipulate that employee representatives be elected by secret ballot, that employee representatives will always adhere to negotiated agreements, will accept the directives of their superiors in the union, and will recommend union members not to take industrial action until specified negotiating procedures have been exhausted. Also, the circumstances in which employee representatives may take time off for union duties will usually be stated.

21. Consequence of recognition

UK law makes a distinction between recognised and non-recognised unions. A recognised trade union is defined as an independent trade union with which an employing firm has at some time or other negotiated on *any* matter, which does not have to involve pay and conditions of employment. British firms do not have to recognise unions if they do not wish to do so, and there is no statutory mechanism for unions to obtain or enforce recognition. However, once a management recognises a union for any purpose, then the union becomes entitled to a number of statutory rights, *even if* the latter do not relate to the purpose for which the union was initially recognised. The main rights conferred on unions following recognition are the right to receive management information (*see* 7: **10**) prior to negotiations, the right of employee representatives to (unpaid) time off work to attend to union duties, and the right to appoint 'safety representatives' to deal with workplace health and safety. The duties of a safety representative include the inspection of premises, liaison with outside inspectors, and the investigation of hazards, accidents and dangerous occurrences. If at least two safety representatives require it, the employer is legally obliged to set up a safety committee comprising equal numbers of management and workers' representatives.

The HSC Codes of Practice

Two codes of practice have been issued by the Health and Safety Commission concerning safety representatives and the information and facilities to be provided to them by employers. The first code recommends that persons appointed as representatives should, if possible, have worked for their firms for at least two years. Representatives should co-operate with employers, take steps to become familiar with legal requirements and potential hazards in their workplaces, and promptly inform employers of any unhealthy or unsafe conditions or working practices. Employers should advise representatives of intended changes in production methods, and regularly update them with accident statistics and news of dangerous incidents. The second code (entitled *Time Off for the Training of Safety Representatives*) suggests that representatives attend an approved safety training course as soon as possible following appointment, and that the course cover legal requirements and the nature of workplace hazards and the possible measures for overcoming them.

22. Derecognition

Derecognition of unions might occur through management's attempts to impose a single-union agreement (*see* 9: **19**) or in consequence of persistent disruptions caused (unreasonably in management's view) by certain unions. Whereas the process of union recognition is usually gradual, the process of derecognition is normally abrupt and traumatic. It has two possible forms: (i) the removal of collective bargaining rights from employees, or (ii) the derecognition of particular unions in certain parts of a firm in consequence of the rationalisation of its overall management/worker negotiation procedures. Derecognition may be appropriate where:

- union density (*see* **23**) is minimal, so that workplace representatives (who might in fact be the union's only members in the firm) are not really speaking for the workforce
- there is much duplication of effort and activity among the firm's various unions
- workplace representatives regularly defy and/or are beyond the control of head office officers
- there is fragmentation of bargaining units (*see* 7: **7**)
- a change in the firm's ownership has recently occurred.

Reasons for derecognition include management's desires to introduce:

- personal contracts (*see* 9:**4**) and performance-related pay

- greater workforce flexibility
- a schism between employee consultation and representation, disciplinary and grievance procedures on the one hand, and union organisation on the other
- an awareness among employees of financial realities confronting the firm
- more direct communications with employees
- a more authoritarian management style
- diversification of the business's activities into new areas
- changes such as the implementation of single status agreements (*see* 9:**18**).

23. Union density

This is the proportion of employees who belong to a trade union in a given country, industry, sector of an industry, or individual firm. Note how figures for union density relate mainly to workers *actually* in employment (the unemployed typically abandon union membership once they have been out of work for a significant period of time) rather than to the propensity of the workforce (many of whom may be unemployed) to join unions were everyone to have a job.

Apart from the factors listed in **10**, union density is known to depend on the average ages and lengths of service of workers: density tends to be highest in situations where older and long-serving employees make up a large part of the workforce. Also, casual and part-time workers are far less likely to join a union than are permanent full-time employees.

Factors known to contribute to total union membership within a country are:

(a) *The average size of business within the economy.* Unionisation is less common in small firms than in large organisations. Interpersonal relations between management and workers are perhaps closer and less formal in small enterprises. Owners know their staff personally and problems can be quickly sorted out.

(b) *The rate of inflation.* There are two possible causes behind the observation that more people join unions when prices are rising sharply than when inflation is low:

(*i*) Workers recognise the adverse effects of inflation on their real wages and see union membership as a means for protecting their living standards.
(*ii*) Inflation is frequently associated with economic expansion, rising employment, labour shortages in certain areas and hence a stronger position for organised labour in all respects. Unions are more active and *seen* to be gaining results.

(c) *Media coverage of employee relations matters.* Unions are frequently blamed by the press and TV for causing strikes and economic disruption. During a dispute, managements may be reported as being conciliatory, making offers, appealing to reason, etc., whereas unions might be depicted as aggressive, making unreasonable demands, inciting violence on picket lines, and so on.

(d) *Laws and government attitudes.* Some governments are pro-union and legislate in order to promote union interests; others are hostile to unions and constantly seek to curb their influence and power.

(e) *The calibre of union management.* A trade union needs to have a strategy and tactics and to be managed just as any other kind of organisation. Wise and efficient stewardship of a union's affairs will help it retain its members.

(f) *The speed of technical change and its effects on economic structure* (shut-downs of heavily unionised industries for example).

(g) *Managerial and governmental attitudes towards trade unions,* resulting from management education and training, culture and ideology. Unions cannot flourish if the overwhelming majority of firms refuse to recognise them and/or if governments restrict their abilities to organise.

EMPLOYEE RELATIONS IN THE NON-UNIONISED FIRM

The absence of a trade union in a company does not mean that it will not experience disputes involving collective action, or that individual workers will cease to express grievances. In recognition of this, certain non-unionised firms have established 'staff associations' to represent the interests of their employees.

24. Staff associations

Staff associations have proliferated over the last quarter century, for a number of reasons:

(a) Managements sometimes prefer to deal with a staff association than with trade unions, perceiving the latter as representing 'their' people rather than interest groups beyond the firm. Recognition of a union raises the possibility of third party intervention in what management might regard as its private internal affairs.

(b) Employees may themselves oppose union involvement with a company. The workers might want to be represented to management, but *not* by an orthodox trade union. Such opposition to joining a union could result from employee perceptions that trade unions are:

(i) political and conspiratorial, wanting only to call strikes and to be disruptive

(ii) bureaucratic and excessively concerned with the ritualistic procedures of collective bargaining, while failing to recognise members' actual working needs

(iii) not interested in equal opportunities, especially for female workers

(iv) more concerned with wider social issues than with mundane matters of pay, pensions, job security, etc.

None of these criticisms need be true, but as long as workers *perceive* them as true workers will be reluctant to join a union. Why, employees might ask, does a union want to enter the firm, especially if the firm has a reasonably good industrial relations record? Will union membership require individuals to sacrifice their freedom of choice? Are there political implications associated with union membership? Will union-inspired collective bargaining cause a levelling out of rewards to employees at the expense of particularly able and/or enterprising employees? These are the questions that workers ask when considering whether to join a union.

(c) Management *and* employees may fear that a union's entry to the firm will disrupt good existing employee relations.

25. Problems with staff associations

Several problems attach to the use of staff associations rather than trade unions to represent workers' interests, from both management and employees' points of view. The major difficulties are:

(a) Elected staff association representatives necessarily acquire first-hand experience of negotiation, disputes procedures, persuasive advocacy and so on through staff association work – ideal training for future trade union officers, organised and financed by the employing firm.

(b) Formation of a staff association might encourage employees to begin looking for things to complain about.

(c) If a staff association is successful this could draw attention to the need for collective representation in the company, thus provoking a trade union to begin recruiting within that firm.

(d) Since management effectively controls a staff association, negotiations between management and staff association representatives are unlikely to cover matters relating to fundamental conflicts of interest between management and employees. Only trivial issues might be discussed, hence weakening the staff association's credibility as a representational device.

(e) To the extent that staff associations are successful in promoting employees' interests they will increasingly behave *as if* they were trade unions, and perhaps give rise to demands for union recognition. So why not simply accept a trade union in the first place?

(f) Unlike unions, staff associations do not (normally) call strikes. Hence crises in confidence in the association's effectiveness in representing employees' interests occur whenever the association feels the need to impose sanctions on management but is unable to do so.

Unions have a great advantage over staff associations where industrial action is concerned. A strike can be organised by head office union officials who are not employees of the firm and thus not subject to threats of dismissal, victimisation, etc., whereas staff association representatives who organise a strike can be quickly identified and dismissed. Negotiations with management during a union strike may be conducted by skilled and independent full-time union officers who have immediate access to legal advice, relevant industry-wide information and contact with union members in the firm's supplying and client organisations. National unions possess the resources to support a strike, while staff associations (which typically charge low membership fees) are rarely able to finance significant industrial action.

THE PROFESSIONS

26. Role of professional bodies

Members of professional bodies (accountants, lawyers, architects, etc.) frequently pursue careers that transcend the individual's affiliation to any one employing organisation. The distinguishing characteristics of a 'profession' are:

(a) Members' activities should be based on an established body of knowledge, the acquisition of which requires several years of substantial intellectual training.

(b) Certain ethical 'professional' standards must be maintained and codes of practice applied to members' work.

(c) Entry should be restricted to persons possessing predefined qualifications, experience and/or characteristics and with common training and perspectives.

(d) Members take a professional pride in the quality of their work, which is seen as an end in itself and not merely a means for earning a living.

(e) The knowledge needed to master the profession is non-trivial and can only be obtained through several years' training and experience, evidenced by passing examinations.

(f) There is a 'community of knowledge' among members who often want to impress professional peers with their ability to undertake higher levels of professional work.

(g) Knowledge obtained during training should distinguish members from other people working in the same field.

The orthodox definition of a professional worker is of someone who belongs to an institute or association the purposes of which are:

(a) to maintain or improve members' occupational status; *and*

(b) to enhance members' standards of performance through training and a system of certification usually (but not always) involving a series of examinations.

Traditionally, professional workers have performed service roles (accountants, lawyers, etc.) and have worked for many 'clients' rather than a single employer. Today, however, the concept of 'profession' encompasses a variety of categories of employee. Teachers and nurses, for example, typically regard themselves as 'professional' workers, despite being normally employed by a single organisation on terms and conditions similar to those of any other category of staff.

The functions of professional bodies are:

(a) Examining, training and education; the production of syllabuses and teaching materials; and the provision of short courses.

(b) Establishment of standards of professional conduct, backed up by disciplinary procedures and the threat of sanctions against those who break the association's rules.

(c) Distribution of information on new developments, practices and other items of interest to members.

(d) Enhancement of the status of the profession via public relations exercises, contributions to debates on topical issues affecting the profession, and generally acting as a pressure group to further members' interests.

(e) Conducting salary surveys among members and publishing summaries of the results.

Not all professional organisations undertake all these functions. Indeed, some exist primarily because of the exclusivity of membership and the prestige attached to current members (the Royal Academy in England for example). However, entry to most professions is 'open' for student membership – provided that minimum basic educational criteria are met. Thereafter, associations set their own examinations, or offer exemption against the examinations in equivalent subjects set by comparable academic or vocational discipline or to further knowledge within a highly specialised area. These turned ultimately into qualifying associations concerned with the maintenance of 'professional' standards. Individuals who had not taken the relevant association's examinations and thus did not enjoy the accreditation of the 'recognised' body in the field would then experience difficulty in practising the profession.

27. Management of professionally-qualified staff

Special problems apply to the management of professionally-qualified staff:

(a) Professionals' talents and qualifications might not be fully utilised by employing organisations, causing resentment among these workers.

(b) Line managers may insist that professionals alter their working methods in order to fit in with bureaucratic organisation structures.

(c) Senior managers might not be competent to appraise the performances of professionally-qualified subordinates.

(d) Separation of professional employees from the normal line of command may undermine the authority of the central administration.

(e) A highly-qualified professional might resent being paid less than line managers on the same grade who have not had to pass professional examinations.

(f) Large organisations often employ members of several different professional associations, who may compete with each other for the favour of senior management. Lawyers, for example, may feel they deserve higher status than (say) accountants.

(g) Often, professionals are engaged on specialist activities and thus fail to acquire the breadth of general management experience attained by colleagues in line management. Hence they cannot advance to the top of their employing organisations.

To resolve these problems, large businesses sometimes apply the following measures:

- Provision of management training to professional employees.
- Widespread use of project teams.
- Creation of 'federal organisation' structures wherein individual professionals are given personal autonomy over how they do their work, but which have separate administrations to perform routine management tasks.
- The setting-up of quasi-independent 'professional support units' that concentrate entirely on the provision of a particular professional service. The legal department of a commercial bank is an example.

EMPLOYERS' ASSOCIATIONS

28. Nature of employers' associations

Employers' associations are organisations consisting wholly or mainly of employers or proprietors whose principal purposes include the regulation of relations between employers and workers or unions. They have the same legal status as a trade union and thus have immunity from civil action arising from bona fide trade disputes (*see* 3: 7).

The early development of employers' associations was due mainly to the advance of trade unionism, seeking to redress the imbalance of bargaining power which many employers perceived to favour the unions. Most employers' associations negotiate with unions at national, local or industry level, though some are only advisory and merely offer advice on industrial relations matters to member firms. Membership of an employers' association implies agreement to abide by its rules, including adherence to pay settlements negotiated by the association with unions. Firms which pay more or less than agreed industry (or national) wage levels are liable to expulsion from the association. The growth of employers' associations stimulated the development of nationwide collective bargaining, and hence the standardisation of wage rates, grading schemes, bonus systems, etc.

Other functions of employers' associations are to:

- provide a forum for discussion of employee relations and other matters of common interest

- co-ordinate members' strategies in relation to multi-firm industrial disputes
- represent members' interests in national and local government and the media
- assist members with the location and selection of expert providers of specialist services, e.g. job evaluation consultancies, lawyers, training consultants, etc.
- prepare model procedures, having regard to government-endorsed codes of practice – for use by members when dealing with grievances, dismissals, industrial disputes, equal opportunities issues, and so on.

29. Problems experienced by employers' associations

Employers' associations face a number of difficulties not encountered by trade unions, as follows:

(a) *Lack of resources.* Associations rely on a relatively small number of member firms each contributing substantial fees. They are not mass membership organisations able to withstand the financial effects of a few members leaving the organisation. Hence they cannot afford to employ many staff or provide extensive ancillary services.

(b) *Representation of diverse interests.* Each member company is likely to have its own expectations of what the association should do and how it should behave. Unions, conversely, have a limited range of clearly defined objectives.

(c) Member firms can easily break pay agreements negotiated by their association through giving employees hidden fringe benefits, extra holidays and shorter working hours, by 'promoting' large numbers of workers into higher grades, etc.

(d) At any particular time it is likely that some association members (possibly the largest firms in the organisation) will be experiencing acute cash flow problems and hence will not wish to stand up to union threats of strike action, preferring to concede to the unions' demands and avoid the destructive consequences of a stoppage.

30. Tripartism

The term 'tripartism' (sometimes referred to as 'corporatism') is used to describe a philosophy of industrial (as opposed to employee) relations that advocates the bringing together of the government, major national trade union organisations and employers' associations. Its aim is to establish mutually acceptable frameworks for the conduct of wage and other negotiations, possibly to conclude collective agreements applicable to a wide range of major industries, and to resolve national labour disputes. Tripartite arrangements occupy a key role in the industrial relations systems of several continental West European nations, and have statutory backing in some cases. Typical duties of a tripartite body include:

- advising government ministers on planned legislation in the industrial relations field
- discussing social matters such as state welfare and pension arrangements
- advising the government on vocational training
- discussing government measures intended to improve industrial productivity.

The basic argument in favour of tripartism is that it integrates all aspects of industrial relations into a common system and obliges employers, unions and the government to adhere to the same set of rules. Also, employers are *forced* to accept the moral legitimacy of trade unionism, while unions themselves are compelled to operate within state-imposed guidelines. Moderation and compromise are encouraged, and the outcomes to discussions can form an important input to a government's national economic plan.

Criticisms of tripartism are that union power (*see* **13**) is undermined, that it interferes with market forces, that unions and businesses lose the ability to act independently, and that it could be used as a device for repressing individual freedom and for enforcing undemocratic state control. Further difficulties are that:

- Tacit union involvement in government wage restraint policies could result in unions losing the trust of their members.
- Governments could use tripartism opportunistically, advocating it during times of economic crisis but abandoning the practice when circumstances change.
- Tripartite agreements only make sense when the the government has a well-constructed overall economic strategy.
- Employers might perceive tripartism as little more than a convenient device to minimise their aggregate wages bill at the national level.

Note, moreover, that many western governments have become increasingly reluctant to enter into tripartite arrangements. In some cases this is due to a political decision to deregulate labour markets and to withdraw from all forms of dialogue and interactions with trade unions, while in others it merely reflects the state's reduced financial capability during (severe) recent recessions to honour tripartite agreements on improved terms and conditions of employment. Also, of course, unions are generally less powerful (and thus more easily ignored by governments and employers) during recessionary periods.

In order to succeed, tripartite arrangements require the full support of the overwhelming majority of employers and workers, otherwise the agreements emerging from tripartite negotiations will be constantly challenged, with frequent unofficial industrial actions, wildcat strikes (*see* 12: **2**), etc.

31. The CBI and the Trades Union Congress

Tripartism in Britain has a patchy and fragmented history and, at the time of writing, is not practised. In the past, however, a number of attempts at bringing unions and employers' associations into the processes of economic planning and policy-making (including the imposition of wage restraint) have been made (with little success some critics would allege). In Britain the main national association of employers' associations is the Confederation of British Industry (CBI), while the national union organisation is the Trades Union Congress (TUC).

The CBI

This is a voluntary confederation of employers' associations. It was formed in 1965 by an amalgamation of some existing employers' federations. Unlike the TUC it deals with other matters besides industrial relations as its general purpose is to promote the prosperity of British industry. The CBI undertakes all the functions of an employers' association (*see* **28**) and is particularly active in the field of promoting the views and interests of the business sector.

The TUC

The TUC was formed in 1868 with the objective of representing the interests of trade unions and their members. To achieve this aim the TUC undertakes a number of activities including:

- lobbying the government on behalf of the trade union movement
- acting as a spokesperson for trade unionism on television, in the press and in other media
- conducting research and giving advice and support to member unions (legal advice for instance)
- attempting to persuade member unions to adopt positions on issues
- helping to settle disputes between member unions
- assisting and supporting the Labour Party which the TUC perceives as sharing the same philosophies and objectives as itself
- liaising with labour organisations in other parts of the world.

32. Problems facing the TUC

Critics of the TUC allege that it is bureaucratic, undemocratic and resistant to change. These disparaging assertions are based on the following arguments:

(a) Individual members of trade unions do *not* directly elect the TUC General Council. Rather the council is composed of trade union leaders elected via a block vote system – votes being cast by union leaders themselves according to the sizes of their unions' memberships. Possibly it would be fairer to have a postal ballot of all members of all unions affiliated to the TUC.

(b) Union density (*see* **23**) in various industrial sectors regularly alters, although the structure of the TUC's ruling bodies in terms of which unions hold most seats is rarely changed.

(c) The TUC is underfunded. It is frequently so short of cash that it cannot afford the specialist research and provision of ancillary services to member unions that are required. Hence, much work has to be done by bureaucratic committees, often on a voluntary basis.

(d) There are no direct communications between the TUC and the individuals who belong to member unions. The TUC is not actively engaged in public relations and does not always project a favourable image to these people, many of whom are not aware of what the TUC actually does.

(e) The dominant event in the TUC's calendar is the annual Congress held in the first week of September. This only lasts for a few days and, some would argue, attempts too many onorous tasks in too short a period. In consequence many important topics are not properly debated, there is much grouping of motions into single 'composites' which might not reflect any of the original motions accurately, and it becomes difficult to *change* (rather than discuss) overall policy in a democratic manner. Decisions are taken using block voting, so that the very big unions invariably get their way.

ACADEMIC THEORIES OF UNION DEVELOPMENT

A number of writers have attempted to explain the origins, development and roles of trade union and labour movements in various countries in Europe and the United States. 'Labour movements' involve trade unions, but also include political parties and pressure groups committed to improving the situation of working people. The ideas of some of the most influential theorists are outlined below.

33. Sydney and Beatrice Webb

This husband and wife team studied British trade unions in the late nineteenth and early twentieth centuries, publishing their best known book, *Industrial Democracy*, in 1911. According to the Webbs, the principal role of trade unions was to extend representative democracy to the industrial sphere via collective bargaining. 'Industrial democracy', in the Webbs' view, meant the determination of wages and other terms and conditions of employment through collective bargaining, because collective bargaining meant that employers and elected employee representatives were able to meet and (according to the Webbs) negotiate as equals.

Union behaviour, they argued, was characterised by two main 'devices' and three 'doctrines', as follows:

(a) The 'device of common rule', i.e. the standardisation of working conditions for all employees in an occupation or industry in order to eliminate individual bargaining. This prevented employers from forcing down wages and working conditions through dealing with employees as individuals.

(b) The 'device of restriction of numbers' whereby unions demanded that entry to certain occupations be open only to those who had served a long apprenticeship, plus other practices designed to reduce labour supply and hence increase the bargaining power of the unions. Such measures were only possible in craft work situations and, the Webbs argued, as mass production and the deskilling of work proceeded they would become progressively less important.

(c) The 'doctrine of vested interests', which involved union opposition to any technological development that threatened traditional skills or challenged workers' control over their jobs.

(d) The 'doctrine of supply and demand', whereby unions would consciously use market forces to their own advantage (rather than seeking to overthrow the capitalist market system).

(e) The 'doctrine of the living wage', i.e. application by unions of the general principle that the basic needs of *all* workers should be satisfied and that employees in strong bargaining positions should use their power to help weaker groups.

34. Selig Perlman

Perlman's book *A Theory of the Labour Movement* (1928) argued that the development of the labour movement in *any* given country could be explained by three factors:

- the strength of the country's capitalist class in terms of its ability to maintain and exercise its power to rule the nation
- the extent and attitudes of a country's 'intelligentsia'
- the objectives and policies of trade unions.

The mix of these factors in a particular nation would, Perlman suggested, determine the nature of its labour movement and how the latter would behave. In pre-First World War Russia, for example, an anti-capitalist intelligentsia had sufficient power to ferment revolution against a weak capitalist class, despite the feebleness of the Russian trade unions. In the United States conversely there were few anti-capitalist intellectuals compared to some other countries and the capitalist class was pre-eminent. Unions responded to this situation by making 'job control' their top priority. Job control involved groups of workers creating labour shortages through apprenticeship restrictions, work rules, demarcation and other practices designed to allocate job opportunities only to union members.

35. Karl Marx

Marx (*see* 1: 8) regarded trade unions as an instrument to be used by the working class in order to seize political power. The essentials of Marx's views on unions can be summarised as follows:

(a) The accumulation of capital in the hands of the small section of society that owned the means of production meant a split between this privileged 'capitalist class' and the overwhelming majority of people who owned neither land nor property but were compelled for economic reasons to offer their labour for bare subsistence wages.

(b) Capitalist systems relied on the exploitation of labour, so that conflict between the owners of industry (employers) and the workers was inevitable.

(c) Unions arose from workers' needs to protect themselves from employers' attempts to reduce wages while increasing output.

(d) The struggle between unions and capitalists would necessarily develop into *political* conflict, so that unions would play their part in the overthrow of the capitalist system and its replacement by socialism.

(e) To the extent that unions focused on mundane day-to-day employee relations issues rather than pursuing broader political goals their leaders would have to be educated in socialist thinking. In general, union interests should be subordinated to revolutionary objectives.

36. American theorists

A number of influential writers examined the development of trade unions in the United States (*see* Chapter 17). Frank Tannenbaum, for example, claimed in the 1920s that US trade unionism emerged as a defensive reaction by workers against machine-based production and the factory system which had disrupted the economic structure of American society. Unions, according to Tannenbaum, were essentially *conservative* organisations that offered to workers a stabilising force in a rapidly changing environment. This was the complete opposite of Marx's interpretation of the unions' role. Tannenbaum predicted (wrongly) that as they grew, unions would begin to purchase and manage big businesses so that corporate and union interests would increasingly merge.

Robert F. Hoxie argued in 1919 that American unions were 'opportunistic' bodies, reacting to whatever labour market situation existed at any particular moment. No general principles underlay the development of the American union movement. Hoxie distinguished four main types of American union, although he offered no theory of why these categories emerged in the first instance. The four types were:

(a) The 'business union', which accepted the capitalist system in its entirety. Members have no 'class consciousness' but see the union simply as a device for improving their terms and conditions of employment. Business unionism would use restrictive labour practices where appropriate, and would exert pressure on political parties if this might help achieve (mundane) union objectives.

(b) The 'uplift union', an idealistic organisation that sought to further the economic and social interests of workers through education and the lobbying of local and federal government.

(c) The 'revolutionary union', the aim of which was to overthrow the capitalist system and implement workers' control of industry. Members have a strong class consciousness and perceive irreconcilable conflicts of interest between capital and labour.

There were, according to Hoxie, two forms of revolutionary union: socialist and anarcho-syndicalist. The former was more pragmatic and prepared to work within the existing socio-political framework. Anarchosyndicalists, conversely, had a contemptuous disregard for orthodox collective bargaining and favoured

41

direct action as the means for attaining goals. Hoxie cited the American Industrial Workers of the World (*see* 17: **11**) as a classic example of an anarcho-syndicalist union.

(d) The 'predatory union', concerned with lining the pockets of union leaders. There were two forms of predatory unionism:

(*i*) 'guerilla' unionism which would ruthlessly use its power to extort money from employers

(*ii*) 'holdup unionism' involving union collusion with employers to enrich union leaders (legally or illegally) at the expense of consumers and/or workers.

Progress test 2

1. What are the implications of individualism?

2. Explain the difference between authority and power.

3. List the main types of trade union.

4. Why does the union workplace representative occupy a crucial role in employee relations?

5. What motivates individuals to become union workplace representatives?

6. List the determinants of union power.

7. State the main points likely to be covered by a union recognition agreement.

8. Define 'union density'.

9. What is a staff association?

10. List the arguments in favour of tripartism.

11. According to the Webbs, what is the principal role of the trade union movement?

3

THE STATE AND EMPLOYEE RELATIONS

1. Voluntarism versus statutory control

Voluntarism is a philosophical approach to employee relations which asserts that employers and unions should be left to resolve disputes and reach collective agreements voluntarily, without the existence of laws governing employee relations or the ability of one of the parties to a dispute to take the other to court. This contrasts with the 'normative approach' to employee relations, which insists that the best way to achieve order and stability in industrial relations is to have clear and binding laws that apply to all parties. Participants then know precisely what is expected of them (although possibilities for flexibility in negotiating agreements are lost). Advocates of the normative approach argue as follows:

(a) As well as employers and workers, the general public has an interest in the outcomes of industrial disputes. This interest may only be represented through elected governments and the legal system.

(b) Legally binding rules and ambiguities and uncertainties can encourage early resolution of conflicts.

(c) The law can be used to force unwilling parties into arbitration.

(d) Individual rights and civil liberties can be safeguarded where these might conflict with the objectives of one of the parties.

(e) Left to their own devices, managements and unions are not capable of self-regulation because market forces and the pursuit of self-interest will *inevitably* cause some participants to break the rules.

(f) Large corporations and unions with huge resources might be able to disrupt normal market mechanisms for determining wages (and hence prices) thus leading to consumer exploitation.

(g) The existence of legislation to control strikes makes striking more costly and risky for unions, hence inducing them not to call their members out on strike light-heartedly.

Arguments against involving the law in employee relations include:

(a) Few laws can be drafted so precisely that they apply to all situations. Industrial disputes are dynamic, circumstances change, legal sanctions might be imposed long after they have ceased to be relevant.

(b) Large numbers of otherwise law-abiding citizens might be involved in illegal industrial disputes. Attempts to arrest, try the cases of and fine or imprison each worker may be beyond the physical capacity of the police and judicial systems.

(c) Legal theory is arguably irrelevant to real-life problems of human relations at the workplace.

(d) Voluntarily signed agreements have greater force, long-run viability and a high likelihood of success.

(e) Negotiators subject to legal coercion may lose confidence in formal bargaining procedures and resort to other methods for achieving their aims.

In practice, it is rare for parties to industrial disputes to take legal action against each other because of the long-run bad feelings and disruptions it might provoke. Existing situations could be made worse, and all litigation is uncertain to some extent. Every dispute has to be settled eventually; legal intervention could hinder the effective resolution of a conflict.

THE STATE

2. Role of the state in employee relations

Apart from its role in enforcing laws, the state may become involved in employee relations in the following capacities:

(a) As the regulator (or deregulator) of labour markets, e.g. by establishing minimum wage levels or requiring that entrants to certain occupations possess particular qualifications.

(b) In the provision of job creation programmes for young workers or the long-term unemployed. This can depress wages, with consequent effects on industrial relations.

(c) As a major employer in its own right. Government incomes policies might be imposed on public sector workers, leaving the private sector nominally free of restriction but using government pay guidelines as an example to be followed by private firms. Also the state can apply equal opportunity policies, codes of practice, etc., to its own employees in order to demonstrate to the private sector how workers should be treated. Indeed, the state can act as a model of good employment practice, e.g. through:

- recognising trade unions and encouraging union membership
- paying above-average wages
- operating occupational pension schemes
- employing physically disabled workers

- implementing fair grievance procedures.

(d) As a participant in tripartite arrangements (*see* 2: **30**).

(e) In the provision of arbitration services to settle industrial disputes (ACAS, for example – *see* **4**).

3. State agencies

Most industrialised countries have government-sponsored conciliation and arbitration services which seek to achieve (among other things) the amicable settlement of industrial disputes. Intervention by an independent third party has a number of advantages:

(a) The staff of such bodies have wide-ranging experience of all sorts of industrial conflict and, in consequence, can often identify solutions, options and compromises that would not have been thought of by the parties involved in the dispute. Additionally, the staff will possess expert knowledge of the legal aspects of employee relations situations.

(b) Government-backed conciliation agencies have access to extensive ancillary services (research facilities, facts and figures on wage levels and terms and conditions of employment in specific industries, neutral premises for the conduct of negotiations, etc.) possibly not available to the disputants.

(c) Use of an independent conciliator enables both sides to claim that the resulting settlement is fair.

(d) Conciliation provides a 'last chance' to reach a compromise following an apparent breakdown in negotiations.

Arbitration, mediation and conciliation

Arbitration means the resolution of disputes via the appointment of independent referees who hear and adjudicate cases. Parties promise in advance to abide by the arbitrator's decision. Each side nominates potential arbitrators, and a mutually acceptable name is chosen. Mediation involves a third party informing each disputant of the other's views and requirements, without the disputants necessarily having to meet face-to-face. Where appropriate the mediator will suggest compromises and ways to reconcile divergent positions.

Conciliation is the use of a third party to act as a broker between disputes, advising each side of the other's feelings and suggesting possible compromise deals. In Britain, the state arbitration, mediation and conciliation service is known as ACAS, which stands for 'Advisory, Conciliation and Arbitration Service'.

4. ACAS

ACAS was founded in 1974 to improve UK industrial relations. The organisation is run by a council comprising a chairperson plus three people nominated by the Confederation of British Industry, three more nominated by the Trades Union

Congress, and a further three independent members. Its staff, who are all experienced in industrial relations, operate through nine geographical regions. ACAS seeks to discharge its responsibilities through the *voluntary* co-operation of managements, unions and complaining employees; it has no independent statutory powers to compel parties to behave in a certain manner. The activities of ACAS are as follows.

Conciliation

ACAS will conciliate an industrial dispute if requested to do so by one of the parties or by the government. Conciliation is voluntary and the eventual values of settlements are determined entirely by the parties to the dispute. Most ACAS conciliation concerns the determination of pay and other terms and conditions of employment.

Securing out-of-court settlements for individuals

All applications to industrial tribunals (*see* 5) involving cases of alleged unfair dismissal, race and sex discrimination, health and safety at work, etc., are automatically referred to ACAS, which tries to achieve out-of-court settlements. Ninety per cent of such referrals relate to unfair dismissal. Information given to ACAS is treated as totally confidential and cannot be used as evidence in an industrial tribunal without consent.

Advice

ACAS will give free advice to any employer, worker, staff association or trade union on any matter concerned with industrial relations or employment. Examples of the areas in which ACAS advice is available include:

- employment legislation, including the law on unfair dismissal, sex and race discrimination, equal pay, recruitment, selection and induction
- disciplinary, dismissal and redundancy procedures
- procedures for settling disputes and grievances
- employee consultation and participation agreements, trade union recognition and the disclosure of information to unions.

Additionally ACAS will provide low-cost help with matters relating to job evaluation, work organisation, ergonomics, motivation, management of change, job satisfaction and stress at work.

Arbitration

ACAS-appointed arbitrators will examine both sides of a dispute and recommend terms for a settlement. Arbitration will not be offered until ACAS is satisfied that all the firm's internal grievance and negotiating procedures have been exhausted. ACAS maintains a list of experienced arbitrators who can be called upon to arbitrate disputes. If ACAS cannot handle a particular case itself, it may refer the matter to another body – the Central Arbitration Committee (CAC) – which specialises in arbitration. Most members of the CAC are experienced union or employer's representatives and are frequently lawyers or academic experts in industrial relations.

Publication of codes of practice

The organisation publishes a number of codes of practice on employment matters. A code of practice is a document issued by a government agency, professional body, trade association or other relevant authority outlining model procedures for good practice in a particular field. Codes give examples of excellent and bad behaviour, and recommendations regarding how things should be done. ACAS codes are not legally binding but will be looked at by an industrial tribunal when determining the procedures that *should* have been followed. Conduct failing to meet standards set in an ACAS code will normally be deemed improper.

5. Industrial tribunals

These are special courts that hear cases concerning unfair dismissal, sexual or racial discrimination, or complaints registered under a variety of other employment regulations and statutes (including health and safety and equal pay legislation). A tribunal consists of three persons: two lay members (one from each side of industry – employers' organisations and trade unions) plus a legally qualified chairperson. Procedure in tribunals is meant to be informal relative to other courts (members wear ordinary clothes, not wigs and gowns), although in practice a large amount of legal jargon unfamiliar to the lay person is used. This is particularly noticeable when one party to a dispute is represented by a solicitor or barrister (or both) while the other is not.

Sometimes the question arises as to whether an industrial tribunal has the legal capacity to deal with a case (e.g. whether the relevant statute actually applies to the person initiating the action). Hence the tribunal will hold a preliminary hearing specifically to determine this matter. Also, the defendant may allege that the plaintiff has brought the case vexatiously – that it has no basis in law and is intended simply to cause annoyance to the other party. Here the tribunal will order a 'pre-hearing assessment' to establish the superficial facts of the case and, if appropriate, advise one of the disputants that it is not worth proceeding. Preliminary hearings, pre-hearing assessments and procedures in industrial tribunals generally are discussed in Chapter 11.

THE STATE AND THE EMPLOYMENT RELATIONSHIP

6. Immunity from legal action

Contracts of employment are *not* subject to the same rules as other contracts since, if they were, workers could never strike. A contract of employment obliges one person to work for another in exchange for a wage. By withdrawing labour, a worker is clearly in breach of that contract, and according to civil law would normally be liable for the financial losses incurred by the employer through the worker's breach. Generally, however, the law recognises the special nature of the employment relationship. In industrial society, work is necessary for survival. It is not an option to be selected or turned down. Thus, except in special circumstances, compensation for breach of contract during strikes is not available to employers. The parties to an industrial dispute are, with exceptions, immune from legal action in respect of breach of contract, conspiracy to terminate an employment contract, or inducing or threatening breach of contract. Note however that certain industrial actions such as general strikes, secondary actions (sympathy strikes for example), picketing of work-places, intimidation, etc., could result in the loss of immunity.

7. Trade disputes

For immunity to apply, the parties must be involved in a bona fide 'trade dispute'. Immunity is only available for disputes concerning terms and condi-tions of employment, dismissal, discipline, negotiation and consultation proce-dures, or other matters strictly related to workers' jobs. Secondary actions, political disputes, sympathy strikes, actions concerning the recognition of trade unions and actions not supported by a ballot of union members do not qualify for immunity.

Independent trade unions registered with the government certification officer (*see* 2: **4**) are exempt from civil liability in respect of damages suffered by employers and third parties during industrial disputes, provided the action is not directed against an employer whose employees are not involved in the dispute. Note that disputes among different groups of workers are not 'trade disputes'.

Unions have a strict legal duty to comply with the technical requirements of all statutes concerning employment, trade union behaviour and industrial rela-tions – on pain of losing their immunity from civil actions brought by employers and other interested parties. If union members do not adhere to statutory requirements the union must immediately, publicly and genuinely dissociate itself from the members' unlawful actions. Also, unions must be made liable for damages caused by unlawful industrial actions committed 'on their behalf' (i.e. endorsed by one of the union's executive committees or by a 'responsible' union officer). Liability could arise from secondary action, from seeking to bring about a closed shop, from actions not in furtherance of a trade dispute or from certain strikes not supported by a secret ballot. There is an upper limit on the maximum damages payable dependent on the size of the union.

8. Employers and employees

An 'employee' is a person engaged under a contract of employment who is not an independent contractor. To distinguish between 'employees' and 'inde-pendent contractors' a court will examine the nature and extent of the control exerted over the work, the degree of integration of the worker with the firm's overall operations, whether the worker determines his or her working hours, whether the person is provided with a uniform, tools or equipment, and whether he or she is subject to internal grievance and/or disciplinary procedures.

Employees have a common law duty (regardless of length of service) to provide work to their employers, to co-operate, to obey safe, reasonable and lawful commands, not to work for any other business during working hours, to respect the employer's trade secrets, and to take 'reasonable care' to protect the employer's property and interests.

'Employers' are persons or organisations responsible for deducting tax and social security contributions from workers' wages. Employers are vicariously liable for the wrong-doings of employees providing the wrongs are committed in the course of the worker's employment.

Vicarious liability

This is the legal rule that responsibility for an employee's breach of a statute or common law duty lies with the employing organisation and not with the employee him or herself, provided the latter was undertaking duties authorised by the employer or incidental to the employee's work.

Vicarious liability does *not* extend to criminal actions or to certain aspects of the Health and Safety at Work Act 1974 which states that any person acting in a managerial capacity may be held personally liable for offences committed against the Act if that person agreed, actively or passively, to the commission of the offence or if it was attributable to his or her neglect.

Legal obligations of employers

These include the duty to pay an employee's wages, to provide work, to take reasonable care to protect the employee, to indemnify the employee against losses sustained in consequence of performing his or her duties, and to treat the employee with reasonable courtesy. In the absence of a specific disclaimer in a worker's contract of employment he or she is entitled to expect these 'as of right'.

9. Contracts of employment

A contract of employment is an agreement whereby one party provides work in return for wages and / or other emoluments paid by the other. Contracts contain **(a)** *express* terms that precisely determine pay, hours of work, etc., **(b)** *implied* terms that arise from the nature of the relationship, custom and practice in a certain industry, and so on, and **(c)** terms required by statute, e.g. the require-ment that the employer provide safe and healthy working conditions. Implied terms cannot override statutory or express terms. A contract may be embodied in a letter of appointment, a written statement of terms, or in other documents (staff handbooks for example). Contracts of employment can be struck orally but have to be confirmed in writing within 8 weeks of starting work.

Employers may not change the terms of an employee's contract of employ-ment without the latter's consent. Unilateral changes imposed by an employer represent fundamental breaches of contract. Hence affected employees are entitled to assume they have been constructively dismissed (*see* 11: **6**).

10. Contracts for services

An important distinction exists between a contract *of* service and a contract *for* services. The former is a contract of employment under which a worker becomes an employee rather than an independent contractor. A contract for services, conversely, is a contract with an independent contractor (e.g. a company or self-employed individual) which is not a contract of employment. Independent contractors provide *ad hoc* services and are paid on invoice. There is no 'wage' and the commissioning business does not deduct tax or national insurance from the payment. Since independent contractors are not employees they cannot claim unfair dismissal, redundancy payments, statutory sick pay or other benefits available to employed workers.

Progress test 3

1. Define voluntarism

2. What is ACAS and what does it do?

3. What is an industrial tribunal?

4. Why are contracts of employment not subject to the same legal rules as other types of contract?

5. What is a 'trade dispute?

6. Explain the consequences of the doctrine of vicarious liability.

4

PUBLIC POLICY AND THE LABOUR MARKET

THE ROLE OF GOVERNMENT

1. The state as an employer

The government of any country is always a significant employer of labour in its own right as it is obliged to ensure the security of the nation, to uphold law and order and administer the system of justice, to run schools, colleges and hospitals, to operate a civil service, and to maintain essential services. Certain governments also become involved in the ownership and management of enterprises, although the last decade has witnessed the widespread privatisation of previously nationalised firms and industries throughout the world. As an employer, the state influences wage levels through affecting the demand for labour and (importantly) sets an example for private sector firms. Also the state can use its investment expenditures to help regulate the national economy. Arguments in favour of state enterprise are that:

- Workers might (but need not) receive a fairer deal than under private employers.
- A government's ability to finance its activities through taxation enables it to operate establishments for long periods, to create a stable environment and hence provide long-term job security.
- The exploitation of workers by private monopolies can be prevented.

Note, moreover, that profit-maximising private businesses are not attracted to industries which require large initial capital investments followed by relatively low-returns. Consequently, private firms might be prepared only to run the exceptionally lucrative parts of public utilities, neglecting low return activities to the detriment of society as a whole.

Disadvantages of public ownership include:

(a) Political interference in managerial decision-taking. On purely commercial grounds, some state-owned firms might need to be closed down. But the social consequences of closure – increased unemployment, loss of manufacturing skills, loss of export revenue, etc. – may cause governments to order them to continue producing at a loss.

51

(b) Large-scale production is not necessarily efficient. Indeed, complex administrative structures can cause big increases in production costs.

(c) Governments can exploit consumers as easily as private monopolies.

(d) State-owned firms that compete with private industry enjoy unfair advantages in their abilities to charge low state-subsidised prices and raise unlimited investment funds through government taxation.

2. Government macro-economic policies

All governments would claim to aspire to attaining four basic economic objectives:

- full employment
- a high rate of economic growth
- a low rate of inflation
- absence of a deficit in the country's balance of payments.

Certain governments would also include such targets as equality in the distribution of the nation's wealth, an even pattern of regional economic development, or making the country attractive to foreign investors – according to the political complexion of the government concerned. In relation to the four primary objectives, however, the essential problem is that economic policies which help achieve the first pair of aims (full employment and a high rate of growth) are usually damaging for the second pair. Expansionary measures such as low interest rates, tax cuts and increases in public spending stimulate the economy and create jobs, but also encourage **(a)** firms to raise their prices and **(b)** workers to demand higher wages (using the threat of industrial action in a labour shortage situation). Also, increased consumer expenditure leads to higher imports and a worsening of the country's balance of trade!

The policy-making problem, therefore, is how best to balance the effects of the policies needed to achieve the four objectives. Of course, the difficulty would be overcome if it were possible to have a separate and *independent* policy to deal with *each* objective in isolation. For example, interest rates could be varied to control inflation; public spending and/or tax rates could be altered to secure economic growth; tariffs, quotas and import controls could be applied to improve the balance of payments; and government make-work programmes and perhaps military conscription could be used to secure full employment. In the real world, however, democracies cannot impose draconian legislative controls (and it is by no means certain that the laws would be obeyed if they did), and international agreements (plus the threat of foreign retaliation) prohibit interference with the flow of foreign trade.

These dilemmas have a number of implications for the labour market, including:

(a) Rates of wage increase are a primary determinant of the level of inflation. In recognition of this, interventionist governments might resort to statutory incomes policies (*see* **14**) in attempts to obtain a separate and independent policy capable of dealing with inflationary pressure.

(b) Governments opposed to intervention and committed instead to the maintenance of a stable monetary environment might restrict the money supply (hence driving interest rates to very high levels) to such an extent that there is an extremely large amount of unemployment (with consequent effects on union membership and union capacities to take industrial action).

(c) Periods of government-induced economic expansion that lead to inflation and balance of payments deficits will need to be followed by deflationary policies which result in economic downturns. Hence 'stop-go' cycles of economic activity are generated, causing firms periodically to increase and decrease the sizes of their labour forces and making it difficult for them to offer security of employment to employees.

(d) Unions and their members may become highly politicised in consequence of their experience of government actions aimed at resolving the policy dilemma.

(e) State-induced economic contractions have an impact on the *quality* of labour as well as the number of people employed. Individuals who are out of work for very long periods may lose their self-respect and feel they are of no further use. This can result in loss of confidence in personal ability and hence a lack of the desire to return to employment. And the longer a person remains unemployed the less likely it is that he or she will ever work again.

THE LABOUR MARKET

Wage bargaining takes place against an economic background governed in most countries by the forces of supply and demand. The labour market comprises all the people seeking work and all the firms, government bodies and other organisations that require employees. Labour markets operate at regional, industry sector, national and (increasingly) international levels. There are sub-markets for various categories of occupation, skill, educational background and other employee characteristics and for different types of task.

Labour is bought and sold just like a physical good, its price being the worker's wage. Hence, wage levels in a market economy result ultimately from the forces of supply and demand.

3. Supply of labour

Labour is the mental or physical effort contributing to the output of goods or services. It is provided by human beings and because humans differ considerably there are many kinds of labour depending on workers' physical capacities, training and skill, innate abilities, attitudes and motivations, and so on. Labour supply is defined as that part of a country's adult population that is available for employment given the opportunity. Factors determining the *total* supply of labour in a country are as follows:

(a) The size of the population: birth rates, death rates, emigration and immigration.

(b) The proportion of the population that actually works, which depends on the age structure of the population, school-leaving and retirement ages, the numbers of working women, and occupational pension arrangements.

(c) The amount of work provided by each worker. This is determined by working habits, number of hours worked per week, the intensity of effort applied, the degree of job satisfaction experienced, and holiday entitlements.

Labour supply to a particular occupation is determined by:

- the length and degree of training necessary
- the kind of ability required and how many people possess this type of ability
- entry restrictions (age or sex barriers for example)
- the attractiveness of the work, whether it is interesting and / or offers career prospects
- the extent of labour mobility (*see* **6**)
- the wage offered, including overtime and bonus payments.

The quality of the labour supplied

This depends on the health and vitality of the workforce, education and training received, the ways in which work is organised, individual initiative, and (importantly) the calibre of the machines and equipment available to the worker.

Natural factors such as climate might also be relevant, as it is easier to work in temperate climates than in hot and humid conditions. Another consideration is that sometimes the quality of the *previous* generation of workers can affect the calibre of today's employees because skills and attitudes can be handed down from older to younger workers.

4. Demand for labour

The demand for labour is a derived demand, depending as it does on the number and types of people needed to produce and distribute goods. Factors influencing the demand for a particular company's products include the rate of growth of total consumer spending, the intensity of competition (including competition from imported goods), changes in tastes and fashion, and possibly seasonal variations in levels of purchases. All these factors affect the volumes and characteristics of a firm's production and hence the labour it needs to employ. Hence the demand for labour within a particular enterprise depends on the firm's competitive advantage within certain markets, and the selling prices of its products.

5. Operation of market forces

The conventional economic theory of wage determination (sometimes referred to as the 'neoclassical' approach) asserts that buyers of labour (employers) will demand small amounts of labour if the wage that has to be paid to labour is high, and large amounts of labour if the wage is low (preferring to use labour rather than capital intensive production methods in the latter situation). More workers will offer themselves for employment at a high wage, so the theory asserts, than at a low wage. If wages are 'too high' then there is 'excess supply' of labour, i.e. more workers will want to work than there are jobs available. Employers will realise this through their receiving very large numbers of applications from well qualified candidates whenever jobs are advertised, and by observing that competing firms paying lower wages are still able to attract good calibre workers. Hence, businesses will begin to reduce the wage at which they hire employees. Otherwise the firms paying excessively high wages will not be able to compete and will go out of business.

If, conversely, wages are 'too low', then a state of 'excess demand' for labour prevails. Firms will receive few applicants for vacant jobs and existing staff will resign and take better paid positions in other companies. Businesses will start offering higher wages as they bid for the labour necessary to maintain operations.

In the case of excess supply, the wage level will be driven downwards; for situations of excess demand the wage is pushed upwards. Eventually a point is reached where the demand for labour is just equal to the amount supplied. Here, the labour market is in balance ('equilibrium') and there is a stable market wage. Any deviation from this market equilibrium wage will trigger the forces previously outlined, which will return the wage to its equilibrium level.

6. Unemployment

Note how there can be no long-term unemployment in the neoclassical model, since any worker can get a job if he or she so wishes. If there is unemployment, a state of excess supply of labour is created. All the unemployed workers need to do is offer their services at a lower wage and firms (as profit-maximising units) will employ them. This means lower wages for everyone, but all workers have jobs. Any person who chooses not to work at the lower wage is, therefore, unemployed *voluntarily*. Hence, the only circumstances in which unemployment can occur are as follows:

(a) *As workers move between jobs*. At any moment in time there will be people who quit their jobs because they wish to change occupation, dislike their current employer, want to live in a different region, or have been laid off following the completion of an *ad hoc* project. This is known as *transitional* unemployment.

(b) *Where there are barriers to the operation of market forces*. The solution in this case, so advocates of the neoclassical theory assert, is for public policy to focus on the removal of the obstacles causing the difficulty. Examples of barriers that might prevent market forces restoring full employment include:

- *Lack of information among workers concerning vacancies* in various industries and regions. This problem might be solved via the provision of state-funded job-finding services and the encouragement of private-sector employment agencies.
- *Inadequate training and retraining facilities*, resulting in skills shortages in

some areas and industries and unemployment in others. Government-sponsored skills training programmes and facilities could help overcome this barrier.

- *Insufficient housing in certain areas.* The free-market solution to this difficulty is to leave firms to suffer the consequences of labour shortages in these regions, so that some of them will have no option but to relocate in places where labour of the type required is available. In the long term, moreover, the housing market should *itself* adjust in an appropriate manner, with more houses being built in the locations where there is greatest demand for accommodation.
- *Trade union activity.* The neoclassical model sees unions as a distorting influence on the free-market mechanism, as they enable groups of workers collectively to refuse to work at anything less than a wage considerably above the market equilibrium level.

Labour mobility

Labour can be mobile (or immobile) between industries, regions or different types of occupation. Factors determining the extent of geographical mobility include workers' family ties, the availability and costs of housing in the areas where there are jobs, whether there are schools and other amenities in these areas, etc. Occupational mobility depends, *inter alia*, on the calibre of the basic education received by workers, training and retraining facilities, employees' willingness to change career, and the transferability of occupational pensions.

Mobility is encouraged by the existence of differences in wage levels between regions and occupations.

7. Pay differentials

Some categories of labour contribute more value to an employer than others. Hence a separate labour market applies to each category, and different wage levels will apply to the various classes. Market forces will equalise the wage *within* each class, since if any job pays more than others of an identical nature then it will attract workers willing to undercut the artificially high current wage. The value to a firm of a category of labour could depend on:

- productivity levels
- the skills and training required to complete the work
- differences in the degree of responsibility attached to the jobs done by these people.

In a fair society, individuals should be able to choose how much to invest in themselves in terms of the number of years of education they undertake, the amount of training completed, acceptance of low wage jobs in order to gain experience, etc. However, not many people have the commitment or ability (or perhaps the opportunity) to make such investments, so there exists relative shortages of employees who possess high level skills, experience and occupational qualifications. Hence the wage rates of these individuals are driven upwards through market forces.

Pay differentials can also emerge from factors not directly related to differences in value added, for example:

- unemployment rates in various regions
- personal preferences for certain types of work, e.g. for a low-paid white collar job rather than lucrative employment in a factory, or a sense of vocation that impels people to work for abnormally low wages.

Wage differentials between men and women

In Britain (and most other western countries) there is a substantial difference between the average hourly pay of men and women, even though EU legislation forbids the payment of unequal wages for work of equal value. The following factors might help explain this phenomenon:

- Prejudice and unfair sex discrimination towards women.
- Women not working as much overtime (at premium rates) as men.
- Less training for higher paid jobs given to women than to men.
- Withdrawal of a certain proportion of women from the labour force in order to bear and rear children (which means that the average age of the female working population is lower than for men, and younger employees generally earn less money than older and more experienced workers).
- Concentration of female employees into part-time jobs that carry less responsibility than full-time positions.
- Lower levels of trade union membership among female employees.

Note, moreover, that to the extent that young females (or their parents) *expect* to have a limited working life they might be reluctant to invest in the training, education, etc., needed to obtain the qualifications for high grade work, so that low expectations become a self-fulfilling prophesy.

8. Effects of unionisation on wage rates

Collective bargaining can secure pay rises for workers, but the benefits will be short-lived in certain circumstances. If wages increase without a corresponding enhancement of productivity or reduction in the size of the labour force then the wage increase must be financed from profits. Economists use the term 'normal profit' to describe the situation where an employer is earning just enough profit to induce the employer to remain in business. Hence, unless the employer is initially making abnormal profits, wage increases in excess of productivity will cause the firm eventually to close down. Abnormal profits may derive from (a) uncompetitive market conditions (where the employer is a monopoly for instance) so that the business can charge an artificially high price, or (b) from the exploitation of labour in the sense that the wage paid is below the true value of workers' contributions to output. In competitive markets a union securing wage rises not backed by improved productivity will have to trade off higher wages against less employment for members.

Any increase in wages, moreover, leads to a decrease in the demand for labour. The extent of this decrease will depend on:

- how easily machines and equipment can be substituted for labour
- the proportion of wage costs to a firm's total costs
- whether the business can simply pass on the wage increase to end consumers via an increase in prices.

In most countries, it has been the case that unionisation has in fact led to higher wages for union members, due perhaps to two major reasons other than employers initially earning abnormal profits.

(a) Without a union, workers have to negotiate with employers individually. To an employer, the loss of the services of one or two workers in consequence of offering them inadequate wages is of little concern. For individual workers, however, unemployment can be a major catastrophe. Hence, in the absence of a union, a firm can play off one worker against another by offering successively inferior terms – relying on each person's fear of unemployment to make them accept lower wages.

(b) Even in highly competitive conditions, long periods may elapse before a shortage of labour in a certain region or occupational field results in higher wages because of lack of information to workers and labour immobility (*see* **6**). Unions are quick to seize the initiative in labour shortage situations.

If *all* workers belong to a union then the union itself becomes the single supplier of labour and thus enjoys monopoly power. This partly explains employers' opposition to 'closed shops' (unlawful in most countries) whereby unions withdraw their labour if a firm employs a non-union member. (Closed shops are also opposed on moral grounds as they interfere with individual freedom not to join a union.) Further criticisms of trade unions implicit in the neoclassical model are that union action:

- can inhibit the use of profitable new equipment through opposing the introduction of new technology, leading to business failures and higher unemployment in the longer term
- causes the equalisation of wages across occupations and industry sections so that individuals are not given the incentives necessary to induce them to obtain the training, skills and qualifications for higher grade work (the wage for which is not much above that for less skilled jobs due to union activity)
- reduces labour mobility (*see* **6**) and hence the market's ability to correctly adjust wages
- encourages demarcations between jobs and occupations thus preventing the application of flexible working practices.

The implication of these problems is clear, according to the neoclassical model: governments should impose binding rules which restrict the extent of union organisation and activity.

9. The case for free markets

Advocates of free markets argue that *laissez-faire* government policies will in normal circumstances guarantee the attainment of a just and equitable society.

Business people, they argue, are in business to maximise their profits, not to make moral judgement about others; thus, through constantly seeking to improve profitability, firms – according to this argument – will increase not only their own returns but also the wealth of society as a whole. In a market economy, prices determine what goods firms want to produce, production costs and the availability of resources determine how they are produced (and the incomes that factor inputs shall receive), while consumer spending determines the market prices which themselves generate production. Goods that are most wanted by consumers command the highest prices. Thus, firms will consciously seek to satisfy consumer demands, and will supply the quantity and types of labour needed to meet this requirement.

Concerns for the environment, social justice, etc., are treated in much the same way as demands for particular goods. For example, it is assumed that if people want the environment to possess certain characteristics they will pay for those characteristics, and organisations will naturally spring up that (in return for payment) will seek to manipulate the environment to satisfy the public's desires. Social considerations, they argue, need not concern individual firms. Managers are not trained or competent in social work, and business is not part of the social security system.

10. The case against free markets

The opposing view asserts that state intervention is essential for ensuring that firms do not behave in irresponsible and socially damaging ways. Large businesses possess enormous economic and – by implication – social power. They can manipulate communities and appropriate for themselves revenues far in excess of those justified by their contributions to the wider society. Firms are able to initiate social change, and it is reasonable therefore that society, through its elected representatives, determine the direction that change should take. Businesses, moreover, are components of a wider economic, social and legal system. As social organisations, they must necessarily be concerned with social issues – education and training, occupational health and safety, incomes and employment, labour relations, equal opportunities and so on. Thus, some managerial prerogatives must be surrendered for the common good. Specific criticisms of the neoclassical model (which is based *essentially* on the free market philosophy) are discussed below.

11. Criticisms of the neoclassical model

The neoclassical model provides a logical and consistent framework for analysing labour market issues, even though its predictions may not be valid. It offers a set of benchmarks against which reality may be compared and, in consequence, furnishes a convenient starting point for the discussion of problems and alternative approaches. Arguably, moreover, it is correct in its *general outline* if not in specific detail.

Nevertheless, the neoclassical theory has attracted a great deal of criticism. The theory that, left to themselves, labour markets will automatically clear and that there will be no involuntary unemployment rests on the assumption that adjustments occur quickly and do not themselves have damaging consequences. Experience suggests that this is not true. If there is high unemployment, the time needed for wages to fall to levels where they do in fact cause firms to hire significant additional labour might be *decades* rather than months or years, and during this period the entire kaleidoscope of national economic activity will have altered (as well perhaps as the political consequences of long-term recession). High unemployment for long periods reduces the total value of consumer spending and causes fewer goods to be produced leading to even more unemployment and lack of consumer demand. Further objections to the neoclassical model are:

(a) To the extent that it is rational for firms and individuals to maximise their returns in a competitive market situation, it is equally rational for firms and individuals to ensure their prosperity by deliberately distorting and/or undermining market mechanisms. Thus, workers will *of course* want to combine in order to raise wages to the highest possible level, while businesses will *naturally* want to create monopoly situations.

(b) Workers cannot retrain themselves; they have to rely on employers to provide the necessary instruction. But the *individual* employer has no incentive to provide (expensive) training because the employees concerned could then be poached by other firms. Hence, no training occurs whatsoever so that technical change leads to widespread permanent unemployment.

(c) Firms and unions can collude to inhibit individuals from negotiating their own remunerations at market levels.

(d) Human behaviour may only be understood in relation to individual *feelings* about particular institutions. People might be attracted to engage in collective action because they enjoy being part of a crowd, experience a sense of excitement when involved in confrontations with employers, etc., quite independent of economic considerations.

(e) The model has little to say about the quality of working life, focusing predominantly on physical output and the level of employment. This can be especially significant in relation to employee health and safety.

(f) Neoclassical analysis, so critics allege, is obsessed with the study of minor problems and small changes *within* the system, refusing to acknowledge the possibility that alternative approaches might be valid and that the fundamental environments and realities of economic and working life are liable to shift periodically.

(g) Implicitly, the model assumes harmonious social relations within the community. It ignores 'class struggle', the influences of political extremism, etc.

(h) Humans have a free will and need not actually behave in the manner predicted by an economic theory. They do not *necessarily* respond to changes in wage rates and other supply and demand factors in the manners posited in **10**. For the neoclassical model to work, individuals must weigh up the advantages of being in employment against the desire for leisure and act accordingly. This may not happen.

(i) The pace of technological change is today so rapid and the effects of the new technologies on employment so far-reaching that long-term unemployment for large numbers of people is seemingly inevitable. It is simply not possible to re-educate, retrain and relocate the entire workforce of a huge industry that collapses in consequence of the introduction of a competing new technology.

These (and other) problems have led a number of analysts to advocate direct government intervention in labour markets. An interventionist approach could involve, *inter alia*:

- forecasting future labour supply and demand at the national level and initiating state-funded training programmes designed to overcome skills shortages
- public investments intended to create employment in certain regions
- government subsidy of various industries
- incomes policies (*see* **14**)
- minimum wage legislation
- tripartism (*see* 2: **30**)
- legislation to protect workers' terms and conditions of employment and to provide employees with redress for unfair dismissal, discrimination, etc.

12. Advantages and disadvantages of interventionism

The *advantages* claimed for interventionist approaches are:

(a) With intervention, employment levels are not dependent on the whims of the market (which can behave in a highly erratic fashion) but rather on a systematic national economic plan that takes into account the needs of *all* sections of society. Economic growth can be stimulated, leading to low rates of unemployment in the long run.

(b) The dignity of labour is recognised. Workers are regarded at the national level as genuine social partners and not merely as another means for producing output.

(c) Environmentally damaging and other anti-social consequences of free-market activities can be avoided.

(d) The state can promote equality of income distribution among the population.

(e) National resources may be directed towards social ends, with social justice and fair living standards for all.

Problems with extensive government intervention include the possibilities that it might:

- put important economic decisions affecting the welfare of millions of people into the hands of a small number of incompetent bureaucrats

- create inefficiencies and overmanning throughout the economy
- cause industries to be inflexible and highly resistant to change (since the profit motive which frequently impels the introduction of new technologies and methods is artificially constrained)
- distort the pattern of competition and give unfair advantages to certain enterprises, industries and employee groups
- restrict personal freedom
- make a country internationally uncompetitive.

Note, moreover, that when governments commit errors the errors they commit are on a grand scale; large numbers of people are likely to suffer following the implementation of an ill-considered policy. A dramatic example of state intervention in labour markets is a government incomes policy.

13. Government incomes policies

These comprise laws or government exhortations which seek to restrict workers' pay rises, typically through establishing a 'norm' for the level of wage increase to be paid in a given period. The aims of incomes policies are:

- to reduce the rate of inflation and hence interrupt a wage–price spiral (i.e. workers demanding higher and higher pay increases to compensate for rising prices caused by firms having to cover their expanding wages bills)
- to prevent powerful unions in key industrial sectors from using their strength unfairly to boost members' pay packets at the expense of the consumer
- to link pay to productivity and/or to redistribute national income towards the lower paid.

Policies can be **(a)** 'flat rate', whereby every employee is only allowed a pay rise of a certain specific monetary amount (usually expressed as so many pounds per week), **(b)** percentage based, so that no worker may receive more than a stated annual percentage pay increase (e.g. 4 per cent per annum), or **(c)** productivity related. In the latter case, firms must demonstrate that their workforces have increased their outputs in line with any pay rises awarded above the norm. Flat rate policies benefit lower paid workers as, over time, pay differentials between lower and higher paid employees are narrowed.

Advantages of incomes policies

Arguments in favour of government incomes policies include:

(a) Unions and large employers, especially those in industries where there is little business competition, can negotiate and agree wage settlements so high that they are not in the national interest. These awards act as an example for employees in the remainder of the economy, which might not be able to afford such high settlements.

(b) Low-paid workers can be allowed higher wage increases than other employees, thus helping to relieve poverty among the very low paid. Note how low-paid workers typically have weak bargaining powers.

(c) General economic planning is facilitated, as the annual increase in the country's total wage bill can be predicted in advance. Unions and employers' associations become involved in the national economic planning process.

(d) The entire labour force is made aware of the country's need to increase its productivity and to exercise moderation when demanding wage rises.

Problems with incomes policies

In practice, incomes policies are frequently ineffectual. They work in the short term, temporarily slowing down the wage–price spiral, but are followed by very high wage increases as soon as the statutory element of the policy is removed. Specific problems with government incomes policies are:

(a) They distort the market mechanisms that otherwise would determine wage and price levels. This could result in an inefficient allocation of resources within the economy.

(b) Incomes policies cannot be applied to the self-employed and are extremely difficult to apply to professional and managerial employees, who typically take a significant proportion of their total remuneration in the form of fringe benefits.

(c) The policing of incomes policies is difficult. Firms might give their workers pay rises without declaring this to the authorities, or circumvent the legislation by 'regrading' large numbers of employees into higher paid jobs, allocating new job titles to individual workers, 'promoting' people, etc.

(d) The norm specified in the policy (i.e. the permitted annual increase) becomes a benchmark for *everyone*, including those groups of workers which otherwise could be asking for pay rises *below* the norm.

(e) Productivity-related incomes policies require the measurement of increases in output. This can be extremely difficult in certain industries, especially in the service sector.

(f) Determination of the norm may be arbitrary. Why, for example, should a norm of 3 per cent per annum be selected rather than 3½ per cent? The norm has to relate to the rate of inflation, but this is not known in advance and itself depends on a wide range of factors (including foreign events).

(g) There will always be 'special cases' to which it would be unfair to apply the policy. Unfortunately, more groups will claim to be special cases than can be objectively justified. Allowing certain groups extra pay rises causes resentments in other areas.

(h) Workers will be reluctant to accept curbs on wages if firms' profits and dividend payments are not controlled in a similar fashion. Even if dividends are statutorily restricted, accumulated profits still represent increased wealth for shareholders and will be reflected in higher share prices.

14. A statutory minimum wage

Many countries have laws that guarantee workers a national minimum wage. Such laws have the following objectives:

- to relieve poverty among low-paid employees
- to protect workers in non-unionised industries and occupations
- to boost the economy by ensuring that large numbers of people have significant disposable incomes (poor people typically spend all their earnings, hence increasing aggregate consumer expenditure)
- to encourage firms to increase productivity in order to compensate for having to pay higher wages.

Also, by introducing a statutory minimum wage, the government of the country openly declares its concern for less advantaged members and for human dignity.

Arguments *against* a legal minimum wage are that:

- It will increase unemployment as firms find it increasingly uneconomic to hire certain categories of labour.
- Higher paid skilled workers who acquired their skills by undergoing training that involved an income sacrifice might resent the loss of their differentials. This could reduce the incentive to undertake training, eventually leading to skills shortages.
- Poverty should be dealt with via the social security system, not by penalising employers and distorting normal market systems.
- Policing and enforcement are extremely difficult. Workers being paid below the statutory minimum might not report their employers for fear of losing their jobs.
- Higher paid workers will insist on maintaining their differentials, causing higher wage bills for firms throughout the economy and hence increasing unemployment.

Arguably, statutory minimum wage rates hurt most severely the groups they are intended to help, i.e. the unskilled, old, young and ethnic minority workers because these are the groups with the highest rates of unemployment in the first instance.

Progress test 4

1. State the basic objectives of government economic policy.

2. What is 'labour'?

3. List the main determinants of the demand for labour.

4. Why can there be no voluntary unemployment in the neo-classical economic model?

5. Define 'interventionism' and state four advantages of the interventionist approach.

6. What are the main objectives of a statutory minimum wage?

Part Two

EMPLOYEE RELATIONS IN PRACTICE

5

EMPLOYEE COMMUNICATION

THE CHALLENGE OF COMMUNICATION

1. Need for employee communication

The need to transmit and receive information is common to all organisations. Management has to pass instructions to the workforce, to explain its policies and objectives, and to tell workers if their jobs are threatened. Specific needs for downwards communication from management to employees relate to such matters as:

- how and when work is to be completed
- employees' duties and obligations
- management's plans and intentions
- changes in organisation structure
- health and safety procedures
- performance standards and company objectives.

Employees need to communicate with management in relation to:

- queries regarding management's instructions and stated intentions
- whether they are able to complete their work effectively, given the resources available
- suggestions for improving working methods and processes
- problems experienced at work.

Sound employee communications are essential for the smooth running of an enterprise for a number of reasons:

(a) Individuals need to be able to behave and take decisions in accordance with company policy. Effective co-ordination of the firm's activities is impossible without good management/employee communications.

(b) Change can only be implemented successfully if the reasons for the change plus its implications for workers are communicated to and accepted by the people likely to be affected.

(c) Employees' basic perceptions of their work and of the company are substantially determined by the quality of its employee communications.

(d) Workers have the chance to respond to communications from management by providing the latter with valuable feedback.

It is important to realise nevertheless that improved communications cannot solve every conceivable employee relations difficulty. Fundamental conflicts of interest need to be resolved by negotiation, not just an increase in the flow of communication. Particularly damaging to the credibility of the employee communication process is management implementing a 'communication blitz' during a crisis situation that requires workers' help and co-operation, followed by complete silence as soon as conditions improve.

2. Costs of bad communication

Inadequate employee communication can impose a number of costs on a company, including:

- bad decision-making consequent to individuals not receiving the correct information
- misunderstandings among sections leading to costly mistakes
- incorrect perceptions of company and personal objectives
- the possible emergence of grapevines (*see* **6**)
- conflicts and industrial disputes resulting from misunderstandings (as opposed to irreconcilable divergences of views)
- lack of employee commitment to the employing organisation
- poorer quality output in consequence of workers not understanding the importance of their role in the quality management process
- employee resistance to change and the possible development of 'them and us' attitudes
- non-implementation of plans and policies
- inconsistent activities and lack of co-ordination.

Note, moreover, that a management's failure to communicate with workers may be interpreted by the latter as management not regarding them as people worthy or capable of receiving and understanding information.

3. One-way and two-way communication

One-way communication (which does not involve any feedback from the recipient) is appropriate for topics that are routine, straightforward and uncontroversial. However, one-way communication is *not* adequate for matters affecting employee welfare or that concern issues about which employees can express useful opinions. Two-way communication (which gives the recipient(s) an opportunity to respond and react) is time-consuming and demands patience and personal skill, but should be used for subjects which are complicated, unexpected, of personal concern to the receivers, or involve matters about which they could make a worthwhile contribution. A better decision may be reached, and it will be accepted more readily.

Autocratic one-way communication is particularly unsuitable for IT-driven computerised workplaces where important decisions have to be taken by lower echelons and where objectives are not attainable without the active *commitment* of employees.

4. Communication problems

Special problems with management/worker communication in employee relations situations are:

(a) Communicators often have ulterior motives when devising and transmitting messages, which frequently express opinions and attitudes as well as facts. Frequently, the purpose of the communication is to persuade and influence as well as to inform.

(b) Many important items of information are transmitted orally rather than in formal written terms.

(c) Recipients of messages may deliberately choose not to understand them and/or to deny they were ever transmitted in the first instance.

Barriers to communication are discussed in 1: **10**.

5. Communication channels

Media for transferring messages include:

- letters and memoranda
- face-to-face oral communication
- telephone conversations
- conferences, committees and meetings
- manuals, employee handbooks, pamphlets
- posters and noticeboards
- house journals.

All these are formal in character, but informal channels are important as well. In particular, the so called 'grapevine' can be a primary medium for the distribution of information.

6. The grapevine

The grapevine is an unofficial, loose collection of communication passages that circumvent and sometimes even replace orthodox communication procedures. Grapevines are common where employees know each other well and exchange information casually without the knowledge or permission of higher authority. They will be particularly virulent if senior management deliberately withholds information that affects employees' welfare. Hence, rumours concerning possible redundancies, confidential personal matters, gossip or scandal will be quickly and widely dispersed through the grapevine system. Although the grapevine is strictly unofficial, people holding key positions within it (namely those who spread the most information) may find that their status in the official system is enhanced because of their grapevine activities.

Although grapevines can sometimes be suppressed through management providing clear, accurate and comprehensive information to employees, certain managements consciously decide to allow a grapevine to survive because it provides a fast and effective means of distributing news. Also, views which management might not want to be made known officially can be made known through the grapevine. The obvious disadvantages of the grapevine system are its tendency to distort reality, and that it can be used maliciously to initiate unsavoury rumours. Even without deliberate malice, grapevines frequently misrepresent issues because the facts behind situations are exaggerated or otherwise altered at each stage in the dissemination process. There is no mechanism for checking the validity of the information transmitted, or for refusing falsehoods.

EMPLOYEE COMMUNICATION MANAGEMENT

People in organisations devote enormous amounts of (expensive) time to communicating with each other, and it is thus essential that communications be conducted in as efficient a manner as possible. Careful attention must be devoted to the questions of *what* and *when* to communicate, *how* to communicate, and *with whom* to communicate, as discussed below. Another important decision is the determination of who is to be mainly responsible for the employee communication function. The possibilities include the personnel department, a public relations manager, line executives, or workplace supervisors. The modern approach is perhaps to shift most of the responsibility for management/worker communications onto first-line managers, who then communicate information to workers on a face-to-face basis.

7. Policies for employee communication

What to communicate depends on management's communication objectives. Does it want to persuade employees to accept a technical change, relate to unions in a particular manner, identify more closely with the company, or some other aim? Specific managerial objectives regarding communication with employees are likely to include:

- encouraging workers to support the aims of the enterprise
- transmitting instructions clearly and in a manner that maximises the likelihood of their being properly carried out
- receiving prompt and accurate feedback.

How and when to communicate will be determined by the amount of information to be communicated and the media available for the process. Media can be written or oral. Written media (*see* 8: **21**) include company handbooks and magazines, newsletters and bulletins posted on noticeboards. Oral media comprise team briefings (*see* **14–16** below), works councils (*see* 6: **14–17**), and joint consultation (*see* 6: **9**). Whichever method is selected it needs to:

- be suitable for and relate to the people receiving the communication
- provide information on important events soon after they have occurred
- be reinforced by management *action*

- be clear and precise
- generate feedback so that communications are genuinely two-way
- inform employees about the matters that concern them most, e.g. planned alterations in company structure or working methods, new payment arrangements or grading systems, overtime requirements, etc.

Typically, an effective system for communicating with employees will involve a mixture of formal and informal channels. Policies for improving the efficiency of management/employee communication include:

- regular communication audits designed to identify communication needs and discover new ways to improve the flow of information
- providing managers with training in communication skills
- developing new systems for canvassing employees' opinions and views.

With whom to communicate

Communication of every piece of information that might be relevant to employees is not feasible, otherwise the firm would devote all its time and energy and resources to transmitting messages, most of which were of little practical use. Thus, choices have to be made.

Correct selection of recipient is also important. An appropriate choice of message recipient will result in an unbroken chain of command. All instructions issued during normal operations will be carried out because those responsible for their implementation will know precisely what they have to do.

EMPLOYEE COMMUNICATION METHODS AND MEDIA

8. Company handbooks

Large enterprises sometimes produce company handbooks/manuals in order to consolidate between two covers a wide range of information of potential interest to employees, plus information that the employer is legally obliged to disclose to its workforce. In Britain the latter includes details of the firm's grievance procedure (if it has one) and its health and safety policy statement. A company handbook provides:

- a handy reference in which employees can look up information they only need infrequently
- a means for enhancing a firm's corporate image in the eyes of its employees
- a convenient location for a written statement of disciplinary rules
- something to discuss during induction programmes for new employees
- an excellent medium for outlining the background to the company, its mission, products, markets, scope of operations and future prospects, an organisation chart and details of senior management.

Further information that could be included are the company's equal opportunities policy, payments methods, availability of welfare services (counselling, crisis loans, etc.), superannuation, the unions recognised for collective bargaining, social club facilities, health and safety information, and so on. Many company hand-books are printed in loose-leaf format so that information can be periodically updated and new sections added as circumstances change.

Advantages to company handbooks are that they:

- can be comprehensive in their coverage of everything the employee needs to know about the firm
- contain clear and (importantly) *written* statements of the business's person-nel and other policies.

A major problem with company manuals is that their subject matter is often extremely boring to the employees who are expected to read them. Accordingly, only that information which is strictly necessary should be included, and it must be presented in the most attractive way possible. Rules and regulations need to be crystal clear, and a convincing explanation of *why* they are necessary should be provided. Generally, the shorter a company manual the better.

9. Company newspapers

Publication of a company newspaper establishes a direct line of communication from the board room to the shop floor and, although they are thrown away unread by many workers, people who are genuinely interested in company affairs are given the opportunity to learn about current developments. They provide a *regular* and systematic medium for transmitting information. Also, routine (though somewhat boring) information can be interspersed with cross-word puzzles, humorous items, 'for sale' advertisements, etc., in order to make the newspaper more readable.

The *disadvantages* of company newspapers include:

- their high production costs (staffing, printing, distribution, etc.)
- possibilities of their being used in attempts to bypass trade unions through making direct appeals to employees to support certain management deci-sions opposed by unions
- situations arising where employees who should already have been in-formed about a certain issue find out about it only when they open the company newspaper!

Role of the editor

A company newspaper will not survive unless it has an enthusiastic editor who is able and prepared **(a)** to chase up various individuals and departments for their contributions, **(b)** to deal with unforeseen production difficulties, and **(c)** personally to write large amounts of material. Further problems can arise over the question of editorial freedom. On the one hand, it is obvious that a publica-tion will soon lose credibility if it contains nothing more than managerial announcements and exhortations to employees to work harder. Equally how-ever, it is unreasonable to suppose that management will allow a company newspaper to be used as a vehicle for propagating hostile anti-company views. The difficulty is especially severe in relation to contentious employee relations situations whereby a published statement by management or a trade union will immediately cause the other side to demand the right to reply. A possible solution is for the publication to devote equal amounts of space to both parties and then invite readers' comments, reproducing the latter in strict proportion to the numbers of comments offered in support of or in opposition to the subject of the dispute.

Newsletters

Company newspapers are expensive to print, especially when print runs are small. Hence, some firms circulate instead desktop published newsletters to their workers. These appear more frequently than house magazines and are less formal in style, concentrating on 'chatty' items – often of a personal nature. Whatever its format, the publication needs to look readable, with an attractive masthead that fits in with the firm's corporate identity and an interesting lead story on the cover page.

Advantages of newsletters include their ease of production, parochial contents, and capacity to transmit large amounts of quite detailed information (far more than a video presentation for example).

10. House magazines

These can fulfil a dual function, acting as an external public relations medium as well as a means for communicating with employees. Their *purposes* are:

- to explain new developments and the achievements of the company
- to encourage feelings of loyalty towards the company among its workers
- to give individual employees an opportunity to contribute features and items of news
- to outline future plans.

Problems with house magazines are that:

- They are not suitable for communicating information about operational difficulties and other bad news.
- The glossy appearance of a house magazine can create the impression that it represents little more than a superficial public relations exercise.
- Employees might not take such publications seriously, discarding them without even looking at their contents.
- Employees' contributions are liable to be censored, leading to disillusion among those who bother to send in opinions and news.
- It might not be possible to fill every issue with interesting items, requiring the editor to 'pad out' certain editions with meaningless waffle.
- High calibre editors (normally company employees) are hard to find.

Magazines are obviously more expensive to produce than newspapers, but **(a)** they provide a vastly superior quality of reproduction (especially for photographs) than is possible in a company newspaper, and **(b)** can be issued at lengthy intervals (once every four or six months for example).

11. Noticeboards

These can be used to transmit news immediately and are suitable therefore for communicating information that cannot wait for insertion in a newsletter or other periodic written media. Information posted on a noticeboard might be confirmed in a more permanent form at a later date. Displays need to be attractive and catch the attention of passers-by. The great advantage of noticeboards is that they are a virtually costless means for transmitting information. They can be used to disseminate 'red hot news' (e.g. the outcome to current management/union pay negotiations) as there are no time delays resulting from elaborate printing or distribution arrangements. Problems with noticeboards are that they are frequently ignored, and tend to become cluttered up with out-of-date material.

Notices in pay packets

These are a low-cost means for communicating with workers (who have to be given payslips in any event so that there is little additional effort in including an additional document). Their main advantage is that they will almost certainly be looked at because nearly everyone opens their pay packet. Such notices are perhaps best used only on occasion (to announce a really important occurrence) since otherwise workers may come to regard all documents in pay packets other than the pay-slip as meaningless management propaganda.

12. Employee reports

Large public companies sometimes issue annual reports analogous to (but generally simpler than) those sent to shareholders outlining the business's performance over the last financial year and its basic competitive position. The *advantages* to the practice are that:

- It is better for employees to learn about these matters directly from management than from press reports following the publication of the company's accounts.
- Such reports demonstrate management's concern for its workers.

Problems are that the report may present a grossly oversimplified view of the firm's affairs, it might appear patronising, and it may be ignored by the overwhelming majority of the firm's workers. Also the figures given might be misinterpreted by employees (e.g. by concluding that profits available for distribution are more substantial than is actually the case, given the need for new investment).

13. Audio visual employee communication

Slides and videos are increasingly used by large companies for employee communication.

Slide shows

Slides can be made quickly and easily and (importantly) a range of slides can be prepared from which an appropriate combination may be selected to meet the specific needs of particular audiences. The problem, perhaps, is the need to train managers in the skills of slide show presentation, since slides and verbal remarks must be carefully synchronised.

Videos

Videos should be interesting to watch and not last too long (not more than about 20 minutes in normal circumstances). Whereas an employee can quickly discard a company magazine or other written communication, he or she is compelled to sit through an entire showing of a video. Thus the video should be entertaining and focus on matters that workers *want* to know about as well as on information that is technically necessary. The *advantages* to preparing and using a video for employee communication are that:

- Workers relate to video presentations because they are accustomed to watching TV at home.
- The combination of sight, sound and movement enables the *demonstration* of things (safety procedures for example).
- They usually have a more dramatic impact than other options.
- Videos can be used to reinforce messages transmitted by other means.
- They are invaluable when a large proportion of the workforce is not very competent at reading.
- A video can include filmed statements by senior managers who cannot attend in person.

The main *disadvantage* is that of cost, since videos need to be well-produced if they are to be credible. Further problems with the use of video are:

(a) Workers might fail to concentrate during the presentation.

(b) Videos cannot be instantly altered to satisfy immediate local requirements (including differences in the audiences watching the presentation).

(c) Videos (and slide shows) need to be watched in darkened rooms which employees may find sleep inducing.

(d) The audience cannot ask questions of a video cassette.

TEAM BRIEFINGS

Oral communication can be more effective than written documents, as it is generally more natural and informal. The pace and tone of the communication can be varied in response to audience reactions to the speaker's remarks, and much more ground can be covered in a short period than when using written remarks.

14. Purposes of team briefings

Briefing sessions can occur at periodic intervals (monthly or fortnightly for instance), or on a daily basis (with each session lasting just a few minutes). The *advantages* of the latter approach are that it:

- is a quick and convenient method of communication
- relates immediately to the workplace situation
- creates a bond between the supervisor and other members of the team
- can integrate fresh ideas for improving quality and productivity with more mundane matters concerning work distribution, training plans, company news, etc.

In longer briefing sessions carried out at (say) monthly intervals, the manager conducting the briefing needs to be concerned not only with imparting information but also with inculcating in employees feelings of participation, security and involvement with the firm. Briefing sessions give managers the opportunity to explain company policy and the implications of recent events.

Unfortunately, managers sometimes err in calling these meetings only when crises arise. Rather they should occur regularly and not just when things go wrong. Sessions should be short and offer:

- brief reviews of progress to date
- the manager's opinions on contemporary problems
- outline proposals (with justifications) for future activities.

Suitable topics for briefing sessions include suggested changes in working arrangements, staff transfers and promotions, results of implementation of new methods, details of available welfare and recreational facilities, and examples of how efficiency has been improved in other departments.

15. Conditions for success

To succeed, briefing groups need to cover *all* levels of the organisation (not just lower grade employees) and to be led by trained and competent people. Restriction of briefing groups to workplace operatives might cause workers to feel that they are being manipulated to make them accept worsening conditions of work. Each session needs to focus on a central theme, should last for no longer than half an hour, and involve no more than 20 people. Employees should be briefed on major company events within two or three days of their occurrence. The information transmitted needs to be relevant to workers' jobs and understandable.

16. Advantages and disadvantages of team briefings

Briefings are normally conducted by line managers (i.e. executives with the authority to take and implement decisions) who thereby disseminate information from the apex of the organisation to its base. Hence, line managers become the major source of information concerning company affairs. This reinforces their authority and helps create a bond between the manager and his or her team. Further *advantages* are that:

- Employees develop wider perspectives on the significance of their work.
- Briefings help prevent the emergence of grapevines (*see* **6**).
- There is face-to-face contact between management and the workforce.

- The information transmitted is necessarily kept short, forcing management to highlight the really important issues.

Problems with team briefings are:

(a) Concrete improvements in performance will rarely occur immediately, leading perhaps to a decline in management interest in the idea in the medium term.

(b) There might not be enough interesting items of company information to pass on during a scheduled briefing session, resulting in its cancellation (with consequent disillusion with the entire process) or in managers 'waffling' during the session and filling out the allotted period with meaningless information.

(c) Administration of a briefing group requires the time-consuming preparation of information, short stoppages of work while the briefing is in progress, expenditures on training for group leaders, etc. This might not be cost-effective if apathy prevails during meetings and no concrete benefits emerge from them. Training costs will be substantial, as the training involved needs to encompass public speaking, the organisation and running of meetings, persuasive skills, motivation, listening and counselling.

(d) Line managers are not necessarily good public speakers. Even with training they might be hesitant, nervous and inarticulate. If so then team members will neither hear nor understand what is being said, and will quickly lose interest in the exercise. A line manager might be particularly inept at answering awkward questions.

(e) There is rarely enough time within a briefing session for any genuinely meaningful dialogue or discussion.

(f) Simply because workers are informed of decisions does not mean they will agree with or accept them.

(g) Trade unions might oppose team briefings on the grounds that through establishing direct communications between management and labour they undermine union authority. Also, briefings can be used to circumvent orthodox joint consultation and collective bargaining procedures.

17. Management by walking around

Objective setting, appraisal, accountability systems, etc., are fine for establishing procedures and monitoring progress, but too often they fail to provide the detailed and accurate information on day-to-day operations and (most important) on staff morale necessary for effective control. Management by walking around (MBWA) is a simple solution to the problem of gathering information about actual behaviour within an organisation. The manager looks and listens, talks to employees and becomes personally involved with happenings at the workplace level. More specifically, MBWA concerns:

- reviewing and appraising sources of information
- looking for new and better contacts

- learning how people (senior managers as well as junior employees) *feel* about the organisation and each other
- finding out how the staff perceive customers, and assessing whether they recognise a personal responsibility for customer care.

MBWA brings managers into daily contact with quality and productivity problems. Managers observe at first hand which jobs are easy and which difficult. Further *advantages* of MBWA are that managers cannot avoid recognising employees' difficulties; that it provides valuable feedback on the success of recently introduced equipment and methods; that it demonstrates management's commitment to genuine employee communication; and that it is likely to result in actual changes designed to overcome workers' problems. It is especially useful for obtaining the 'gut reactions' of employees to management's proposals.

Visits should not be at fixed times or dates, or employees might 'prepare' for the visit so that an unrepresentative impression is generated. The system should operate at all levels within the organisation and a variety of managers need to be involved – not just a handful of interested individuals. *Problems* with MBWA include:

- Managers might engage in the practice simply to waste time.
- Workers could learn how to manipulate the system in order to present to their bosses favourable but untrue images of their work.
- Visits could become little more than friendly social chit-chats that add nothing to the company's efficiency.
- Managers are taken away from possibly more important duties.
- In a large company a senior manager cannot visit *all* sections on a regular basis.

Progress test 5

1. What are the main costs that bad employee communication can impose on an organisation?

2. Explain the difference between one-way and two-way communication.

3. List the main channels available for employee communication.

4. What is the grapevine and how does it operate?

5. List the purposes of house magazines as a medium for employee communication.

6. What are the advantages to management of preparing employee reports analogous to those sent to shareholders?

7. List the purposes of team briefings.

8. Explain 'management by walking around'.

6

EMPLOYEE PARTICIPATION

THE PROS AND CONS OF PARTICIPATION

1. Meaning of participation

The term 'employee participation' covers a wide range of institutional arrangements and workplace activities, each possessing its own particular set of implications. Among the various possibilities are:

- joint consultation (*see* **9–11**)
- quality circles (*see* 14: **25**)
- worker directors (*see* **19**)
- workers' control (*see* **2–3**)
- employee involvement in the setting of personal objectives
- works councils (*see* **14–16**)
- financial participation (*see* **13**)
- suggestion schemes (*see* **8**)
- autonomous team working (*see* 14: **13**).

Participation may or may not include elements of industrial democracy, i.e. joint decision-taking between management and employees with the latter being empowered to initiate and (importantly) veto proposals on certain matters.

Procedures for implementing employee participation can involve direct contact between managers and subordinates (usually in a group work setting), or indirect *representation* of workers' interests via individuals elected to serve on various committees and/or the company's board. Indeed, collective bargaining (*see* Chapter 9) can itself be regarded as a form of 'employee participation'. Usually, however, the term is used to describe workers' involvement in management decisions that are not normally subject to collective bargaining as such. Note, moreover, that it is possible to have active employee participation within firms where there is no collective bargaining.

2. Workers' control

In its extreme form, workers' control could mean the overthrow of the capitalist system and the management of enterprises being undertaken by the elected representatives of the workforce. Otherwise, the workers' co-operative movement could be regarded as a form of 'workers' control'. Workers' co-operatives are governed according to the principle of one vote per *member* (i.e. employee), rather than one vote per share held by outside shareholders. Workers own the co-operative and divide its profits among themselves. In theory, employee relations within a workers' co-operative should be harmonious because workers own the business so that conflicts of interest between workers and management ought not to arise. All members have one vote regardless of how much capital they contribute or how much work they do for the co-operative. Surpluses belong to members and must be distributed equitably; business is conducted for the *mutual benefit* of members. Hence the integration of work, ownership and democratic control should – advocates of industrial co-operatives argue – enhance workers' job satisfaction, improve efficiency and (since workers and owners are one and the same) remove the conflicts of interest between capital and labour that lead to industrial strife.

3. Problems in co-operative management

A common problem with worker co-operatives is that while employees are competent and willing workers, they might dislike assuming responsibility for others and be unable to reconcile co-operative principles with the robust commercialism needed for business success. Note, however, that through being forced into confrontation with business realities members may be encouraged to work even more energetically for the success of their firms.

Special organisational difficulties sometimes experienced by co-operatives include:

(a) Lack of commitment by some employees to the long-term well-being of a co-operative, seeing it as a means for short-term gain rather than long-run development.

(b) Breakdowns in communications among members, and between members and the co-operative's management committee (if it has one). Good communications are essential since each member has one vote and shares equal responsibility for the co-operative's success. Regular meetings – at which all members can freely express their views – are especially important.

(c) Difficulties in finding new members who possess much needed technical and/or business skills and who are sufficiently interested in joining (and perhaps investing in) a co-operative. This might result in the business having to hire skilled workers either as non-voting employees or as subcontractors. Hence the co-operative starts to act as a conventional employer, and becomes involved in industrial relations disputes, dismissal and appeals procedures, wage bargaining, etc., at the expense of pursuing co-operative ideals.

(d) Disagreements over the business's goals. Members may have differing perceptions of the objectives of the enterprise, ranging from social amelioration through to the maximisation of financial profit whatever the human cost (people might belong to co-operatives without being committed – or even aware – of co-operative principles).

(e) Better qualified or experienced members may resent having the same management authority as junior colleagues, especially when some members have contributed more capital, time and/or equipment than the rest.

(f) Various members may hold different views about how each member should be paid, about working hours, conditions of employment, etc., and about how the more interesting aspects of the co-operative's work should be divided. Yet all members share equally in management and must jointly determine such matters.

4. Purposes of participation

These include the improvement of the quality of working life (*see* 14: **15**) plus increased business efficiency. Participation should enhance employee motivation and reduce industrial strife. At the national level, governments sometimes see worker participation in management decisions as a means for improving overall corporate productivity and hence for enhancing the nation's international competitiveness. The European Commission has always supported the involvement of employee representatives in management decisions on the grounds that it develops social cohesion, underwrites the principle of fair treatment for labour and acts as a counterbalance to the concentration of power in the hands of a small number of business organisations. Hence the Commission has proposed a number of schemes for involving employee representatives in the management of firms (*see* **20–21**).

Other purposes of participation include:

- increasing workers' job satisfaction
- providing employees with a means for relating their own self-interests to those of the firm
- inculcating in workers the belief that management wishes to be fair and just, and that management is taking employee welfare seriously
- enhancing workers' feelings of job security. Decisions on new equipment, rationalisation, mergers, etc., can create great anxiety among the workforce. Involving employee representatives in these matters helps remove the fear of the unknown as workers will at least be kept fully informed of the latest developments.

5. The case for participation

The principal argument in favour of participation relates to its mobilisation of the talents, resources, experiences and expertise of employees, who are positively encouraged to develop their decision-making capacities and to become more involved with the efficient management of the firm. People can influence the events that determine their working lives. Note how society accepts that individuals are capable of rational behaviour when electing governments, so why should not equal responsibility be exercised in electing representatives to help manage a firm? Managerial accountability to workers' representatives can, through forcing managements to think long and hard about the welfare implications of their actions, encourage analytical approaches which improve the overall efficiency of the enterprise. Further benefits could be greater willingness by workers to abide by decisions they helped to make, and the fact that bad, unworkable decisions are less likely because those who would have to implement them receive opportunities to point out potential difficulties.

Additional *advantages* are that participation:

- encourages responsible and flexible attitudes among employees and positive responses to change
- assists staff development
- enables management to receive valuable feedback from employees about day-to-day operations
- involves a greater number of people in taking decisions and hence a lower risk of important factors being overlooked
- fits in with modern education philosophy, methods and policies which encourage independent action and thought.

Participation can also be defended on the grounds of social justice and the promotion of the democratic ideal within a nation.

The main *advantages* to management are:

- Efficiency should increase as employees become involved in decision-making.
- Loyalty and commitment to a trade union may be replaced by greater employee loyalty to the firm.
- The management of change is facilitated, since employees are made aware of the environmental circumstances that create the need for change.
- The machinery of participation (committees, works councils, quality circles, etc.) provides a means for channelling conflict into peaceful institutional procedures.

6. Conditions for effective participation

For participation to be meaningful and effective a number of conditions need to be satisfied:

(a) Managers and workers must both want participation to succeed. Hostility from either side will guarantee failure.

(b) Employees should actually be able to *influence* managerial behaviour. Otherwise the situation is one of 'communication' rather than participation *per se*.

(c) It must extend to significant issues that genuinely affect employees' working lives.

(d) It should not involve bargaining, with various parties haggling for bigger shares in the profits of the firm.

(e) Employees need to be competent to offer sensible and useful ideas to management.

(f) Management should make available to employees whatever information is necessary to enable them to form a considered opinion on relevant issues.

(g) All participants should be clear about the scope and objectives of the scheme.

(h) The institutional mechanisms for participation should be cost-effective and not absorb too much management or employee time.

(i) Participation should only apply to matters that the organisation and its workers can control. For example, there is no point in management and employee representatives meeting to discuss government policy or the propriety of proposed new legislation.

Note the problems sometimes created by differences in perception over what is meant by participation that sometimes arise between managements, which regard themselves as *allowing* workers to become involved in decision-making, and employee representatives who might demand the *right* to help determine matters that affect their working lives.

7. Arguments against employee participation

Those opposed to worker participation emphasise that employees do not own firms. Owners or their representatives have the right to administer their property in whatever ways they think best – without time-wasting interference from workers' representatives. Management, they argue, is a specialised skill acquired through training and experience: workers have insufficient knowledge of administrative procedures to be good managers. Other criticisms are that:

(a) Much managerial information is confidential in nature, involving personal matters relating to individuals. This should not be disclosed to employees' representatives.

(b) Conflicts of interest between management and labour necessarily occur. These are best resolved through collective bargaining: workers cannot simultaneously represent their colleagues and be part of management. Sooner or later workers' representatives must support unpopular managerial decisions, causing them to lose the confidence of the rank and file.

(c) Participation does not alter fundamental realities or a firm's prospects for the future – businesses fail despite having extensive worker participation schemes.

(d) Workers sometimes adopt short-term, mercenary approaches to issues which really require long-term solutions.

(e) Decision-making becomes slow and possibly inefficient.

(f) Employees might not be competent to comprehend the complex issues sometimes involved in managerial decision-making.

(g) Managers and union representatives could become immersed in the *mechanics* of participation (committee procedures, determination of the scope of the subjects to be discussed, etc.) and lose sight of its fundamental purpose.

(h) Arguably, participation interferes with managerial prerogative (*see* 8: **14**): managers should not have to consider employee interests when making important decisions. According to this view, management's job is to manage; the worker's role is to complete whatever tasks are assigned. Employees have unions and staff associations to protect their interests via collective bargaining and this should be all that is required.

(i) Individual employee participation could undermine collective action and hence a union's ability to organise industrial action. It might be better, therefore, systematically to extend the scope of collective bargaining to include matters currently subject to unilateral management decision-making.

(j) Certain forms of participation (quality circles for example) could require extensive changes in a company's communication system, especially where the firm is organised as a tall hierarchy with a long chain of command.

FORMS OF PARTICIPATION

Autonomous work groups, quality circles, and joint management/employee target setting are discussed elsewhere (*see* 14: **13, 16, 25**). The following sections examine employee suggestion schemes, joint consultation, financial participation, works councils, and board room level employee participation.

8. Suggestion schemes

Suggestion schemes operate in many companies and are generally popular with both management and employees. The topics typically covered by a scheme include safety at work, use of materials, efficiency and cost saving, organisation of production and administrative procedures, and the invention of new equipment and techniques. Normally the firm will have a committee consisting of representatives of managers and employees to assess the suggestions and recommend whether they should be adopted, perhaps after taking expert advice.

Advantages to suggestion schemes include the financial benefits that accrue both to the firm and to the employee making the suggestion. There will be higher productivity and less defective production, fewer accidents, and enhanced communication between management and the workforce. Use is made of the employees' ingenuity and creativity; job satisfaction should increase.

The difficulties involved

The basic problem with suggestion schemes is deciding who will receive the benefits from suggestions that result in large financial savings. In most countries the patent rights of a new invention are vested in the firm which employs the inventor, and not the individual concerned. Workers may be discouraged from suggesting improvements unless they are guaranteed a substantial return. Related problems are that:

(a) Once a suggestion is submitted it becomes known to the firm. How can the inventor subsequently prove his or her claim to be the true initiator of the idea?

(b) If a firm offers a reward of a fixed percentage of the financial returns from a suggestion, how can the individual employee obtain access to the company's records to check the accuracy of the firm's estimate of the financial benefits obtained?

(c) If a firm rejects an employee's suggestion, what can prevent the firm subsequently taking it up when the employee has left the firm, and not rewarding the inventor?

If it is to succeed in the long term a suggestion scheme must be well publicised within the organisation (photographs of participating workers in company newsletters, formal presentations of awards, etc.), the monetary rewards to individuals need to be substantial, and a convenient yet secure mechanism for submitting suggestions should exist. Occasional 'suggestion campaigns' focusing on specific issues may be necessary in order to maintain interest in the scheme. Unsuccessful contributors must have the reasons for the rejection of their ideas carefully explained to them.

9. Joint consultation

With joint consultation, management retains control over the decision-making process, but seeks to utilise the energy and initiative of the workforce by involving it in decision-making activities. Management informs employees of its plans and opinions on various issues and invites comments from workers' representatives. The essential difference between joint consultation and straight-forward communication (through briefing groups for example) is that management hears employee criticisms and suggestions and stands ready to reconsider its decisions in certain circumstances. Also management is prepared to give reasons for not accepting employee representatives' proposals.

Note how joint consultation might develop as a precursor to a firm fully recognising a trade union. Indeed, a management strategy of using joint consultation as a device for preventing unions gaining a foothold in a company could backfire through its raising of collective consciousness among the workforce. The factors discussed in 2: **24** and **25** concerning managerial relations with staff associations are relevant in this regard. Objectives of joint consultation include:

- creation of a forum for exchanges of views on matters of mutual interest to management and the workforce
- the critical examination of problems and the determination of solutions acceptable to all the parties involved
- provision of an efficient channel of communication for management to announce its future plans and to receive workers' comments on them.

10. Advantages to joint consultation

The basic advantage of joint consultation as far as management is concerned is that expert advice is obtained from employees who possess detailed knowledge of workplace procedures and conditions. Also workers who, through consultation, are able to exert limited control over their working environments are likely to be more co-operative, with resulting benefits to efficiency. Further advantages are that:

- The implementation of new methods might be facilitated as the need for change is explained and discussed.
- Employees are given the opportunity to draw management's attention to their concerns (including grievances) in a forum not connected with (possibly confrontational) collective bargaining machinery.
- Management/worker communication is generally improved.
- Management and labour come to see issues from each other's points of view and to understand each other's problems.
- It provides management with valuable information from the workforce.

11. Drawbacks to joint consultation

Problems with joint consultation can include:

(a) Managements might raise issues at a joint consultation meeting that should really be the subject of collective bargaining.

(b) Employee representatives may wish only to discuss immediate workplace problems whereas management might want only to discuss long-term plans.

(c) Management may see the consultation process as little more than a device for passing on information, while employee representatives might want the opportunity to examine various options and recommend a decision.

(d) Bureaucratic joint consultation procedures are perhaps outdated in the modern world where progressive companies apply a range of more sophisticated means for involving employees in management decisions (group problem-solving, quality circles, etc.).

(e) Joint consultation might be used by management as a device for minimising union influence within the organisation. Arguably, joint consultation becomes redundant in firms with comprehensive and effective collective bargaining machinery.

Joint consultation, moreover, is not suitable for discussion of issues where management and unions have fundamentally conflicting interests.

The use and acceptance of joint consultation implies a unitarist perspective on employee relations (see 1: 3) and that management has the ultimate right to determine which matters shall and shall not be discussed.

12. Techniques of joint consultation

Techniques for joint consultation vary from consultative committees containing employee representation, through to briefing groups (see 1: 3) with two-way communication. To succeed, a joint consultation system requires from management a genuine willingness to listen sympathetically to divergent views, to explain and justify proposals and to enter into genuine discussions. Obviously, a joint consultation scheme will fall into disrepute if management persistently listens to employee representatives' opinions and then proceeds to ignore them. Joint consultation must not be seen to *compete* with normal management/ employee bargaining procedures.

Meetings should be held within working hours and convened on (at least) a monthly or bi-monthly basis. Some schemes rotate the chair of the joint consultation committee annually between management and employee representatives. All levels of employee and major sections within the firm should be represented.

Joint consultation procedures require decisions concerning:

- how it will be done (institutional and organisational arrangements), where and when
- whether consultation is to occur *before* decisions are made or *during* the decision-making process
- the scope of the issues that will be subject to consultation
- whether separate joint consultation bodies will exist for differing occupational categories or divisions within the company.

Institutional and organisational arrangements need to encompass such matters as who will chair meetings, periods of office, numbers and constituencies of employee representatives and their method of election, periods of office, voting procedures (where appropriate), and so on.

Failure of joint consultation

Reasons for the collapse of joint consultation procedures are many and varied, and might include:

- unclear objectives
- poor performance by the chairperson
- lack of trust and commitment on the part of the participants
- apathy resulting from the amount of time and effort devoted to discussing minor issues
- deliberately disruptive behaviour by management or union representatives
- breakdowns in communication between union members of a joint consultation committee and the workers they are supposed to represent.

13. Financial participation

Workers can become part-owners of limited companies through being allocated shares in their firms as supplements to wages. As part-owners, workers may be motivated into greater effort because they now have direct interests in their employer's profitability. Arguments against the issue of shares to workers include:

(a) If workers really want to become shareholders in a company they are free to buy shares on the open market. That they choose not to do so is evidence of unwillingness to be financially associated with the business.

(b) Shares not allocated to employees would presumably be sold to outsiders, possibly at lower prices. Employee share distribution schemes, to the extent that they are alternatives to higher wages, can thus be interpreted as backdoor methods for firms to raise additional long-term finance.

(c) Financial participation is sometimes used as an alternative to participation schemes that involve workers in management decision-making, creating thereby an impression of participation while not in fact allowing employees any influence over matters relating to their working lives.

(d) There is no immediate link between individual effort and reward.

(e) To the extent that workers accumulate benefits over a long period (as occurs in certain share ownership schemes), they stand to lose this money *as well as* their jobs if the company collapses.

WORKS COUNCILS

Works councils (referred to as works committees in some countries) are an important feature of the continental European business scene, though not in the United Kingdom. The latter situation is likely to change, however, in consequence of **(a)** the European Commissions's encouragement of the works council system, and **(b)** the growing influence of successful continental EU businesses' organisation structures and management methods as an example to be followed by British companies.

14. Works councils in EU countries

These are compulsory for certain sizes of firm (normally defined in terms of a minimum number of employees) in all EU nations except for the UK (the latter situation resulting from the UK's opt-out from the Maastricht Agreement) In countries where they are required, councils are normally legally obliged to *discuss* particular (specified) matters, and entitled to *take decisions* (effectively giving employee representatives a right of veto) on others according to the particular laws of the relevant nation.

The ranges of issues involved differ substantially from country to country. Decision-making powers vary from internal works rules (e.g. the operation of grievance procedures) to recruitment methods and whether the firm is to take on part-time or temporary workers. In Germany and the Netherlands, employee representatives on works councils have the legal right to delay certain important management decisions (on company mergers for instance). Examples of issues that are subject to decision-making by works councils are:

(a) Criteria for hiring temporary staff and for selecting workers for redundancy (Belgium)

(b) Profit sharing agreements (France)

(c) Changes in working hours, training agreements, recruitment and disciplinary procedures (Germany)

(d) Operation of job evaluation schemes, appraisal and grievance procedures, working hours (the Netherlands).

Matters subject to *discussion* by works councils in various EU countries include:

- financial plans and company structures
- acquisitions, physical investments and divestments
- working practices and the introduction of new technology
- proposed incentive schemes and wage payment systems
- company sales, profits and prices
- personnel policies (including recruitment methods)
- health and safety at work.

In Belgium, members of the works council are (legally) bound by confidentiality, and can be prohibited from disclosing sensitive information to other employees. Employers can apply to the Belgian Ministry of Labour to withhold certain information from the works council, although in practice this is extremely rare. German and Portuguese works council members are also statutorily bound by rules on confidentiality.

15. Advantages of works councils

Benefits claimed for the practice of having works council in firms include:

(a) The existence of a works council compels management to seek consensus with employee representatives on many important issues, hence avoiding conflicts and disruptive industrial action.

(b) Employees assume *obligations* for the operation of the business as well as rights to consultation. Works councils come to execute certain management functions (allocation of overtime, decisions on working methods, determination of promotion criteria, etc.) that otherwise would have to be undertaken by alternative (and perhaps more costly) management committees. Also, discussions between management and labour encourage the latter to propose new ideas, offer alternative solutions to problems and generally adopt constructive and useful perspectives.

(c) Change can be introduced more easily, since a works council provides a useful forum for explaining the needs for and implications of new methods.

(d) Management benefits as it is quickly made aware of any problems relating to intended developments that are likely to provoke hostile opposition from the workforce and hence can alter its plans in order to remove or minimise employee resistance.

Although it is known that employee apathy frequently results in works councils not operating within many companies in countries where employee representation is legally required, the *existence* of legislative procedures itself can create an environment in which managers are extremely sensitive to the need to consult with and win over the workforce, leading perhaps to greatly improved management/labour relations.

16. Criticisms of the works council system

Opponents of works councils argue as follows:

(a) Wages and conditions of employment in firms with active and influential works councils tend to be higher than elsewhere, possibly causing companies operating works councils to lose competitive advantage.

(b) The administrative costs of running a works council (executive time, rooms, secretarial support, etc.) can be substantial.

(c) Employees may adopt short-term perspectives, and might oppose decisions that would benefit the company in the long run but do not offer many rewards to employees in the immediate future. Innovation and enterprise may be discouraged.

(d) Decision-taking can be slow, and many employee representatives will not have the technical knowledge upon which they can base decisions.

(e) Efficiency improvements that involve shedding labour might be impeded.

(f) Councils can easily degenerate into vehicles for plant-level collective bargaining, undermining normal management/union negotiating machinery.

EMPLOYEE REPRESENTATION AT THE BOARD-ROOM LEVEL

17. Worker directors

These are directors elected to the board directly by all employees, or appointed by existing union officials. They may or may not be excluded from major decisions on capital investment, organisation structure, appointment of key management personnel, and so on. The essential argument for having worker directors is that since many employees devote much of their working lives to a particular firm, they are entitled, through elected representatives, to some say in how the firm is run. Against this is the fact that firms are owned by entrepreneurs and/or shareholders who put their personal capital at risk. Owners of firms may resent the imposition of worker directors who, in part, will control the owners' assets without having been elected by the owners themselves. Specific problems facing worker directors could include:

(a) Reluctance of other board members to disclose confidential information to employees' representatives, in case it is passed on to union negotiators. But if worker directors agree not to reveal sensitive data, they face criticism from union colleagues who expect them to divulge information gained in board meetings. To whom does the worker director owe loyalty, management or the union?

(b) Hostility and social ostracism from other board members, who might conduct secret board meetings to decide key issues without the presence of worker directors.

(c) The fact that special privileges afforded to worker directors – higher status, preferential treatment, expenses, time off for board meetings, perhaps even higher wages – might cause them to lose contact with the workers who elected them. Hence they might become integrated into the management system, adopt management perspectives and become reluctant to challenge management decisions. Effectively the worker director's role disintegrates to being nothing more than explaining, justifying and/or apologising for management's actions.

(d) Although a company's board of directors is nominally the most powerful body in the enterprise, real power might in fact lie elsewhere.

(e) To the extent that a worker director can influence the board's decisions, he or she will be presenting arguments *as an individual* and not as an employee representative as happens with collective bargaining: there is no question of negotiation occurring during board meetings.

(f) Worker directors may be patronised but effectively ignored.

(g) Company boards take *strategic* decisions the outcomes to which might not be visible for several years, so the employees the worker director represents may not see any tangible short-term benefits to electing worker directors.

(h) Boards of directors have to deal with a wide variety of issues, not just employee relations. Board members other than worker directors will have been selected for their knowledge of and ability to contribute to these wider discussions. Worker directors who have no experience of practical management but who wish nevertheless to express opinions on all matters could impede effective decision-making.

(i) Worker directors may not be able to relate their immediate workplace concerns with the need to adopt an overall perspective on the enterprise. Can worker directors realistically be expected to think strategically?

Perhaps the most immediately useful functions of a worker director are to voice criticism of management's stated intentions and to articulate the workplace point of view. Management is confronted with new and different interpretations of issues. Also, the presence on the board of employee representatives underlines senior management's commitment to employee welfare, and a climate of mutual confidence and co-operation between management and labour may emerge.

Employee representation on company boards is compulsory in Belgium, Germany, Luxembourg and the Netherlands. In France, voluntary arrangements on this matter are possible which, once entered into, can thereafter be enforced by law.

18. Supervisory boards

In Germany, Belgium and the Netherlands there exist legal requirements compelling large companies to have two-tier boards of directors. The lower tier is an 'executive board', comprising managerial employees of the firm responsible for the day-to-day operational management. Above this is a 'supervisory board', which takes strategic decisions in relation to the overall direction of the enterprise. By law, employee representatives must sit on the supervisory boards of companies in these countries. The functions of supervisory boards include:

- the appointment and dismissal of executive managers and the determination of their remunerations
- deciding the overall direction of the enterprise (its products, markets, major new investments, etc.)
- matters concerning mergers and takeovers and how the company is to be financed.

Two-tier boards were first used in Germany in the 1860s, when the German banks began making large financial investments in industry and demanded representation at board-room level in order to protect their interests. The *advantages* claimed for having a separate supervisory board are that:

(a) General policy-making is undertaken objectively and independently without interference from executives with vested interests in outcomes.

(b) Interpersonal rivalries among lower level managers can be ignored.

(c) Employee interests may be considered in the absence of line managers who control workers.

(d) Tough decisions that adversely affect senior line managers can be taken more easily.

Problems with supervisory boards are that:

- The people who determine basic strategy might be remote from the day-to-day realities of executive management.
- Decision-making is slowed down by the need to go through two separate boards for decisions on certain issues.
- Confusions could arise between executive and supervisory boards, with the decisions of each not being properly understood by the other.

19. Worker directors on supervisory boards

The general advantages and disadvantages of having employee representatives on company boards are discussed in **17**. Specific implications of having worker directors on supervisory boards are:

(a) The knowledge and experience of employee representatives can be directly applied to *strategic* decisions without employee representatives having to argue with line managers.

(b) Matters concerning human relations are automatically elevated to the highest level of decision-making within the organisation. Note that since the supervisory board appoints and dismisses senior managers then the latter will be highly sensitive to worker directors' views, and to human relations issues generally.

(c) Arguably, the presence of employee representatives on a supervisory board facilitates the financial stability of the company, because worker directors' concerns for employees' continuity of employment invariably cause them to argue in favour of profit retention and the accumulation of reserves to guard against temporary economic downturns. Also, employee representatives will oppose any merger or takeover that could result in redundancies.

EUROPEAN UNION INTERVENTIONS

The European Commission has initiated two major proposals concerning the compulsory participation of employee representatives in board-room decisions. These are Draft Directive V on Company Law, and the European Company Statute.

20. The Fifth Draft Directive on Company Law

The initial version of this proposal stipulated that all European Community based companies with more than 1,000 workers would have had to set up a two-tier board of directors with compulsory employee representation on the supervisory board, or worker participation in management through a separate works council with representation on the board, or an equivalent body established by collective agreement (provided the body affords at least the same rights as alternative devices). However, the Draft was subsequently amended to offer companies the option of a single board with a majority of non-executive directors (empowered to appoint and dismiss executive directors) instead of having a two-tier board. Between one third and one half of a single or supervisory board would consist of employee representatives.

Benefits possibly resulting from this arrangement are discussed in **19**. A number of objections have been raised against the proposal (particularly within the UK), including:

(a) Agendas of board meetings could become dominated by personnel management and industrial relations issues, at the expense of considering strategic and operational matters.

(b) Businesses affected by the Directive would need to train employee representatives in the principles of management, company structure, finance, market environments, etc., in order to enable them to understand board-room discussions.

(c) Companies operating in several EU countries would experience severe practical problems resulting from their boards having to include employee representatives from several countries, speaking different languages (thus requiring the presence of interpreters at board meetings), from widely disparate trade union backgrounds, and with contrasting cultural perspectives.

(d) Conflicts might be created between agreements reached by worker and other directors at the board level, and settlements concluded via plant-level collective bargaining in divisions and subsidiaries of the firm.

21. The European Company Statute

This EU proposal provides for the establishment of a new type of limited company, the Societas Europea (SE), governed not by the laws of any one member country but by a set of fresh rules and procedures applicable throughout the EU. The European Commission proposed that these companies will have compulsory workers' participation. Three options are to be available for this purpose, as follows:

(a) between one third and one half of its supervisory or administrative board must consist of employee representatives; or

(b) a separate works council could be established, meeting at least once every three months; or

(c) the SE may adopt the employee representation model of the country in which it registers, provided this model offers *at least* comparable participation rights to worker representatives as those embodied in the SE proposal.

Regardless of the precise form of participation, employee representatives would have to be informed of any proposal with 'significant implications' for workers, and to be consulted about any planned takeover or disposal of part of the business valued at more than 5 per cent of the SE's share capital (this percentage may be increased to up to 25 per cent in certain circumstances). Consultation would also be necessary prior to the conclusion of major loan agreements or supply contracts.

An SE will require a share capital of at least ECU 100,000. This figure represents a big reduction on the original proposal (of ECU 250,000) in order to make the SE format accessible to small businesses. SEs will register in Luxembourg and thereafter be subject only to the European Company Statute and *not* national company legislation.

Progress test 6

1. What are the purposes of employee participation in management decisions?

2. List the benefits to employers of employee participation in management decisions.

3. State five arguments against employee participation.

4. What are the main problems associated with the implementation of suggestion schemes?

5. In what circumstances is joint consultation unlikely to succeed?

6. What are the functions of works councils?

7. List the major problems that might be experienced by worker directors.

8. What is a supervisory board?

9. State the implications of having worker directors on supervisory boards.

7

NEGOTIATION

1. Meaning of negotiation

Negotiation is a method for joint decision-making that, in the context of employee relations, involves bargaining between management and workers' representatives. The objective of negotiation is to obtain *mutually acceptable* agreements concerning wages, working conditions and other aspects of employment. Thus, negotiation implies compromise. A willingness to negotiate presupposes that each side is prepared to forgo some of its demands: there is no point in either party entering into negotiations if it is not ready to make concessions. Negotiation differs from 'consultation' in that, whereas the latter results in a unilateral decision imposed by management (possibly taking into account the views of the persons consulted), negotiation requires *agreement* and leads to decisions which all parties to the negotiation are then obliged to respect.

2. Outcomes to negotiation

Agreements emerging from negotiation may be substantive or procedural. The former determine employees' actual pay and working conditions (annual leave, wage rates, shiftwork arrangements, overtime pay, etc.). Procedural agreements specify the methods that are to be applied to the settlement of grievances and disputes and the resolution of other employment issues. Hence, procedures might be negotiated for the processing of employees' complaints, for implementing redundancies in an equitable manner, for introducing new technology, for discipline, for joint consultation, and so on. Typically a procedural agreement will specify the range of topics that may be discussed under the procedure, who will chair the meetings, who is to be allowed to participate, voting powers of the parties, etc. Most procedural agreements contain a 'preamble' which states the intentions and (importantly) the *spirit* of the agreement, plus time limits for processing matters arising under the agreement and details of any third party that might be called upon to arbitrate a dispute.

Need for sound procedures

Well constructed procedural agreements are essential for the long-term success of the enterprise. The benefits of having robust procedures are that:

- Day-to-day problems that could flare up into destructive conflicts are defused through their being dealt with in an orderly and agreed manner.
- Disputes and other matters are handled consistently. Precedents are set, hence speeding up the processing of future cases. Also, the availability of written records means that the existence of agreed decisions cannot later be disputed.
- All parties to the discussions will (hopefully) be committed to decisions reached via mutually acceptable procedures.

3. Negotiating strategies

Negotiators need to predetermine how far they are willing to go in order to accommodate the other side's position. In multi-party negotiations it is also important to identify potential allies and the issues that could turn a current enemy into a friend. Negotiating objectives must be specific, and the following matters clarified:

(a) The strengths and weaknesses of the other party's case, and the resources at its disposal.

(b) The implications, costs and benefits of the various possible outcomes.

(c) The accuracy of the facts the opposition is likely to put forward in support of its claim. What does the opposition *really* want and how far is it prepared to go in securing its objectives?

(d) Which issues are 'primary' and not open to negotiation, and which are 'secondary' and hence subject to compromise. No negotiator can realistically expect to achieve all his or her demands, so priorities must be established and some objectives relegated to a subsidiary role.

Tactics

A negotiator must try to understand the feelings and motives of the other side, to empathise and see the issue from the opponent's perspective. This may require an analysis of the personal characteristics of the individuals representing the opposition, including their attitudes, knowledge of the issue and levels of competence.

4. Successful negotiation

Research into negotiation has revealed:

(a) Mutually agreeable outcomes are most likely when points of difference between each party's position are clearly defined and fully understood by all participants.

(b) Negotiations are most efficient when conducted dispassionately. There should be no personal abuse, each party's case should be stated precisely and politely.

5. The negotiating team

This needs to consist of more than just the people who actually sit at the table and conduct the negotiation. A team might comprise:

- a representative of the firm's senior management (or of the upper levels of a trade union or staff association) authorised to determine overall negotiating strategies and objectives
- one or more researchers who will analyse the validity and strengths and weaknesses of the opponent's case plus (where appropriate) the characteristics of the individuals acting for the other side
- spokespeople to present the case
- someone to record comments and decisions. This is an important function as the two sides might subsequently disagree over what was actually decided. Usually both sides will have their own notetaker.

Roles of the participants

Note how the skills, personalities and competencies required of each of the above categories of member of a negotiating team might be completely different. Researchers need an eye for detail and the ability to unravel complex information at short notice. Spokespeople must be articulate, persuasive and good at selling a proposition. A spokesperson might adopt either of two approaches: 'spearhead' or 'conductor'. *Spearhead* negotiators are individuals who intentionally do most of the speaking during a negotiation and generally dominate the proceedings. This contrasts with the *conductor* negotiator, who calls upon other members of his or her team to contribute to discussions while personally co-ordinating their efforts. A problem with the conductor approach is that team members might make contradictory statements. The advantage is that it shares the stress of negotiating among several people, each of whom can make an expert contribution.

Skills needed by the spearhead negotiator

These include the abilities to:

- respond quickly to changing situations
- identify in opponents aspects of behaviour (including body language) that reveal clues to their feelings about issues
- summarise large amounts of information in short statements
- withstand stress
- exercise judgement and discretion
- predict the objections that the opponent will raise
- empathise with the opponent's position
- recognise and deal with 'red herrings'.

6. Competitive advantage in negotiation

What is meant by the term 'strong bargaining position'? A number of factors help determine the extents of the power of the various parties to an employee relations negotiation:

- the state of the labour market (levels of unemployment, skills, shortages, etc.)
- how badly a sanction imposed by one party (a strike for example) will affect the other side
- the skills and persuasiveness of individual negotiators
- the nature of the procedural agreement (*see* **2**) governing the negotiation, which might contain rules constraining the activities of one of the parties
- unity within the negotiating team
- legal rules surrounding the conduct of negotiations and the abilities of the parties to apply sanctions
- the intrinsic value of a case and the degree to which the opponent will perceive it sympathetically.

7. Negotiating conventions

There are three types of negotiating situation: conjunctive, where parties have no alternative but to settle, distributive, involving the sharing out of a fixed amount of resources or rewards; and 'integrative', whereby the parties seek jointly agreed positions. Differing negotiating techniques might be used for each of these situations, but in all cases a number of common conventions have emerged to facilitate efficient bargaining without damaging the interests of any of the participants:

(a) Offers, once made, should remain open unless circumstances change significantly.

(b) A target date for concluding the agreement should be specified.

(c) All items on the agenda should be negotiable, unless one of the parties has previously indicated its unwillingness to discuss certain matters. If necessary a preliminary meeting should be held to decide the topics to be included in the negotiations.

(d) Negotiators should negotiate only with each other and not make secret appeals to the people the other side represents Also, confidential conversations between opposing representatives should not be repeated during formal negotiations.

Bargaining units

A bargaining unit is the domain to which a collective agreement applies, e.g. a division of a firm, a subsidiary of a company, an entire business, an industry, etc. The size of a bargaining unit should depend on its ability to implement agreed decisions. For instance, there would be little point in, say, a workplace union representative negotiating with his or her head of department for a pay rise for union members in a certain section of a business if wage increases can only be sanctioned by the firm's top management. Matters for which a bargaining unit will be responsible should be predetermined.

8. The process of negotiation

Usually, proceedings begin with one of the parties (normally the side which initiated the negotiation) making an opening statement outlining its objectives and offering facts and opinions designed to convince the opponent of the justice of its case. An outcome will be suggested, and haggling ensues. Neither side will normally be prepared to indicate at this stage how much it is prepared to concede. Negotiations rarely involve 'all or nothing' situations, so even when one party has a much stronger case than the other it will try to find a means whereby the latter can 'save face'.

Having defined fall-back positions beyond which they are not prepared to retreat, negotiators usually make bids in excess of what they are prepared to accept. If settlements do not emerge, the particular items preventing agreement might be isolated and set aside while other matters are discussed. Precise definition of a stumbling block can generate fresh insights into its substance and stimulate new ideas on how it might be overcome.

Failure to agree

Unsuccessful negotiations should conclude with a written statement formally recording the fact that the parties to a negotiation have not been able to settle their differences. The statement will specify the precise reasons for the breakdown in negotiations and detail each party's current position.

The problems involved

Parties to a negotiation share common experiences, interact socially and develop personal relationships. This may expedite negotiations but might not benefit the negotiators' principals: friendships between individuals could cause them not to extract the maximum possible concessions from the other side. Other problems with negotiation include:

(a) Negotiators might personally disagree with the settlements their principals (senior management or union bosses for example) expect them to achieve.

(b) Principals might alter their expectations of outcomes as the negotiations develop.

9. Organisational politics

The term 'organisational politics' is used to describe negotiations and settlements within organisations made necessary by the existence of contrasting interests and the differing perceptions of various organisation members. Political activities lead to compromises, toleration, and a stability of relationships which enables the organisation to survive.

Organisational politics typically involve the building of coalitions around issues, persuasion and advocacy, and the skilful deployment of resources and power. Control over information is a key tool in the process. Coalitions rise in consequence of bargaining among various interest groups, and a dominant coalition will emerge. Organisational politics affect which issues assume prominence within the organisation and how they are discussed and interpreted. The manner in which a problem is diagnosed may be determined primarily by the self-interests of influential individuals and coalitions. Hence organisational politics influences how decisions are taken as well as the decisions themselves. Note how certain rules, procedures and interpersonal relationships might develop outside the official management system.

A company's political power system can affect its organisation structure, even to the extent that the latter becomes unsuitable as a means for realising the enterprise's goals. Internal politics helps shape the ideas about organisation structure that are deemed acceptable and, once implemented, the organisation design most favoured by the dominant political group might perpetuate itself indefinitely. Organisational politics can affect business planning in the following respects:

- disputes over who should undertake corporate planning activities
- the status of the planning function in the overall company hierarchy
- possible misuse of planning mechanisms by individuals wishing to pursue their own personal objectives
- resistance to planning on the grounds that it could pose a threat to vested interests within the firm and/or may expose personal weaknesses
- conflicts between various functions (marketing and finance for example) regarding which department's plans are to be paramount
- use of a corporate plan as a means for making redundant people who otherwise would be dismissed for underperformance.

Organisational politics are perhaps most likely to develop where:

(a) The organisation faces severe resource constraints, so that individuals and departments are compelled to fight hard for their budget allocations.

(b) Environments are fast changing and uncertain.

(c) There is a lack of leadership at the top of the organisation.

(d) The firm does not have clear objectives.

(e) Key managers have fundamentally different opinions about the basic purpose of the organisation.

(f) There is little accountability and inadequate management control.

Organisational politics can damage a company in a number of respects:

(a) Certain individuals may come to act as 'gatekeepers'. An organisational gatekeeper is someone who (i) communicates with the outside world on behalf of an organisation (formally or informally), (ii) gathers information from external sources and (iii) through being able to withhold this information from certain of the organisation's members is able to influence the decisions it makes.

(b) Departments are encouraged to seek to make other sections dependent on them, regardless of whether these inter-relationships benefit the firm as a whole.

(c) Sectional goals might be inconsistent across the organisation and not shared by all individuals and departments.

(d) Managers may become obsessed with ideological struggle, conflict and gaining the upper hand, at the expense of getting on with their work.

(e) Bad decisions might result from the internal political bargaining process.

(f) Interpersonal relationships may deteriorate.

(g) Inaccurate information might be deliberately circulated.

(h) Decision processes can become disorganised and disorderly.

10. Information for bargaining

A major function of the researcher (or 'analyst') member of the negotiating team is to assemble information that will be useful during the negotiation. Unions will want to know the firm's financial position and, for quoted public companies, the sensitivity of its share price to possible industrial action, the wages paid to all the various categories of the firm's workers, market prospects, etc. Hence, if the business is a limited company the researcher will examine the company's annual accounts (which by law must be available for public inspection), possibly have a credit agency conduct a check on the business, and go through past issues of newspapers and magazines looking for articles that mention the firm. A commercial computerised database host (Textline or FT Profile for example) might be used for the latter purpose.

Managements will want to know about the motives, commitment and track records of the employee representatives involved in the negotiations, about levels of pay and conditions for workers doing comparable jobs in other firms and industries, relations between union negotiators and workplace union representatives, and so on.

Disclosure of information

Employee representatives in negotiating situations frequently complain of not having sufficient information to bargain effectively. Most of the information relevant to negotiating situations is in fact management information, for example:

- organisation structure
- manning levels
- costs of various activities
- sales forecasts
- investment plans and future prospects
- proposed dividends
- profitability and productivity levels.

11. The case for disclosure

Arguments in favour of management disclosing large amounts of information to employee representatives are as follows:

(a) If information is not revealed, employee representatives may suspect that management is deliberately withholding relevant facts and will *assume* that the firm's position is much healthier than might actually be the case. Disclosure can help dispel workers' misconceptions about the company's affairs, especially its profitability and the extent of competition.

(b) Lack of sound management information encourages the circulation of rumours amongst the workforce. Such rumours can confuse employees, leading to feelings of insecurity and resentment that could cause conflict and (unnecessary) industrial disputes.

(c) As business operations become increasingly complex and subject to rapid technical and other changes so too does it become necessary for management to keep its workers fully informed about current developments. Employee representatives should not have to bargain in ignorance of the firm's future prospects, investment plans, etc.

(d) Joint consultation (*see* 6: **9**) is facilitated. Employees and their representatives may come to feel a sense of involvement and participation in the organisation. Worker participation in management decisions is discussed in Chapter 6.

The arguments *against* the free disclosure of management information are that:

- It might give union negotiators an unfair advantage.
- The information disclosed could be passed on to third parties, including employees of competing businesses.
- It could interfere with managerial prerogative (*see* 8: **25**).

Further problems are that:

- The costs and inconvenience of preparing detailed information for employee representatives could be substantial.
- Employee representatives might demand information vexatiously.
- Some employee representatives might not be able to understand financial and management control data.
- The information passed on might be deliberately inaccurate and presented in a manner intended to deceive.
- The fact that information is disclosed does not mean it will be believed.

12. Legal considerations

Some countries have laws compelling managements to disclose information needed by employee representatives for the purposes of collective bargaining. Britain's Employment Protection Act 1975, for example, empowers the representatives of recognised trade unions (but not staff associations – *see* 2: **24**) to demand information without which union representatives would be *materially* impeded in pursuing collective bargaining plus information that should be disclosed 'in accordance with good industrial relations practice'. Under the Act, management may if it wishes insist that the request for information is stated in writing. Union representatives can similarly insist that the information be provided in written form. The information requested must be 'relevant and important' to a collective bargaining issue over which the union has *recognised* negotiating rights: there is no compulsion to disclose information to a union that an employer does not recognise.

Exceptions to the Act

Union representatives are not entitled to information which:

- would be against the interests of national security
- would be illegal to disclose
- had been obtained in confidence
- relates to an individual (unless consent has been given)
- had been obtained for the purpose of legal proceedings
- would be likely to cause substantial injury to the employer's undertaking.

The ACAS code on disclosure

ACAS (*see* 3: **4**) has issued a code of practice, *Disclosure of Information to Trade Unions for Collective Bargaining Purposes* (HMSO, 1977), which suggests that 'relevant' information should include matters relating to pay and benefits, conditions of service, manpower performance and the firm's financial position. Under the code, employers need not provide cost information on individual products, or details of intended investments, price structures, marketing or tender data, or about suppliers, customers or financiers, provided the disclosure of such information would cause 'substantial injury' to the firm. The burden of establishing that substantial injury would occur should lie with the employer.

Appeals

A union which believes it has not received adequate information may complain to the Central Arbitration Committee, which may then refer the matter to the Advisory, Conciliation and Arbitration Service. If conciliation fails, the Committee will hear the case and make a declaration on whether or not the complaint is well-founded.

Then the union can apply to the CAC for the terms and conditions of employment of affected workers to be amended in appropriate ways (e.g. that their pay be increased). These new terms and conditions will be deemed to be part of employees' contracts and are thus legally enforceable.

13. Information agreements

The ACAS code recommends that management and unions reach some sort of consensus concerning the precise extent of the information that management will disclose to employee representatives on a regular basis. Such an agreement should cover the following issues:

- The headings under which information is to be disclosed and the timing of declarations.
- How the information may be used, including restrictions on the use of confidential information.
- Who is to be responsible for gathering and disclosing information.
- The formats in which the information is to be disclosed.

- Procedures for seeking clarification and further and better particulars.
- Facilities for discussing the information.
- Procedures for resolving disputes over the adequacy of the information divulged.

Progress test 7

1. Explain the difference between negotiation and consultation.

2. What is the difference between a substantive agreement and a procedural agreement?

3. In what circumstances are negotiations most likely to succeed?

4. Outline the role of the spearhead negotiator.

5. What is a bargaining unit?

6. List the arguments in favour of firms disclosing to trade unions large amounts of management information.

8

MANAGERIAL APPROACHES TO EMPLOYEE RELATIONS

1. Management theory

There are three major schools of thought in management theory: classical, human relations and contingency, each possessing its own particular implications for the conduct of employee relations. A school of thought is a collection of writers, thinkers and practitioners of a subject who all adhere to the same fundamental principles and doctrines and/or follow similar working methods where that subject is concerned. Members of a school may be separated geographically (proponents of the school might reside in different countries), or by time – new enthusiasts for a school can emerge many years after the deaths of its founders.

THE CLASSICAL SCHOOL

The classical school has macro and micro dimensions. At the macro level it involves the structuring and control of organisations; in its micro aspects it analyses the efficiency of day-to-day workplace operations. The leading writer on the latter (micro) dimensions of the classical approach was F.W. Taylor (1856–1917) who, together with subsequent followers, developed a complete and self-contained theory of work and workplace management. Taylor's approach is commonly referred to as 'scientific management' or, more colloquially, as 'Taylorism' after its founder.

2. Taylorism

Taylor believed that workers are motivated primarily by the prospect of high material reward. Thus, if employees' wages are closely related to the volume of work done, and if working methods are designed to generate high levels of output, then people will work as hard as their physical attributes allow and high quality production can be expected as a matter of course. The fundamental features of Taylor's approach were as follows.

(a) The division of labour should be applied to its maximum extent, following the detailed and 'scientific' study of work and the timing of physical movements.

Hence, operatives would require minimal (costly) training and could develop great speed and dexterity in the completion of simple and narrowly defined operations.

(b) Tasks should be executed under standard conditions involving the most efficient working methods. Working environments should be carefully controlled. No time should be wasted in fetching raw materials, arranging tools, or transporting finished work.

(c) Operatives should be set relatively high targets to stretch them to their maximum capacities.

3. Implications of Taylorism for employee relations

According to Taylor, management should plan, standardise, direct and closely supervise all the worker's efforts, leaving little discretion for individual operatives to exercise discretion. Job specifications should be clear, simple, precise and logical.

As the application of scientific management methods was genuinely expected to raise workers' incomes to unprecedentedly high levels, its advocates did not believe there could be any fundamental conflicts of interest between management and labour. The worker, it was assumed, would willingly accept the system. Workers are given the opportunity to earn high wages, which are assumed to constitute the primary employee motivator. High wages provide access to physical goods, services and lifestyle greatly valued by the majority of people. Also, the imposition of wages directly related to performance would prevent 'soldiering' by workers, i.e. only putting minimal effort into the completion of tasks in order to stretch work out and ensure continuity of employment.

A 'revolution' in employee attitudes was needed, so Taylor argued, if scientific management was to be successful. Management and labour would have to recognise the existence of a common interest in achieving higher productivity, and thus not engage in quarrels and industrial disputes over relative returns to capital and labour. Also they should willingly co-operate with management and accept its imposition of the best 'scientifically correct' methods.

4. Contributions of scientific management

The major contributions of scientific management to later approaches to organisation and management are:

(a) It demonstrated the need to define clearly the patterns of authority and responsibility within organisations.

(b) It provided a rational basis for separating and analysing organisational functions.

(c) It emphasised the role of target setting and the need for logically determined standards.

(d) It stimulated interest in the design of incentive systems and the analysis of the role of money in the motivation of employees.

5. Work measurement

The timing of work was a principal feature of scientific management. Taylor himself would break down the cycle of a major operation into small groups of motions, which he called elements. These elements were then timed and analysed separately. Taylor's objectives were: (*i*) to cause work to become routine and easy to complete; (*ii*) to minimise physical effort; and (*iii*) to eliminate duplicated operations.

Followers of Taylor developed this approach. Of particular importance was the work of F.B. and L. Gilbreth, who conducted detailed analyses of human body motions in work situations. The Gilbreths began their investigations with a study of all the body movements required for bricklaying, extending the analysis to other types of work and eventually compiling a complete taxonomy of all the human body motions used in manual labour.

6. The scientific management revolution

Taylor stated that the effects of scientific management would be revolutionary. Everyone would have a job (eventually, if not in the immediate short term); incomes would be high and all the material benefits of mass production and a consumer society would be obtained. However, if scientific management was to succeed then, he argued, a fundamental change in managerial and employee thinking was required. Management and labour would have to:

(a) recognise the existence of a common interest in achieving higher productivity, and thus not engage in quarrels and industrial disputes over relative returns to capital and labour

(b) accept the need for a clear division between mental and manual work

(c) replace *ad hoc* rules and approaches with 'scientific' analysis of working situations.

7. Union reactions to Taylorism

In fact, organised labour and many individual workers did not share this view and many serious industrial disputes followed the introduction of Taylor's methods, both in the United States and in Britain. Unions saw scientific management as a challenge to their role, influence, credibility and position. Specific complaints were that:

(a) Traditional work organisation practices whereby employees themselves determined how work should be completed were abandoned.

(b) Application of the division of labour meant (*i*) the loss of craft skills, (*ii*) little training of long-term benefit to the individual operative, and (*iii*) the 'dehumanisation' of work, i.e. jobs became repetitive and boring.

(c) Although it is possible to measure how long, on average, a task takes to complete, there is no truly scientific way of estimating the time in which the task *ought* to be finished.

(d) Attention is focused on efficiency at the workplace rather than at higher levels within organisations. The existing environment in which firms function is assumed constant and accepted without question. In reality, however, business enterprises are microcosms of society as a whole, and if conflicts between owners and organised labour exist within society they may equally exist within firms.

(e) Unemployment can result from increased industrial efficiency. Fewer people are needed to produce a given amount of goods. This, together with the loss of individual control over working practices and procedures implied by the scientific approach, naturally arouses distrust, fear and antagonism among organised labour. Moreover, the bulk of the additional wealth generated by the adoption of scientific management seemed always to accrue more to shareholders rather than to workers.

Social factors

Through its concentration on the mercenary and economic aspects of human nature the scientific approach tends to ignore the social and psychological needs of employees. In fact, these psycho-sociological factors exert powerful influences on behaviour. Arguably, moreover, the application of scientific management created 'them and us' attitudes that have plagued industrial relations right up to the present day.

Note that Taylor's ideas were formulated in the United States at the turn of the twentieth century, during a severe skills shortage in that country and hence the need to deskill operations. Yet as industry developed it became increasingly important for workers to be creative and to exercise discretion, especially where quality control was concerned. Scientific management removed all responsibility for quality and product and process improvement from the worker.

On a wider level, opponents of Taylorism argue that the treatment of human beings as little more than adjuncts to mechanised production and the factory system is inappropriate in a modern democratic society which values personal development as well as the creation of physical wealth.

8. Macro-organisational aspects of the classical approach

The classical approach to organisation rests on two basic propositions:

(a) People should be selected and trained to fit into the organisation; the organisation itself need not be structured to suit the human needs of particular individuals. Rigid organisation patterns are specified and people are allocated to particular positions according to their perceived suitability for those jobs.

(b) The *same* set of organisational principles should be applied to *all* enterprises, regardless of cultural, historical and / or technical circumstances. These principles, which derive mostly from the work of Max Weber (1865–1920) and Henri Fayol (1841–1925), can be summarised as follows (for further details see the M&E text *Organisational Behaviour*):

- formal rules and procedures (recorded in writing)
- a 'tall' hierarchy created by narrow spans of control (i.e. each manager having only a small number of immediate subordinates) and hence many levels of management within the firm
- a clear line of authority running from the top of the organisation to its base
- unity of command, i.e. application of the principle of 'one person one boss' in order to avoid employees receiving conflicting instructions from different superiors
- management decision-making based on expert advice received at the top end of the organisation rather than employee participation at the workplace level
- application of the managerial division of labour, specialisation of functions, and the precise definition of authority and responsibility structures
- creation of job security for personnel
- the setting of objectives throughout the organisation and the centralisation of plans to provide a 'unity of direction' for the entire firm.

9. Implications of classical approaches to organisation for employee relations

Employees of an organisation modelled on classical lines are expected to adopt a passive attitude, to do as they are told and consciously to fit in with the system. Management seeks to provide security of employment which (in a paternalistic way) can improve employee relations. However, the structure can stifle individual initiative and (crucially) be highly resistant to change.

Teamwork, project task forces, etc., with overlapping responsibilities and employees reporting to the team leaders of the groups to which they are assigned as well as to a functional head of department are not easily accommodated by the classical approach to organisation. Organisation charts, precise job descriptions and formal rules and procedures, moreover, can encourage parochial attitudes among employees and discourage flexibility. Ritualistic work routines may be accepted (indeed welcomed) by employee representatives, but the detailed minutiae of these routines can become ends in themselves and discourage workers from exercising initiative and wanting to become fully involved in the work of the enterprise.

Possibly the classical approach (which is unitarist in perspective – *see* 3) was suitable for the nineteenth and early twentieth centuries (when technologies were simpler and organisational hierarchies more precise) but is not suitable for today's complex and fast-changing business world, especially wherever interpersonal relations and possible conflicts of interest are involved.

HUMAN RELATIONS THEORIES

The human relations approach to management theory emerged **(a)** as a reaction against the moral implications of the classical school, and **(b)** from the observation that the practical application of classical principles failed disastrously in many situations. Taylorism – so the human relations movement alleges – does not bring out the best in people. Thus it is necessary for managements to seek to satisfy workers' personal needs in such a way that workers will respond by giving their total commitment to the organisation.

Human relations (HR) theory shares two things in common with the classical approach:

(a) Like the classical school, HR approaches are *universalistic*, believing that certain basic principles should always apply regardless of circumstances. However, the HR principles advocated (*see* below) differ radically from those of the classical school.

(b) Human relations theory is unitaristic in orientation (*see* 1:3). Workers are assumed naturally to want to relate to their employing organisation rather than to a trade union. Accordingly, advocates of the school perceive little need for the institutionalisation of conflict. Rather, emphasis is placed on the minimisation of the potential for disputes and the development of communication between management and workers.

10. Origin of the human relations school

Human relations theories originated with the work of G. Elton Mayo (1880–1949) who in the 1920s and 1930s observed with academic colleagues the behaviours of small working groups and experimented by altering the environmental circumstances in which work was undertaken. This important research (for details see *Organisational Behaviour*, published in this series) suggested that group relationships were far more important in determining employee behaviour than were physical conditions and the working practices imposed by management. Also, wage levels were *not* the dominant motivating factor for most workers. Rather, behaviour depended on norms and standards established through contacts with other people within and beyond the working group. Leadership style, interpersonal and organisational communications, employee morale, group norms, group cohesion and job satisfaction are deemed especially important.

11. Propositions of the human relations approach

According to human relations theory, organisations should be constructed to accommodate the social and human needs of employees rather than expecting individuals to fit into a predetermined organisational form. Specific conclusions were that:

- Employees work better if they are given a wide range of tasks to complete.

- Standards set internally by a working group influence employee attitudes and perspectives more than standards set by management.
- Application of the division of labour can make work so boring, trivial, and meaningless that productivity actually goes down.
- Non-economic rewards can motivate workers more than high wages – feelings of happiness and security often result from factors independent of pay.
- Individuals perceive themselves as members of groups. Norms of behaviour emanate from standards set by the groups to which workers belong, and not from standards imposed by management.

The HR school further recommends flexible organisation structures with overlapping responsibilities, employee participation in decision-making, and joint determination by manager and subordinate of the latter's targets.

12. The work of Douglas McGregor (1906–64)

Douglas McGregor, a leading HR theorist, asserted that classical theory made unrealistic suppositions about employee attitudes. McGregor outlined two alternative sets of assumptions. Theory X was the set of assumptions likely to be adopted by autocratic managers who believed that the average person dislikes work and must therefore be coerced, directed and threatened with sanctions. According to McGregor, theory X assumptions are that:

(a) People will avoid work if they can. Hence inducements, sanctions, and close supervision are necessary to stimulate effort.

(b) Workers are naturally reluctant to assume responsibility, preferring the security of control by management.

(c) People are happier with clearly defined tasks than broadly defined objectives.

In opposition to theory X McGregor recommended the adoption of an alternative set of assumptions about human nature. These he referred to as theory Y. The major propositions of theory Y are that:

(a) Workers will normally devote as much effort to their work as to their home and recreational activities. Individuals will work hard without coercion.

(b) Generally, employees will exercise self-direction and self-control.

(c) Industrial society constrains the realisation of individual creative potential. Such potential exists in most people – it has only to be extricated and developed.

McGregor condemned the theory X suppositions that the average employee will not work hard unless coerced into doing so, and that workers require continuous supervision and detailed specification of tasks. Work, argued McGregor, is natural to the human species, and those who perform work will normally devote their full attention, effort and interest to its completion. Thus, management's primary concern should be to harness the innate energy and willingness to co-operate of the workforce – managers do not have to coerce and threaten workers to make them work hard, employees are capable of self-control.

13. Advantages and disadvantages of the HR approach

The implications of the HR approach for employee relations are obvious: worker participation in management decisions, sound employee communications within enterprises, teamwork, and so on. Human relations theories recognise explicitly the role and importance of interpersonal relations in group behaviour at work, and reject the presumption that society consists of a horde of mercenary individuals each attempting selfishly to maximise his or her personal self-interest.

HR theories have been attacked, however, for being unrealistically altruistic, and for failing to recognise the inevitability of conflicts of interest in business affairs. Arguably, the HR approach overestimates the motivation, the desire to participate in decision-making, and the occupational self-awareness of many employees. Not everyone wants to exercise initiative or to control their work. Indeed, many people have little idea of what they actually expect or desire from the employment experience and thus welcome directions imposed by a higher level of authority. And it perhaps focuses too much attention on the influence of small groups while neglecting the effects of the wider social structures within which groups are embedded. HR theories have little to say about the influence of trade unions on employee attitudes and behaviour.

14. Neo-human relations approaches

A number of sub-schools have emerged within the human relations framework. The various sub-schools differ in respect of the following:

(a) The content of the material studied. Some insist that leadership style is the major determinant of employee behaviour, others emphasise individual psycho-social differences, the role of job design, etc.

(b) Whether they study the effects of external variables (political systems, for example).

(c) How they view the role of empirical research in relation to abstract theory, e.g. whether they believe that the basic forces that motivate workers can be observed and accurately measured.

(d) How they interpret the relationship between the way people feel and what people actually do, particularly as this affects patterns of interaction between individuals.

(e) The mechanisms that researchers believe contribute to the formation and change of attitudes.

15. Structuralism

The structuralist school is a derivative of the human relations approach. It regards conflict between individuals and their organisations as inevitable and (importantly) not always undesirable. In particular, structuralists argue that:

(a) Each organisation is to some extent unique and has therefore special problems requiring specific approaches.

(b) Large organisations are usually complex and contain many groups with disparate and incompatible interests.

(c) Frustrations and disagreements between factional interests inevitably arise.

(d) Formal procedures based on pluralistic assumptions (*see* 1:**4**) are necessary to resolve conflicts.

SYSTEMS THEORY AND THE CONTINGENCY SCHOOL

16. Definition of the systems approach

The systems approach views organisational behaviour as the consequence of the interaction of social and technical factors both within the organisation itself *and* between the organisation and its environment. The school emerged from dissatisfaction with the rigid intellectual straitjackets imposed by the classical and human relations approaches.

Every aspect of the organisation is regarded as interrelated and interdependent. Thus, management's task is to:

- identify the key parts of the wider system
- determine the nature and extent of the interdependence of one part (subsystem) with others
- establish procedures for co-ordinating the system in order that it may achieve its organisational goals.

17. Origins and nature of the systems approach

In the 1930s Chester Barnard noted that, in addition to official structures, organisations typically possess powerful informal systems. Within an organisation there is upward and downward communication and unofficial leaders emerge. The organisation is a system inside which several networks of individuals interact, and which itself interacts with the wider social and economic environment. Many other writers have developed the theme of the organisation as a system dependent on interrelations between its component parts and with the outside world.

Systems theory emphasises the significance of interrelations between the various internal components of an organisation, and relations between the organisation and its environment. Firms, for example, exist in 'open' systems (*see* **19** below). They have relations with customers, suppliers, neighbours, and local and national governments. The usefulness of a particular management style might be affected by such relationships. For instance, laws exist to govern the conduct of industrial relations between firms and employees; limited liability companies are required to apply certain rules regarding rights and duties of shareholders; there are laws to protect customers from untruthful advertisements, and so on.

Systems factors

The systems approach enables changes in environmental conditions and their effects on management to be analysed methodically. An example of a systems factor might be an alteration in the individuals to whom an organisation is accountable; the structure and management style of a firm which must account for its actions to only one or two people will probably differ from the approach adopted by a firm that is accountable to a large number of shareholders. Again, a firm that must explain its behaviour to the government is likely to act in particular ways. Managements which are required to justify their actions to employees will have different attitudes from those which are not.

Systems theory emphasises the need for those in control of a system to define its boundaries clearly. Are, for example, customers to be considered an integral part of the organisation, or does the system end at the point of the sale? Often, a system can be accurately described through specifying where its boundaries lie, and many insights into how a particular system operates can be obtained by analysing what happens at the boundaries between the system in question and others.

18. Objectives of systems theory

The aim of systems theory is to bring together and integrate several approaches to and aspects of organisation. Individuals are known to possess attitudes, beliefs and perspectives deriving from a multitude of sources. As employees of organisations, moreover, people continually interact with others and with their wider environments in attempts to fulfil their material and psycho-social needs. The accurate analysis of how individuals pursue these interactions, their causes and their effects on the working of the overall system, is the main goal of systems theory.

19. Closed and open systems

A *closed* system is one that (*i*) is independent of its environment; (*ii*) determines its own destiny; and (*iii*) controls its own internal relationships. The continuing existence of a closed system does not depend on it entering transactions with the outside world.

Open systems, conversely, are in continuous contact with their environments, and the boundaries of such systems are neither rigid nor easily defined. They have the following characteristics:

(a) They transform inputs obtained from the environment into outputs returned to the environment (e.g. a firm transforms labour, materials and capital into goods and services).

(b) They must enter transactions with their environments (e.g. a firm must recruit workers and persuade customers to purchase its goods).

(c) They need to be able to adapt to external change.

Inputs and outputs

Inputs include human resources (i.e. how many workers are available, their skills and ability levels); physical resources, such as plant and equipment, raw materials, land and buildings, machines, tools, etc.; and financial resources, such as cash, loans, trade credit, and other monetary assets.

The process that transforms inputs into outputs involves:

- organisational policies and procedures
- decision-making systems
- control mechanisms
- the culture of the organisation.

Outputs might be in the form of physical goods, improved services, enhanced efficiency of the system, higher wages for staff and/or greater profits for shareholders.

Constraints on a system could include technical factors, actual or potential behaviours of competitors, resource limitations (skills shortages, for example), and the wider macroeconomic and political situation of the country in which the organisation is located.

Organisations as open systems

An organisation is a collection of people with a set of objectives and a number of sub-systems, usually including a technical sub-system for producing goods and a psycho-social sub-system for regulating social relationships and helping individuals attain their personal needs. Clearly, organisations are open systems since they: (*i*) operate within a wider society that impinges on their freedom to behave as they would like (through laws, social conventions, etc.); (*ii*) have flexible boundaries separating them from the wider society; (*iii*) undertake exchanges of information and resources with the outside world.

Specific issues of interest to systems theory include:

- whether the organisation should recruit its senior managers externally (open systems approach) or promote from within (closed system approach)
- where and how to raise finance, e.g. from retained earnings or from outside sources (share issues, for instance)
- the extent to which the organisation should use external agents or consultants
- attitudes towards after-sales service, provision of product guarantees, customer care facilities, etc.
- the degree of the organisation's involvement with trade associations and outside professional bodies.

20. Advantages and criticisms of the systems approach

Advantages of the systems approach include:

(a) It is *holistic* in that all aspects of an organisation's activities are considered.

(b) The effects of changes in one element of a system can be traced through to changes in others.

(c) Environmental influences are explicitly recognised.

(d) Relationships between inputs and outputs are examined.

(e) Models depicting cause and effect within particular systems can be constructed.

The main problem with systems theory is that it suggests few tangible propositions about how exactly managers should behave. It is one thing to think about businesses in systems terms, but quite another to translate these thoughts into concrete action. Systems theory is abstract and lacks immediately discernible applications. Further criticisms of the approach are:

(a) Organisational systems consist of and are run by people. Accordingly, interpersonal relations might be more important than particular input/output structures and organisational forms, which in any case are subject to human control.

(b) Systems theory has little to say about the causes of motivation to work hard within various types of system.

(c) The boundaries of a system might change according to circumstances and over time (changing patterns of distribution, for instance).

(d) Different members of the same system may have entirely different interpretations of its structure and aims.

(e) The actions of a single individual can instantly transform the nature of a system.

(f) Systems theory cannot of itself explain organisational behaviour without taking other considerations into account.

(g) Often, organisational relationships are highly complex. In these cases the application of the systems approach might naively simplify what in fact is an enormously complicated problem. There is a vast range of variables potentially relevant to organisational performance so that the specification of just a few inputs and constraints is bound to be arbitrary to some degree.

(h) Some advocates of the systems approach have used it to justify centralisation of administrative procedures (see Chapter 20) in circumstances where this might not be entirely appropriate. The tendency to centralisation follows from the adoption of a holistic perspective: hence the desire to concentrate decision making at the apex of the organisation.

21. The contingency school

This emerged from the systems approach and emphasises the need for flexibility in both organisational design and leadership style and asserts the impossibility of generalising about appropriate management behaviour for differing situations.

Each set of circumstances is regarded as unique. For example, a military exercise might require the coercion of large numbers of unwilling soldiers to perform dangerous, unpopular tasks. A management style relevant to this situation will not be the same as one suitable for managing a business! Similarly, circumstances within particular organisations vary between departments and over time.

The contingency approach is diagnostic rather than prescriptive, suggesting that the role of management is to identify characteristics which define situations and then apply management techniques appropriate to specific circumstances. The obvious problem is the vast range of variables – environmental, social, physical, economic, legal, technical, industrial – potentially relevant to each situation.

Inadequacy of human relations prescriptions

Whereas feelings of contentment, happiness and job satisfaction can improve workers' performances, not all working environments can be made satisfying or even interesting for the staff involved. Some work is necessarily unpleasant but still has to be done. The human relations approach relates operational efficiency to worker satisfaction. Unfortunately, it might not be possible to create pleasant working environments or adjust conditions to meet the social needs of employees. In this case, financial reward is probably the key motivator, and a contingency theorist would recommend payments which directly relate wages and effort, as would an advocate of the scientific management school.

22. Problems with the contingency approach

Adoption of the contingency approach releases managers from the rigid straitjackets imposed by other schools. Managers simply dovetail their behaviour to the needs of various situations. However, the contingency approach does involve certain problems:

(a) A manager who behaves in this manner may appear insincere and inconsistent to colleagues and (particularly) to subordinates. One approach is adopted today, and possibly an entirely different approach tomorrow, according to circumstances. Subordinates and others never know what to expect from the manager. Advocates of the contingency approach might object to this assertion on the grounds that management's role is to allocate different managers to the roles and situations for which they are best suited. In practice, however, most managers will necessarily experience a variety of situations and need to occupy several roles in the course of their work.

(b) The individual manager may not be sufficiently skilled or mature to be able to change his or her approach from one situation to the next, especially if the manager has not been trained in the techniques of contingency management.

(c) It may be entirely appropriate to apply certain basic principles regardless of circumstances, particularly where professional ethics and moral issues are concerned.

23. Post-Fordism

The term post-Fordism is sometimes used to describe the changes in working methods necessitated by the shift from standardised mass production associated with classical scientific management techniques and towards customised production using flexible manufacturing (*see* 14:**6**), total quality management (*see* 14:**21**), and so on (Sorge and Streeck 1988; Warde 1990). 'Fordism' involved the application of the division of labour to its maximum extent, low-cost production for mass consumer markets, and standardised work routines offering employees little discretion over how they completed their duties. The term arose in consequence of the Ford Motor Company's adoption of scientific management (*see* 2 to 7 above) in the 1920s. Key elements of post-Fordist production systems are:

- Labour flexibility, with employees undertaking a wide range of tasks.
- Batch production for multiple niche markets. Firms react quickly to changes in customer tastes and preferences.
- Widespread use of the latest information technology and manufacturing techniques.
- Greater need for trained and qualified labour.
- A large peripheral workforce (*see* 15:**9**) with little job security.
- Extensive use of sub-contracting, as opposed to company takeovers and mergers.
- Output that increasingly competes in international markets in terms of quality and product design rather than the price of the item.
- Teamwork and the empowerment (*see* 14:**8**) of working groups and of individuals.
- Decentralised collective bargaining (*see* 9:**5**), performance-related pay and the hiring of large numbers of workers on individual contracts.
- Employees themselves deciding how to complete jobs.
- Intense concern for quality management.

Several wider economic and political changes are said to have accompanied the move to post-Fordism, notably the privatisation of state-owned enterprises, a reduction in the level of state intervention in industry, less legally enforceable employment protection for workers, and a rise in corporate concern for employee welfare. Post-Fordism production requires different approaches to job design; the recruitment, selection and training of workers; work supervision and employee reward systems; than for standardised mass production technologies.

Criticisms of post-Fordist theory are that:

- It only applies within a limited number of companies. Mass production is still common, while the latest IT and flexible manufacturing systems are simply not available to numerous small businesses.
- Governments continue to intervene in private sector economic activity.
- Extensive state-sponsored employee welfare and social security programmes are to be found in all economically advanced countries.

MANAGERIAL IDEOLOGY

24. Nature of managerial ideology

The term 'managerial ideology' describes the totality of the ideas, opinions and perspectives of those who exercise formal authority (see 2: 2) in business situations and which seek to explain and justify that authority. No single managerial ideology is universally held by business executives, since ideology is heavily interconnected with general approaches to management and the latter vary from country to country and time to time. The main managerial ideologies are:

- unitarism, which (together with its opposite, 'pluralism') is discussed in 1: 3
- social Darwinism, which relies on *laissez-faire* and the idea of the 'survival of the fittest' in competitive employment situations
- paternalism (see 29), whereby the employer is assumed to have a moral responsibility for employee welfare
- classical and human relations approaches (see above).

Functions of managerial ideology

A manager's ideology will influence his or her sentiments, actions and expectations of how the workforce should behave. Ideologies filter information (downgrading the significance of any facts or occurrences that contradict the predictions of the ideology), and simplify (perhaps naively) complex issues. Possession of a distinct ideology helps the individual to cope with **(a)** uncertainty, **(b)** stress and other psychological demands of work, and **(c)** the strains that arise from ambiguities concerning the legitimacy of a manager's role. The latter is especially important because a manager's perception that his or her position in the social hierarchy is right and proper enables that person to give orders, expect them to be obeyed, and generally to exercise power. Managerial ideologies might be communicated to workers in attempts to inspire the acceptance by employees of management's 'right to manage' without interference from employees. The concept of 'management's right to manage' is referred to as 'managerial prerogative'.

25. Managerial prerogative

Belief in the propriety of managerial prerogative (i.e. management's *moral* right to manage in addition to the fact that management has control over resources and the ability to hire and fire) rests on a number of assumptions, namely that:

- Managerial perspectives and activities should focus on serving customers, *not* pleasing employees.
- Only management possesses the information, training, skills and resources needed to make effective decisions.
- Since management either owns the firm or has been appointed by its owners then management represents the organisation's fundamental interests and aspirations.

- Managers are able to take a more objective view of the needs of particular sections and departments than workers and hence can make decisions which maximise the well-being of the *entire* organisation.
- Employee representatives frequently lack the professionalism, training and basic education needed to assess the implications of important management decisions.

Workers are expected, therefore, to trust management to make wise decisions and to be impartial and objective. Individual managers' specialist knowledge and competencies should be recognised and respected, and management itself is deemed to know when and in what circumstances it is appropriate to consult with employees.

MANAGEMENT STYLE

26. Definition of management style

The term 'management style' has two (related) meanings. One is the demeanour that a manager adopts when dealing with employees; the other is the collective approach of the management of an entire organisation to questions of leadership, worker participation in management decisions, control of employees, and interpersonal relations between managers and basic grade workers. In the former context the particular style chosen will depend on personal inclinations, training and experience and on environmental factors. It will affect managers' relations with their subordinates, group productivity, and patterns of interaction among employees. In the macro-organisational sense, management style helps determine formal structure, line and staff relationships, whether the firm uses project teams, the frequency and character of interactions with workers, and so on.

27. National differences in management style

Significant differences in the management styles predominant within various nations can be identified. In some countries the prevailing style is highly formal and authoritarian, in others it is the reverse. National disparities result from:

(a) *Cultural* factors such as religion, attitudes towards industry and towards management as an occupation, and community views on efficiency, the role of profit, savings and investment. Achievement in business is rewarded more in some societies than elsewhere. Willingness to accept risk also differs markedly between countries.

(b) *Social* factors such as:
(*i*) Whether there exists a *work ethic* in the country. Higher incomes and increasing productivity create possibilities for greater amounts of leisure, yet in some communities managers (and others) choose to work extremely hard and take little time off regardless of their large remunerations.

(ii) *Social class systems*. A high degree of class and / or occupational mobility results in individuals from a wide variety of class and income backgrounds reaching the top in management positions. Class systems affect recruitment policies and procedures and promotion and salary grading schemes. Rigid class structures cause an oversupply of trained, educated and competent people in lower level management jobs, since social barriers prevent their moving up the hierarchy.

(iii) *Attitudes towards authority*. Paternalistic management styles and highly formal interpersonal relationships between managers and subordinates are likely in countries where deferential attitudes are valued for their own sake. The psychological distance between managers at different levels affects communication, problem-solving and decision-making systems.

(iv) Existence or otherwise of *strong desires to accumulate wealth*.

28. Types of management style

A continuum of management styles is available, ranging from complete autocracy on the one hand to a totally democratic approach on the other. Autocratic styles, which involve the issue of precise and detailed instructions covering all employee tasks, can be dictatorial or paternalistic. The dictatorial approach involves rewards and penalties (often in the form of a steeply progressive bonus system), threats of sanctions for under-performance, highly formal interpersonal relationships and, generally, strict control. Paternalistic styles similarly involve detailed supervision, though the manager tries consciously to capture the allegiance and respect of employees through the force of his or her personality. Favours are bestowed on those who adhere to the leader's wishes; dissent is tolerated, thought not condoned. Workers are not expected to exercise initiative – indeed they are actively discouraged from doing so. Consequently, workers are never allowed to develop their decision-making potential, so that work ceases whenever managers are not present to insist that it be done. Also, autocratic approaches can easily degenerate to dominance and unpleasant aggression.

The advantages of directive autocratic styles are:

(a) They are appropriate when quick and / or unpopular decisions are needed.

(b) Arguably, many employers prefer being told what to do rather than being consulted and expected to participate in taking decisions.

(c) Management takes the initiative in developing activities, in defining problems and suggesting solutions.

(d) Management is proactive rather than reactive, consciously seeking out new information and ideas and issuing instructions based on *facts*. Issues are clarified, there is co-ordination of events, employees are helped to complete their tasks.

29. Democratic approaches

These can be consultative or *laissez-faire*. Workers participate to varying degrees in planning, decision-taking and control, and there is much consultation and

121

communication. Whereas the autocratic manager 'tells' workers about decisions (possibly 'selling' decisions as well), the democratic manager involves workers in the decision-taking process. With *laissez-faire* leadership, workers are left completely alone to make whatever decisions they deem necessary to achieve their objectives. Consultation implies (but does not guarantee) joint decision-taking between workers and the group manager, though the latter will try his or her utmost to persuade workers to accept a particular point of view.

The *advantages* of the democratic approach are that it can improve workers' morale, stimulate their initiative and, through broadening their responsibilities, increase workers' job satisfaction. It improves employee motivation and sense of involvement; there is consensus on what should be done and general commitment to decisions reached.

Disadvantages are that decisions might fail through the lack of experience and expert knowledge of those contributing to them, and procedures for taking decisions may be long-winded and inefficient. Continual disagreement and lack of positive direction might prevent objectives being attained. Note, moreover, that the application of participative styles to *trivial* issues, while simultaneously refusing consultation on *major* decisions, may be bitterly resented by employees.

DESIGN OF ORGANISATIONS

Modern management theories strongly suggest that there is no unique organisational structure that is always applicable to every situation. Rather, choices are necessary and organisations need to be *designed* to suit the requirements of specific sets of circumstances. In particular, management must resolve the following issues:

- the extent to which individual employees should specialise and how precisely the division of labour should be applied
- whether and to what extent employees' responsibilities should overlap
- the spans of control (*see* **8**) of various managers
- how individual and departmental activities are to be co-ordinated and controlled
- whether to organise the firm around products, functions or people.

Four major factors affect these choices:

1 *How much information flows through the firm.* If information flows smoothly through the business and if interpersonal and interdepartmental relations are good, a relatively complicated organisation structure may be appropriate.

2 *Employees' attitudes, morale, abilities and educational attainments.* Organisations which use highly qualified staff for specialist tasks may need to adjust their organisation structures to meet the emotional requirements of this type of worker.

3 *The firm's goals.* A change in objectives might create the need for a new organisation structure. Consider, for example, a business which operates in a fast-moving, technically sophisticated industry and finds that a competitor introduces a new product which renders all existing models obsolete. The firm must react instantly by altering its own product line. This can involve complete reorganisation of methods of production, marketing and administration. A flexible structure that can be quickly altered is most appropriate in this case.

4 *The nature of the external environment.* Examples of variables affecting wider commercial environments are the laws and/or customs of society, market structures, the degree of market uncertainty, local business practices, perhaps even the local political system.

30. Organisation theory

To organise work is to break it down into units for allocation to people and departments. The system for distributing tasks constitutes the 'organisational structure' of the enterprise. This structure defines the framework within which activities occur. *Organisation theory* is the study of organisational structures, of how organisations function, the performance of organisations and how groups and individuals within them behave.

Organisations are composed of people. Control of an organisation, therefore, necessarily involves the regulation of human activity and the arrangement of people into hierarchies and working groups. Patterns of authority, responsibility and accountability must be fashioned and employees made aware of their duties. Individuals need to know the extent of their personal authority and whom they should obey.

31. The classical approach to organisation theory

This cannot be attributed to any one person; rather it is a conglomeration of the ideas of many people developed over several decades. The fundamental proposition is that people should be selected and trained to fit into the organisation – the organisation itself need not be structured to suit the human needs of particular members of staff. Rigid organisational patterns are specified and individuals are allocated to various positions according to their perceived suitability for those particular jobs. The principal tenets of the classical theory are outlined below.

Specialisation and the division of labour

Resolution of a job into simple, routine operations usually increases the speed and precision of the work. Less skill is needed for easy and repetitive tasks, so fewer highly qualified employees are required.

The concept of the division of labour can be applied to managerial work. Advocates of the classical approach would recommend that managers be responsible for a single function and not assume overall control of a wide range of activities. Hence, specialised skills are developed and individual performance improves.

In the managerial context, division of labour creates the need for a pyramid structure of authority and control. At the apex of the pyramid is the managing director (or equivalent chief executive), then come senior executives, line and staff managers, supervisors and, finally, operatives. Higher managers must co-ordinate the efforts of subordinates. The lower the manager's position in the hierarchy, the more specialised the duties performed.

Unbroken chain of command

There should be a clear line of authority running from the top of the managerial pyramid to its base. A break in the chain of command means that instructions issued by senior managers will not be implemented: chaos and disruption might then ensue.

Unity of command

A subordinate should be directly responsible to one superior only. Instructions to the subordinate should not be issued from different sources, otherwise orders received could conflict and the subordinate would have to choose which to obey.

Application of this principle is difficult in practice because of the strong influences sometimes exerted by informal authority systems. A person might in theory be responsible to a single superior, but in reality may behave according to standards determined by someone else.

The classical theory recommends narrow spans of control (see **8** above). It assumes that only small numbers of immediate subordinates can effectively be managed by one superior.

Management by exception

F.W. Taylor (see **2**) recommended that subordinates should submit to their superiors only brief, condensed reports on normal operations but extensive analyses of deviations from past average performance or targets set by higher management. Routine matters should be dealt with at low levels, leaving senior managers free to devote their time to unusual problems and major policy issues.

Delegation

The assignment of duties to subordinates, accompanied by the devolution of authority necessary to implement decisions, is essential for the efficient administration of large organisations because top management does not have the time or specialist knowledge to take all important decisions. Care is necessary in the choice of duties for delegation, and higher management must ensure that subordinates selected to receive delegated work are competent to complete it successfully. Recipients of delegated authority must be given all necessary resources and information. Systematic delegation is crucial for management development programmes. Work of increasing difficulty can be delegated thus gradually improving a subordinate's capacity to act independently.

32. Reactions to the classical approach

All organisation theorists have asked the same questions – how best to structure and administer working groups – but their answers have differed according to the schools of thought to which they belonged. The basic disagreement concerns the extent to which universal prescriptions – the idea that there is always one best way of organising a business (or other administrative unit) regardless of circumstances – may reasonably be applied.

The human relations approach

According to the human relations school (*see* **10** to **13** above) organisations should be designed to accommodate the social and human needs of the people who work within them. They should encourage personal initiative and release creative potential. Rigid organisation forms are said to inhibit the innate enthusiasm of junior managerial staff, hence reducing efficiency. Advocates of this theory recommend participative management. Targets jointly determined by subordinate and superior will be more readily accepted than those arbitrarily imposed.

Contingency theories

The contingency school (*see* **21**) insists that the general application of any of the previously discussed principles will, in practice, be doomed to failure. Instead, organisations should be individually structured to meet the requirements of specific circumstances. The contingency approach is therefore the antithesis of the classical proposition that authority and responsibility systems should be constant and predetermined. Rather, management should examine the influence of a number of key variables and then select an organisational structure that provides the 'best fit' to the needs of the situation. The variables to be examined include:

technology
environments
nature of employees' work duties
the firm's labour and product markets.

33. Line and staff organisation

Line managers are directly responsible for achieving the organisation's objectives, and exert direct authority over their subordinates. Line authority flows through the chain of command (*see* **31**), from the apex of the organisation to its base. Often, the chain of command is illustrated by means of an organisation chart.

Typical line management positions are: managing director, production director, general manager, works manager, sales manager, first line supervisor. Each position in the line system identifies points of contact between manager and subordinates, showing the authority of its occupant and to whom that person is responsible. Vertical communications proceed only through the line system; if a manager cannot handle a problem it is referred upwards to superiors. Equally, work may only be delegated to the subordinates of a specific position.

Staff managers

Staff managers advise line managers but do not possess authority to implement important decisions. Line executives might ask staff managers for advice, but are not obliged to accept their recommendations. Examples of managers likely to occupy staff rather than line positions are lawyers, researchers, industrial relations specialists, or technical experts.

Often, staff and line organisations are mixed. Such a combination is called a 'functional' organisation. It means that staff managers are empowered to implement their own decisions within carefully specified areas of activity. A personnel officer, for example, might be authorised to choose media to carry job advertisements, but not to select candidates for particular posts. Another example would be a training officer who is empowered to insist that members of other departments attend certain training courses, even if the line managers in charge of the individuals concerned are not keen on the idea.

Hence, 'functional authority' in this context means a specialist staff manager's right to control the activities of other departments within the limits of the function. Line managers are *obliged* to accept the staff manager's advice in certain prespecified matters relating to the relevant function.

34. Personal staff

Note the distinction between a 'staff manager' and a manager's 'personal staff'. The former is a position in the managerial hierarchy (e.g. company lawyer or training officer), whereas the latter consist of helpers who assist a manager (line or staff) to fulfil his or her duties. Personal staff are adjuncts to the line or staff manager concerned, who is solely responsible for his or her activities regardless of the inputs of personal staff. Examples of personal staff are personal assistants, secretaries, research assistants, etc., who provide services to one person, section or department rather than to the organisation as a whole.

35. Advantages and disadvantages of various systems

In practice it is frequently difficult to distinguish between line and staff organisation and to define who exactly is a line executive as opposed to a staff manager! However, advantages and disadvantages apply to each system. The *advantages* of line organisation are that:

- There is an unambiguous chain of command.
- Each person's area of responsibility is clearly defined.
- Everyone knows to whom they are accountable.
- It is coherent and easy to understand.
- Decision taking can be fast and effective (orders have to be obeyed immediately).

Disadvantages of line systems include:

- Staff advisers are relegated to subsidiary roles which, as highly qualified specialists, they may resent having to occupy.
- Line systems rely heavily on a small number of key personnel whose resignation or illness may cause great disruption.
- Power is concentrated into the hands of a few line managers who might

not be sufficiently mature, experienced or competent to exercise it responsibly or effectively.
- Line managers might be overworked, have to take too many decisions, and thus be subject to excessive amounts of stress.

For staff organisation the *advantages* are that:

- Line managers do not become immersed in detailed analysis of what to them are secondary issues.
- Staff specialists are left free to develop their personal expertise.
- Executive decisions are taken by people who have been trained and are sufficiently experienced to take them.

The *disadvantages* are:

- Possible confusion over who is responsible for what and who has authority over whom.
- Line managers might rely too heavily on staff specialists' advice.
- Line managers may receive so much advice from staff specialists that vital points are missed.
- Experts are not able directly to implement their expert recommendations.

'Functional' organisation has the following *advantages*:

- It lifts the burden of routine decision making from line executives.
- Expert decisions can be implemented immediately.
- Fewer line managers are required.

The *disadvantages* of a 'functional' organisation are that:

- Organisational structures become extremely complex.
- Much co-ordination of activities is required.
- Duplication of effort may occur.

36. Conflicts between line and staff managers

Conflicts between line managers and staff managers may result from the following factors:

- line managers' jealousy of staff specialists' superior knowledge and qualifications
- staff managers giving their advice in unintelligible technical jargon
- line managers not implementing staff managers' recommendations
- differences in the backgrounds and lifestyles of line and staff managers (the latter might be younger and more outward looking than line managers)
- resistance to change by line executives
- staff managers' possible lack of concern for wider organisational objectives beyond the confines of their particular specialisations
- employees perhaps taking more notice of staff managers' recommendations than line managers' directives
- staff managers giving advice that is theoretically sound, but impractical.

37. Tall versus flat structures

Narrow spans of control create numerous levels of authority within the organisation and therefore long chains of command. The advantages of a 'tall' organisation with many levels between top and bottom are:

(a) Managers may devote their full attention to the demands of their subordinates.

(b) It recognises that an individual's capacity to supervise others is limited and that it is better to deal with a small number of subordinates properly than to have contact with many subordinates but only in casual ways.

(c) There is less need to co-ordinate the activities of subordinates than in a flat structure.

(d) Duplication of effort among subordinates is unlikely.

(e) Communications are facilitated.

(f) Employees are presented with a career ladder and thus can expect regular promotion through the system.

(g) It facilitates specialisation of functions and the creation of logically determined work units.

'Flat' organisations have the following advantages:

(a) Managers are forced to delegate work; hence, subordinates acquire experience of higher-level duties.

(b) Morale may improve on account of the majority of employees being on the same level.

(c) Low supervision costs.

(d) Subordinates are given more discretion over how they achieve their objectives.

(e) Few personal assistants and staff advisers are necessary because there are fewer levels.

(f) Managers and subordinates meet directly without having to communicate through intermediaries. Thus, information will not be lost or misinterpreted as it passes up and down the organisation.

(g) Managers remain in touch with activities at the base of the organisation.

38. Organisational size and employee performance

The size of an organisation exerts several influences on the relevance of a particular organisational structure and on the attitudes and behaviour of its employees. Specifically, large organisations:

- have more extensive and complex communication systems
- contain a wider variety of interest groups
- require more co-ordination
- project relatively authoritarian images to their employees

- are perceived to offer greater opportunity for employee development and promotion
- have access to many specialist support services
- possess a large number of levels of management
- require much delegation of authority
- have many departments
- tend to be more bureaucratic than smaller organisations.

39. Structure and technology

The technology an organisation uses affects its structure and operations in the following ways:

(a) An organisation that operates in a high-technology environment must (normally) be involved in research and development.

(b) High-tech firms need to employ large numbers of technically qualified staff.

(c) Substantial amounts of training are necessary in high-tech organisations.

(d) Technology affects the nature and extent of the division of labour within the organisation and hence employee job satisfaction and morale.

(e) Complex technology may require narrow spans of control.

(f) A high-tech organisation will usually require a sophisticated management information system.

40. Structure and markets

The markets in which a firm operates can influence its structure. A number of market characteristics might affect organisation structure, including:

(a) *Number of customers and their location*. This will help determine whether the firm is organised by product or by market.

(b) *Extent of competition*. Fiercely competitive environments require organisational structures that can be quickly and easily modified (in order to introduce new products and/or change distribution systems).

(c) *The degree of market segmentation*. Market segmentation means splitting up a total market into sub-units (e.g. for teenage consumers, middle-aged men, consumers with different income levels, lifestyles, etc.) and then modifying product characteristics and promotional methods to fit in with the needs of each market segment. This affects the size of production runs and the number and structure of departments within the firm.

References

Fayol, H. (1916), *General and Industrial Management*, English translation Pitman 1949.

Gilbreth, F.B. and Gilbreth, L. (1914), *The Psychology of Management*, Sturgis and Walton.

Gilbreth, F.B. and Gilbreth, L. (1916), *Fatigue Study*, Sturgis and Walton.

McGregor, D.V. (1960), *The Human Side of Enterprise*, McGraw-Hill.

Mayo, G.E. (1945), *The Human Problems of an Industrial Society*, Harvard University Press.

Sorge, A. and Streeck, W. (1988), 'Industrial relations and technical change', in Hyman, R. and Streeck, W. (Eds.), *New Technology and Industrial Relations*, Blackwell, 19–47.

Taylor, F.W. (1911), *The Principles of Scientific Management*, Harper.

Warde, A. (1990), 'The future of work', in Anderson, J. and Ricci, M. (Eds.), *Society and Social Science*, Open University Press.

Weber, M. (1947), *The Theory of Social and Economic Organisation*, The Free Press.

Progress test 8

1. What are the three major schools of thought in management theory?

2. On what grounds did trade unions object to the introduction of Taylorism?

3. How did the human relations approach to management originate?

4. State four problems associated with the contingency approach.

5. Define (i) managerial ideology and (ii) managerial prerogative.

6. List the advantages of an autocratic management style.

9

COLLECTIVE BARGAINING

FUNDAMENTALS

1. Nature of collective bargaining

With collective bargaining, representatives of groups of workers seek to negotiate with and influence employers on matters relating to pay, working hours and conditions, indeed on any issue that affects working life. It recognises the weakness and ineffectuality of the individual worker as a negotiating unit and, implicitly, accepts the existence of conflicts of interest between management and employees.

Collective bargaining can be regarded as a means for the *joint regulation* of terms and conditions of work by management and employee representatives. Although collective bargaining has traditionally been concerned with wage determination, its scope has widened considerably over the years and today encompasses working hours, holiday entitlement, sick pay, promotion policies, pensions, the pace of work, maternity and paternity leave, and many other matters.

2. Outcomes to collective bargaining

These comprise 'substantive' agreements covering pay, hours and conditions of work, etc., and 'procedural' agreements which regulate the methods applied to settlements of industrial disputes. Procedural rules covering consultation methods, arbitration and grievance regulations, recognition agreements and so on can help defuse sudden conflicts through forcing parties to meet, discuss and negotiate. Each side will have time to reflect and reconsider its attitude and position. Responsible, flexible, compromising behaviour is encouraged.

Mutuality

The term 'mutuality' is sometimes used to describe a trade union's 'right to bargain' with management. In its extreme form, mutuality is an ideology (*see* 8: **24**) which asserts that:

- certain conditions of work and trade union privileges are non-negotiable
- workers have no responsibility for the competitive position of the employing organisation

- employees have the *right* to improved terms and conditions without being required to make major concessions.

Status quo clauses

These sometimes appear in grievance procedures, technology agreements (*see* **22**) and agreements concerning the conduct of work study exercises. A status quo clause represents a guarantee given by management to trade union representatives that none of a firm's existing workers will be made worse off in consequence of changes in working methods and that new systems will not be implemented without either **(a)** union agreement, or **(b)** a decision in management's favour by an independent arbitrator to whom the matter has been referred.

3. Advantages to collective bargaining

The existence of a collective bargaining system creates *rules* and *institutions* for handling disputes in a systematic manner. Norms of behaviour are established and the parties to a dispute can consider issues dispassionately and examine fully all their aspects and implications. As a technique of decision-taking collective bargaining offers several advantages: it encourages compromise, opposing viewpoints are openly discussed, and participants are drawn together in a common activity.

Collective bargaining between managements and trade unions can provide benefits to employers as well as employees, as follows:

(a) Negotiation with unions is an effective way of determining pay and working conditions and for settling disputes. If each employee were to negotiate his or her own pay individually, the firm's personnel authorities would need to spend enormous amounts of time in individual negotiations. Since every worker could earn a wage different to those of other employees, numerous petty difficulties would arise causing frictions and resentments among employees. Agreements negotiated with recognised, official, trade unions will normally be accepted by all union members, and can be expected to stick until the next round of negotiation.

(b) Meetings between management and unions provide a useful forum for discussion of wide issues concerning the progress of the firm, and for presenting workers' views to management.

(c) If unions are not allowed to bargain on behalf of the workforce, labour will still make its opinions known in some way, possibly with disruptive consequences – such as absenteeism, lack of effort, non-cooperation, perhaps even industrial sabotage.

(d) The existence of collective bargaining procedures might cause workers to feel more secure and hence be willing to co-operate with redeployment and alterations in working practices.

Another argument for collective rather than individual bargaining is that the latter is not in keeping with modern approaches to team working (essential for the operation of certain new technologies) at the workplace level. Group cohesion may suffer badly if each employee has to negotiate his or her own wage independent of other members of the team, resulting perhaps in significant differences in pay for employees who perform identical duties.

Long-term pay deals

Most negotiated pay agreements are for a 12-month period. Sometimes however pay deals extend to longer durations (two years for example). Long-term agreements are said to stabilise industrial relations, reduce the time spent conducting negotiations, and enable the firm to implement long-run strategies and to prepare meaningful labour cost budgets. The problem from the employees' point of view is that a sudden rise in the rate of inflation can drastically reduce their living standards. Hence, long-term awards may include measures to deal with upswings in inflation, e.g. via automatic cost of living pay increases or through provision for *ad hoc* second-stage wage increases.

4. Problems with collective bargaining

Against the benefits of collective bargaining are (from management's point of view) the strong possibilities that managerial prerogative (*see* 8: **25**) will be reduced, and that labour costs will increase. Further problems with collective bargaining are that:

- The setting of standard terms and conditions that apply to everyone prevents market forces from allocating labour resources in the most efficient manner.
- Certain individuals who could command higher wages if they negotiated their own pay are prevented from doing this, hence possibly reducing their motivation and productivity.
- Arguably, collective bargaining helps promote the interests only of those who are a party to it, at the expense of the welfare of the general community.
- The institutions of collective bargaining support the status quo and can be highly resistant to change.
- The need for collective bargaining might in fact represent little more than failure of management and workers to establish harmonious relations and work together as a team, so that it would be better to concentrate on improving teamwork rather than on collective bargaining.
- Collective bargaining might encourage 'them and us' attitudes.
- Management/labour relations become highly formal and bureaucratic, with a loss of personal communication between managers and the people who work for them.
- The rituals that surround collective bargaining could cause union representatives to lose touch with the 'rank and file'.

Collective bargaining is effectively useless if one of the parties is not prepared to compromise, since compromise is the essence of negotiation (*see* Chapter 7). Without compromise, collective bargaining becomes little more than a communications exercise, but without the participants necessarily realising that this is so. Also it is often the case that one of the parties to a dispute has much more power than the other, and is participating in collective bargaining just to enable the other side to 'save face'. The outcomes to negotiations are actually predetermined so that the time spent in collective bargaining is wasted. In multi-union situations, moreover, simultaneous negotiations with several different unions can be tedious and difficult, and the unions might not agree among themselves.

Wage drift

The term 'wage drift' is used to describe the situation that sometimes occurs whereby the average *actual* earnings of a group of workers consistently rises faster than basic pay rates. Explanations for the phenomenon include overtime working, merit pay increases, bonuses, shift premiums, grading increments and other incentive payments. Wage drift is important because it determines employers' real wage bills, irrespective of the wage levels negotiated via collective bargaining.

Personal contracts

A personal contract is the result of an individual bargain between the firm and the employee. It will specify a wage and terms and conditions of employment for that *particular* worker. Often the pay and conditions stated will differ from those pertaining to other employees. Personal contracts are more common for managers than for basic grade workers, although the practice of issuing personal contracts to manual workers is increasing throughout the industrialised world. Reasons for putting employees onto personal contracts include:

- the ability to pay higher wages to workers in occupational categories where there are skills shortages, and *vice-versa*
- moves towards short-term contracts
- facilitation of the introduction of performance-related pay
- removal of certain grades of labour from the process of collective bargaining
- partial or complete derecognition of trade unions (*see* 2:**22**).

Problems with personal contracts are that in aggregate they might be no cheaper for the employing firm than the outcomes to collective bargaining and that:

- Workers could still join unions and collectively fight for improved pay and conditions.
- The administrative costs and time involved in negotiating individual contracts may be very substantial.
- As employees discover they are earning less than colleagues doing comparable work they become demotivated and agitate for improved terms and conditions.

DECENTRALISED COLLECTIVE BARGAINING

5. Nature of decentralised bargaining

The term 'decentralised bargaining' is used in two contexts:

(a) To describe the situation where managements and unions in different firms in different areas conclude independent collective agreements at the establishment ('plant') level, rather than a panel of representatives of various firms and/or employers' associations negotiating with a panel of representatives of different trade unions in order to settle terms and conditions for workers in an entire industry or occupational group at the national level.

(b) To denote the practice that occurs in some very large enterprises (with numerous divisions, subsidiaries, units and sections spread throughout the nation) of empowering the management of each subsidiary, division, etc., to conclude separate deals with the union(s) in that unit, independent of agreements struck by 'local' managers and unions in the firm's other subsidiaries and divisions elsewhere.

Situation **(a)** is discussed below; situation **(b)** in **8** to **11**.

6. National and local agreements

Bargaining can occur at national, industry or plant level. At national or industry level a combination of employers will negotiate with a panel of unions to establish national wage rates and conditions of work. Quite often, however, these national agreements are looked on as representing minimum rather than actual terms. Thus, local union branch secretaries and employee representatives try to negotiate extra bonuses and better conditions with managements in individual workplaces.

Frequently, national agreements are formal and in writing, whereas local agreements are informal and unwritten. A major problem with national agreements is the difficulty of drafting them in sufficient detail to make them applicable to all firms and circumstances. Hence, they are usually formulated in very general terms. Note also that national agreements can quickly become out of date as business conditions change. Another difficulty with national-level collective bargaining is that since it typically involves a large number of employers and trade unions there is a significant probability that some members on either side will subsequently renege on agreements, or at least not enforce them enthusiastically. Negotiating panels often lack cohesion and are badly organised.

Local agreements have the advantage that they are immediately and directly relevant to existing circumstances and may be altered at short notice. Agreements negotiated by local union officials should enjoy the backing of local employees who, after all, elected local officials to office. However, the informality of local agreements might encourage negotiating parties to break agreements soon after they have been reached. Further problems with local bargaining are that:

- It is usually disjointed and disorderly, lacking the formal rules of procedure applied at national or industry level.
- It encourages unofficial industrial action within particular enterprises.
- Productivity and pay are not linked at the national level, possibly leading to inflation.
- There is leapfrogging of settlements among enterprises in the same industry sector or geographical area.

7. Factors determining bargaining levels

Whether bargaining occurs at industry, national or plant level depends on a number of factors, especially the current state of the labour market. Traditionally, unions have favoured plant-level collective bargaining during periods of economic expansion and labour shortage, when threats of local-industrial action are sufficient to compel profitable firms with full order books to grant large pay increases to the employees of a particular department or enterprise. Employers, conversely, usually prefer plant-level bargaining in times of high unemployment, so that firms in hard hit areas do not have to pay their workers nationally negotiated wage rates above the local level. Other determinants of variations in bargaining level include:

- cultural and historical factors such as whether an industry sector is concentrated in a geographically small area, or the degree of skill involved in the job
- technology, since the diffusion of advanced techniques is likely to carry with it a harmonisation of the wage levels of the people doing the work.

8. Decentralised bargaining within the same firm

This occurs when there is a shift in the level at which collective agreements are concluded from the level of the overall company to individual divisions or other sections within it. Reasons for single-employer decentralisation of collective bargaining include:

(a) Management's desire to relate employee remuneration to productivity levels achieved in *local* operations.

(b) The trend towards overall decentralisation and diversification of activities in large companies, with quasi-autonomous profit centres, budgetary control by local managers, decisions on industrial relations management being taken at the establishment level, etc.

(c) Increasing competence in the human resources management field of the line managers employed by large blue chip companies, consequent to more extensive training and better staff development than in the past.

(d) Effective teamwork within a local unit can be accompanied by team-based bonus systems.

(e) Local circumstances can be taken into account during collective bargaining.

(f) From management's point of view, decentralised bargaining has the advantage that unions find it more difficult to organise industrial action at the enterprise level because of the need to arrange ballots at each place of work, and the fact that workers in at least some decentralised units are likely to vote against and hence not become involved in strikes, etc. With centralised bargaining, conversely, a union need gain only an overall majority of votes in favour of industrial action at the *company* rather than individual workplace level.

(g) Increasing competition among businesses, recession and declining profit margins have led many enterprises to overhaul entirely their negotiating procedures in order to try and cut costs.

9. Advantages to single-company decentralised bargaining

These are as follows:

(a) Local factors can be taken into account during negotiations.

(b) Operational managers in divisions, subsidiaries, etc., become closely involved in employee relations decision-making.

(c) It is suitable for large companies with divisions that conduct differing types of work and hence employ disparate categories of employee, each with its own set of terms and conditions of employment.

(d) Unit-level performance-related pay can be introduced more easily.

(e) The firm's most highly valued groups of employees can be properly rewarded.

(f) Plant-level management/employee representative communications are facilitated.

(g) It might strengthen managerial authority at the local level.

10. Disadvantages of single-company decentralised bargaining

Decentralised plant-level bargaining tends to be informal, fragmented, heavily dependent on unwritten rules, and often undertaken by individuals without any training in negotiation or employee relations. The specialist expertise that a head office industrial relations unit may provide is sacrificed. Other problems are that:

- Whereas managements are often keen on decentralised bargaining when there is high unemployment and little union activity, their enthusiasm can wane when the situation is reversed and unions in local units successfully leapfrog each other's pay settlements.
- Changes in working methods and terms and conditions of employment might be introduced to local units in an uncoordinated and haphazard manner.
- The stability of a firm's relationships with national trade union officers could be endangered.

- To the extent that a company uses job evaluation, this will have to be applied at the local rather than company level leading perhaps to many inequalities in the pay of employees doing similar work but in different establishments.
- There is duplication of effort within the bargaining process.
- Regional labour shortages can enable unions to exploit the situation and obtain large wage increases, which then become benchmark figures for unions negotiating in other areas.
- The issues discussed during decentralised negotiations are likely to become parochial, ignoring matters relating to corporate strategy, planning and investment.

11. Use of decentralised bargaining

Decentralised bargaining is more likely where:

- There is little integration between the production systems of decentralised units (as sometimes happens when a business has expanded via mergers and acquisitions of other firms).
- The company has many products and operates in multiple markets.
- The impact of technical change is felt predominantly at the local workplace than at the company level.
- There is no overall corporate identity to which workers in decentralised units can relate.
- The skills and competencies needed to undertake a decentralised unit's work are found in local rather than national labour markets.
- There are big regional disparities in wage levels.
- A company's activities are spread over a wide geographical area.
- There are poor communications between workers in various decentralised units.
- Different unions operate in different units.
- Disputes and grievance procedures operate at the local and not the company level.
- Major changes in working practices need to be introduced in some sections of the company but not in others.

Decentralised bargaining in practice

Single-company decentralised bargaining can be arranged on product lines or labour market lines. The latter involves negotiations with particular occupational groups at the local level; the former requires single-table bargaining (*see* **14**) for *all* categories of worker concerned with a particular operational unit. Sometimes, companies introduce two-tier decentralised bargaining systems, with basic pay levels being determined centrally and leaving bonus rates, working hours, holiday arrangements, etc., to local determination.

Note how decentralised bargaining within a company requires a more active personnel department than otherwise might be the case. In particular, the personnel department needs to:

- provide expert help and advice to decentralised units
- develop schemes for training local managers in the skills of negotiation
- implement disciplinary, grievance and disputes settlements procedures at the local level.

ENFORCEABILITY OF COLLECTIVE CONTRACTS

12. Personal contracts and collective contracts

Contracts of employment are discussed in 3: **9**. In Britain, outcomes to collective bargaining in the form of collective agreements can only be incorporated into an individual employee's contract of employment if the affected person has previously agreed to this happening. Thus, for example, a worker's contract may state that levels of pay and conditions of employment negotiated between management and trade unions shall apply to that individual. If so, union pay rates will be imposed on the worker concerned *regardless* of whether he or she is a union member or not. Otherwise, collective agreements will not apply to all the firm's employees unless **(a)** there exists a statute compelling acceptance (as in the Health Service for example), or **(b)** there has been long-standing acceptance of collective agreements by everyone involved.

13. Collective agreements and the law

In the UK, collective agreements are binding 'in honour only', and special legal immunities cover unions and workers who break a collective agreement (albeit one incorporated into employees' contracts of employment) during an industrial dispute. This differs markedly from the practice in most other EU countries, where:

(a) Collective agreements are legally binding, so that workers who break a collective agreement can be sued for damages by the other side (this is the case in all EU nations except for the UK and Ireland, and in the latter country case law has held that certain collective agreements bind those who are party to them).

(b) In some countries it may also be the case that national collective agreements *automatically* extend to and legally bind other firms and workers who were not party to the agreement. Hence, such agreements could cover the bulk of the workforce, even though trade union membership is minimal in the industry or country concerned.

Collective agreements concluded within a certain sector can be extended to bind non-signatories at government discretion in Belgium, France, Germany, Luxembourg, the Netherlands and Portugal. In Spain they *automatically* apply to all firms in the same trade in the same local area. Italian law provides for collective agreements to apply throughout the relevant industry, while in Greece a collective agreement can be extended by ministerial discretion provided at least 51 per cent of workers in an industry are already covered by the agreement.

Arguments in favour of collective agreements being legally enforceable are that:

- It creates medium-term stability in management/worker relations.
- Firms are able to plan ahead in the knowledge that wage rates will not alter.
- Legal enforceability encourages the parties to an agreement to specify its terms clearly and precisely in case the agreement has to be interpreted by a court of law.
- Co-operative attitudes are encouraged, with both sides having to ensure that the terms of the agreement are strictly satisfied.
- Unofficial strikes are less likely as they might result in the strikers being sued for damages.

The arguments *against* enforceability include:

(a) Experience suggests that in countries where collective agreements are legally binding, concentrations of strike activity occur when agreements are being renegotiated for the next period. These strikes can be bitter and protracted.

(b) Workers can easily find other ways of being disruptive apart from striking (and hence making themselves potentially liable to pay damages).

(c) Enforceability only applies to formal written agreements. In practice many workplace 'agreements' emerge from *ad hoc* deals struck between sectional managers and workplace employee representatives. It is extremely difficult to establish whether a collective agreement even exists in such circumstances. Thus, enforceability could encourage widespread resort to unofficial, unrecorded, *ad hoc* workplace bargaining.

(d) Trade union power is reduced, which is arguably unfair in view of employers' command over financial and physical resources.

(e) Collective agreements can become out of date and irrelevant shortly after they have been negotiated, yet they legally bind the signatories for substantial periods.

DEVELOPMENTS IN COLLECTIVE BARGAINING

The range of issues subject to collective bargaining has widened and could today include equal opportunities, single status, the introduction of new technology, and procedures for removing workers' capacities to strike. Increasing public awareness of environmental factors, moreover, could lead to ergonomic issues (less noise on production lines, brighter and airier offices, etc.) occupying a leading position on the negotiating agenda. The major recent developments in the scope and nature of collective bargaining are discussed in the following sections.

14. Single-table bargaining

The term 'single-table bargaining' (STB) is used to describe the situation where the pay and conditions of *all* groups of workers employed by an establishment are determined around a single table in a single set of negotiations. This might involve a single union representing both manual and non-manual employees, although it is more common for single-table bargaining to mean several unions negotiating at a single table in order to bargain as a single unit.

Implications of STB

Bargaining arrangements are unified and usually relate to a common pay and grading system, which encompasses all employees from unskilled labourers to junior managerial staff. STB makes sense in single-status situations (*see* **17**) where all workers have the same hours, holidays, sick leave and pension entitlements, etc., so that alterations in these can be settled for (nearly) everyone in the organisation at a single sitting. It is interesting to note that British trade unions have been generally supportive of multi-union STB because it represents a credible alternative to the single union deals (*see* **19**) increasingly imposed by managements on their workers. Often, STB is offered by an employer as part of an overall package intended to streamline the firm's employee relations. Hence STB might only be available if accompanied by the introduction of flexible working practices, teamworking, new quality assurance procedures, etc.

15. Advantages of STB

The benefits of STB are:

(a) Less time and other resources need be spent on the negotiating process.

(b) Unions are induced to adopt a common position and resolve inter-union conflicts *before* negotiations open.

(c) STB is an excellent medium for introducing major changes in working practices.

(d) Demarcations in working practices encouraged by fragmented bargaining can be avoided.

(e) STB creates a forum for the discussion of wide-ranging matters connected with business policy and the future of the firm.

(f) All the company's collective bargaining activities are completed at the same time of the year.

(g) The firm's employee relations structure is greatly simplified.

(h) Effective management/worker communications are facilitated.

16. Problems with single-table bargaining

STB might not improve the efficiency of bargaining in cases where important differences in terms and conditions of employment apply to white collar and blue collar (manual) employees, since separate discussions will be necessary on the hours, bonus payments, leave entitlements, etc., of each group. Further problems are:

(a) Managements lose the ability to change the conditions and working practices of specific groups of employees independent of the remainder of the workforce – management cannot easily reward those whose skills, motivation and commitment make their contributions to the firm especially valuable.

(b) Workplace union representatives in certain sections of the organisation might not be able to represent their members effectively.

(c) Rivalries between manual and non-manual unions can still occur at single-table negotiations.

(d) STB might be accompanied by a common job evaluation system covering all grades and types of worker, yet the nature of the work undertaken by various employees could be fundamentally different leading to numerous possibilities for disputes and conflict.

(e) The voting rights of the unions sitting at the table need to be established. Should the union with the highest number of members within the establishment have the majority of votes on the union side of the negotiations, or should a 'one union, one vote' situation apply?

(f) The system can become overloaded with work as diverse employee groups raise more and more issues for discussion at the single table. Yet if separate procedures are established to deal with matters that are specific to particular groups then the entire STB arrangement might lack credibility.

(g) Single-table bargaining may be said to go against approaches to management/worker relations which emphasise concern for individual values and motivation rather than collectivist trade union action.

(h) STB requires higher levels of skill and maturity among negotiators than does separate bargaining, particularly where strategic matters concerning training, human resources planning, and the overall direction of the business are concerned. Management and union representatives might not be competent to undertake this work.

Critics of STB allege, moreover, that it undermines union power through restricting a union's ability to improve its members' conditions via separate negotiations, and that it prevents managements from 'playing off' one group against another. Responsibility for reconciling divergent interests among the workforce is transferred from management to the firm's unions. And it could be extremely difficult to ensure that all parts of the workforce are properly represented.

17. Single status

STB is frequently connected with agreements providing for single status within an enterprise. Single status is the practice of managers and all other categories of employee (including basic grade operatives) sharing the same canteen, using the same car park, wearing similar clothes, having equal access to company superannuation schemes and enjoying similar welfare and fringe benefits. In Britain, a number of legislative and other environmental factors have encouraged the introduction of single status, notably:

- European Union Directives on aspects of employee protection (health and safety for example) that apply to *all* categories of employee
- Laws on equal pay for men and women doing work of equal value
- Technological advances that call for working practices which cut across traditional occupational boundaries
- Increasing recognition of the importance of the production operative's role and of the need to motivate production workers (via teamwork, quality circles, etc.)
- Trade union mergers which mean that many white collar and blue collar workers now find themselves in the same union.

Other factors militating towards the adoption of single status are:

(a) Many manual jobs that (normally) do not carry 'staff' status (with superannuation and so on) in fact require more skill and longer periods of training than certain non-manual jobs which automatically attract 'staff' benefits.

(b) The availability of mechanical handling devices has removed many previously important distinctions between 'light' and 'heavy' labour.

(c) It is no longer the case that white collar staff necessarily earn more than production operatives (as was invariably the case in the 1800s and the early years of this century).

(d) The terms 'white' and 'blue' collar workers are themselves not *literally* applicable today because (compared to the past) relatively few contemporary manual jobs need be physically dirty. There is no reason in principle why operatives and managers in most modern firms should not dress in a similar manner.

(e) A century of public education has created a labour force that, for the most part, is literate and capable of communicating meaningfully with people from other backgrounds and in higher level occupations.

(f) The values to the firm of manual and non-manual occupations have narrowed in many areas.

(g) Nowadays, skill shortages are just as likely in manual as in non-manual occupations so that it is no longer necessary to offer higher status to non-manual workers as a recruitment incentive.

The major effects of single status on manual workers' terms and conditions are usually:

- Hours of work are shortened.
- Fringe benefits, particularly pensions and sick pay, are improved.
- Control becomes less strict; for example, manual workers are no longer required to clock on.

- Overtime is paid at a lower rate; the natural resistance to this change is often dealt with by a simultaneous productivity agreement which abolishes or greatly reduces the amount of overtime worked.

18. Advantages of implementing single status

Differences in working hours, eating places, modes of dress, etc., contribute to a sense of class distinction within a company, perhaps encouraging adversarial attitudes towards industrial and employee relations. Specific advantages to single status include the possibilities that it can:

- improve the organisational climate of an enterprise through underpinning management's concern to be fair to all employees
- promote positive attitudes towards flexible working
- help the firm recruit top quality workers through the creation of a progressive corporate image
- encourage workers to adopt a responsible approach to their jobs, willingly participate in workplace group problem-solving and decision-making, exercise initiative, etc.
- induce unions to accept productivity agreements that improve the economic efficiency of the business
- increase the firm's ability to redeploy workers. (The existence of numerous status differentials makes it difficult to move people into jobs that do not carry the same status privileges as previously.) Thus, single status necessarily encourages the acceptance of change.
- cause individual employees to identify with the company *as a whole* rather than with a particular grade within its status hierarchy.

In adopting single status, management transmits a strong and clear signal that it values and respects all its workers. The sight of senior directors carrying their own trays in the company canteen, of heads of department having to turn up early in order to guarantee a parking space in the firm's car park, of directors clocking-in alongside all other grades of staff, etc., tells the world that top management is genuinely committed to working as an integral part of a company-wide team and is not concerned with petty status differentials.

Barriers to single status

Although common terms and conditions of employment can be introduced within a company, psychological perceptions of differences in what constitutes correct attitudes and behaviour for various employee groups might continue unabated. To some extent this is proper and inevitable, because managers, supervisors and operatives have differing duties and responsibilities and hence disparate prestige and 'status'. More concrete barriers to the introduction of single status include:

- interest groups (white collar employees or skilled workers for example) seeking to maintain their existing privileges
- the potentially high cost of applying common terms and conditions

throughout the organisation, especially in view of the tendency to 'harmonise upwards' in borderline situations

- the pride that some workers feel in being recognised as undertaking a certain occupation
- unions possibly regarding single status as a *starting point* for further improvements in members' pay and conditions, rather than as the final outcome to a package involving concessions by both sides to a negotiation.

Not surprisingly, single status has been adopted most successfully in 'greenfield' business start-up situations where operatives, supervisors and junior managers are recruited fresh and where the single status arrangement applies from the outset.

19. Single-union agreements

Employers in countries that have many different trade unions face a number of problems. They might have to deal with several unions covering the same category of manual worker (maintenance staff, for example, could belong to an electrical trade union, an engineering union or a general union), while white collar employees might be members of a separate division of an industrial union or members of a union that only recruits white collar staff. Employees of various levels of skill could belong to different unions. Each union possesses its own perspectives, rules, and expectations of how management should behave and typically will demand separate negotiations on pay and conditions. Unions representing skilled workers will probably wish to maintain pay differentials between their members and those of unions recruiting unskilled operatives.

Multi-unionism has been criticised for encouraging demarcation ('who does what') disputes, for increasing the cost and complexity of collective bargaining, and for the leapfrogging of pay claims by various unions. A further difficulty is that as technologies change, so too do the skills requirements of workers – meaning that a previous trade union affiliation may no longer be appropriate. In particular, computerisation and the widespread use of robotics has cut across conventional occupational boundaries, and multi-union negotiation of agreements for the workers in establishments using these technologies is *extremely* troublesome. There is a duplication of effort within the company's unions, possible conflict between unions as employees transfer from one type of work to another, and so on.

Firms confronting such problems could derecognise certain unions in favour of others (a somewhat drastic policy that may provoke adverse reactions) or, more commonly, may seek to negotiate a single-union agreement, i.e. a deal whereby an employer will only recognise one union for the purpose of collective bargaining. Workers who wish to belong to a trade union must join this single union.

20. Advantages and problems of single-union agreements

The *advantages* to a firm having a single company union include:

- greater acceptance of change by the workforce
- less scope for demarcation disputes
- a more adaptable workforce capable of undertaking a wider variety of tasks
- identification of the firm's employees with the overall activities of the company
- administrative convenience and cost effectiveness
- the fact that the union as well as management becomes irrevocably committed to the well-being of the enterprise
- the ability of full-time union officials to specialise in negotiating with a single firm, hence developing a deep knowledge of its staff, operations, management personnel, working practices, etc.

Critics of single union deals have alleged that:

- The union recognised will not be genuinely independent and will inevitably become subject to management control.
- They are only relevant where the firm offers its workers long-term security of employment.
- Arguably, a union that represents manual workers is not necessarily the best union also to represent managers, supervisors and engineers.
- Union ability to impose serious sanctions to defend members' interests is weakened.
- The unions competing to be the one recognised are required to participate in demeaning 'beauty contests' that involve their throwing away many of their traditional weapons in order to gain recognition.

21. Pendulum arbitration agreements

Pendulum arbitration is a method for fixing the level of pay increase to be awarded to a group of workers. Management and (usually) a trade union each submit to an independent arbitrator figures they believe to be reasonable. The arbitrator selects one figure or the other: the parties are not allowed to haggle. The settlement is binding on both sides.

The *advantage* claimed for pendulum arbitration is that it forces the parties to be realistic in their demands; there is no 'splitting the difference' as commonly occurs with conventional collective bargaining. Thus, a union which claims a ridiculously high pay increase (as an opening gambit prior to accepting something less) is bound to lose under this system provided management does not submit a proposal that is equally absurd. Management also must take care not to offer too little or the arbitrator will 'swing the pendulum' towards the union's more reasonable demand.

Acceptance of pendulum arbitration means the assumption of risk by both the parties to a dispute, since it is an 'all or nothing' method of conflict resolution which involves a gamble that the arbitrator will agree with one side's proposal. Not surprisingly, therefore, pendulum arbitration is invariably preceded by intense 'behind the scenes' in-house discussion and negotiation prior to recording a failure to agree and subsequent referral to the arbitrator, which (perhaps advantageously) will be avoided if at all possible.

Problems with pendulum arbitration include:

(a) There is no *guarantee* that the disadvantaged party will actually accept the arbitrator's decision.

(b) It might encourage one of the parties not to negotiate as sincerely as otherwise might be the case, and not to offer concessions.

(c) There is outside interference with the enterprise's work.

(d) The arbitrator may not understand the complex circumstances surrounding demands and offers, especially where the negotiations involve a package of pay rises, holiday entitlements, working hours, pension benefits, etc. Hence 'all or nothing' awards could be unfair in relation to certain elements of the package.

(e) Where there are preliminary negotiations, the parties to the initial negotiations might make 'last minute offers' to prevent an issue going to pendulum arbitration, thus encouraging negotiators to keep back certain concessions until the last moment – as occurs with conventional negotiations.

(f) The cost of losing could be much higher than with conventional 'concession' bargaining – so high that the loser might have no alternative but to refuse to accept the arbitrator's decision.

(g) Each party to the dispute might be hopelessly over-optimistic regarding its chances of winning over the arbitrator, leaving the arbitrator to choose between two utterly unreasonable positions.

22. New technology agreements

A new technology agreement is an accord whereby management and unions jointly consider, negotiate and agree procedures for the introduction of major technical innovations. In Britain they were introduced in a number of industries in the 1970s, at a time when the rate of change of technology began increasing. Since then, however, they have become less common, possibly because of higher unemployment and a weakening of unions' abilities to demand such agreements, and probably because the idea of technical change is today more readily accepted without challenge.

The purposes of new technology agreements are to facilitate the application of new equipment and working methods, reduce uncertainty and involve unions directly at the time a significant change is contemplated. Bargaining then ensues over the amendments to job specifications, working practices and employee reward structures implied by new methods and systems. The contents of a new technology agreement typically include:

- predictions of the consequences of the technology to be introduced for existing employees
- arrangements for discussing problems
- a statement of management's commitment to avoiding compulsory redundancies

- retraining, regrading and redeployment policies
- possibly a status quo clause and details regarding arbitration in the event of a failure to agree
- the extent and character of the management information to be disclosed to workers' representatives.

A problem with new technology agreements is that the rate of technical change is today so rapid that it is frequently impossible to disentangle 'new technology' from alterations in working methods brought about by a whole range of related factors. Hence the specific matters that are covered by the agreement might be unclear. Further difficulties are that:

- The implementation of new technologies essential for the firm's survival could be impeded.
- Managerial prerogative (*see* 8: **25**) is constrained.
- Inefficient working methods might result from the application of the agreement.
- The document could be out of date as soon as it is concluded.

23. No-strike agreements

These are clauses in workers' contracts of employment which forbid the worker from going on strike. In Britain, no-strike clauses may be included in contracts only if they are in writing, made known to the worker, and agreed by independent trade unions. Because UK collective agreements are not legally binding, a no-strike deal is worthless in a technical sense because a union can break it at will without fear of legal consequences. The real significance of a no-strike agreement lies in the *commitment* of all parties to settle disputes via means that exclude industrial action. Operation of a no-strike deal requires:

- provision of a working environment that as far as possible eliminates the need for industrial action
- solemn commitment to the use of independent arbitration if all else fails
- extensive application of in-house grievance and disputes procedures prior to external arbitration
- high quality communication channels between management and labour.

In the UK, most no-strike agreements automatically refer a dispute to ACAS (*see* 3: **4**) once internal procedures have been exhausted.

Critics of no-strike deals allege that:

- Unions entering into them are weakening their bargaining power and generally 'selling out' to management.
- They only apply to *formal* relations between management and the workforce, ignoring unofficial 'wild cat' strikes at the workplace level. To the extent that shopfloor workers perceive their union to be collaborating with management at the expense of employees' interests, such unofficial action is likely to increase rather than diminish.

24. Equality bargaining

Under the Treaty of Rome discriminatory terms in collective agreements that disadvantage either of the sexes are illegal throughout the European Union. Employers can be taken before industrial tribunals for imposing on individuals unfairly discriminatory contracts of employment, and trade unions can be sued for encouraging firms to practise unlawful sex discrimination. It should follow, therefore, that managements and unions have an incentive to purge their collective bargaining machinery of unfair discrimination and to amend existing collective agreements to make them non-discriminatory. Examples of unfair clauses in collective agreements include:

(a) Length of service requirements prior to employees becoming eligible for certain benefits where this disadvantages women who have taken time out of the labour force in order to bear and raise children.

(b) Job evaluation procedures which fail to generate equal pay for men and women undertaking work of equal value in terms of the effort, skill, decision-making and responsibility involved in their jobs. For example, tribunal cases have determined that the work of a factory nurse was of equal value to that of a skilled fitter, that a secretary's work was equal to a data analyst's, and that the demands made on a seamstress were of equal value to those made on a fork-lift truck driver.

(c) Rules concerning the availability of overtime, access to training, promotion systems, etc.

25. Problems of application

A number of difficulties arise in the application of equal opportunities considerations to collective bargaining, including:

(a) Most business executives, trade union negotiators, personnel managers and employers' association representatives are male, so that sex equality issues might be discussed without any female participation.

(b) Equality matters could be regarded as peripheral to the main content of a negotiation and hence dealt with quickly and superficially at the close of the discussions. Indeed, there might even be separate machinery to discuss equality issues, thus further 'marginalising' the consideration of such matters.

(c) Sexual stereotyping and pre-assumptions about the sorts of work that are suitable for men and women are still common in many organisations.

(d) Women continue to lack influence in trade unions. Branch meetings may take place at times and in locations not convenient for them, and equality issues rarely figure prominently on the agendas of union branch meetings.

(e) Because many powerful unions and occupational groupings are male dominated, whereas occupations undertaken predominantly by females tend to be less powerful (in terms of their ability to take destructive industrial action), then managements may be more likely to seek to pacify male-dominated interest groups at the expense of female workers.

Many difficulties arise from the fact that large numbers of women work part time, resulting in their ineligibility for pension and sick pay schemes, bonus arrangements, training, promotion, etc. Note how an agreement to increase bonus rates rather than basic pay could indirectly discriminate against female workers, who may not have access to overtime and other categories of work that qualify for bonus payments.

Practical measures for improving sex equality in the context of employee relations could include:

- establishment of a company working party to deal with equality issues
- analysis of current agreements to identify sources of possible unfair discrimination
- monitoring the earnings, extent of overtime working, bonus payments, etc., of male and female workers
- close examination of job evaluation systems and their implications for sex equality
- extending negotiations to include discussion of enhanced maternity leave, career-break opportunities, flexible fringe benefits (e.g. the ability to trade off longer maternity leave against pension rights), the retraining of women in traditionally 'male' occupations, etc.

Progress test 9

1. Define collective bargaining.

2. What is meant by 'mutuality' and what are its philosophical foundations?

3. List four problems associated with collective bargaining.

4. What factors should determine the extent of a bargaining unit?

5. State six advantages of single-company decentralised bargaining.

6. How does British and continental European law differ in relation to the enforceability of collective agreements?

7. Define 'single-table bargaining'.

8. What are the major effects of single-status deals on manual workers' terms and conditions of employment?

9. List the main criticisms of multi-unionism.

10. What is pendulum arbitration and how does it operate?

11. Define 'equality bargaining' and state the problems associated with its introduction.

10

HANDLING GRIEVANCES

1. Causes of grievances

Employee grievances can arise from the actions of management or from the behaviour of other employees (as in the case of sexual harassment for example). They might result from external circumstances, such as the employer imposing detrimental working or other conditions or treating a particular employee less favourably than others, or from internal feelings of unhappiness within the individual even though no formal employment rule or obligation has been breached (interpersonal conflicts for instance).

Grievances caused externally can be resolved (assuming they are well-founded) through altering environmental circumstances: restoring a contractual right, improving conditions, increasing a benefit or whatever. Grievances resulting from the worker's hurt feeling might best be resolved through counselling (*see* 1: **11**). Common causes of employee grievances are:

(a) *Conflicts of interest*. These might be cleared up by defining more carefully the authority and responsibilities of specific people and departments, and by generally promoting co-operation between sections.

(b) *Misunderstandings*. Here a simple statement of facts may be all that is required to resolve the matter causing difficulties.

(c) *Breakdowns in communications* (*see* 1: **10**). The solution in this case is to increase the flow of information within the organisation.

(d) *Interpersonal rivalry and petty jealousies*. Teamwork and group cohesion (*see* 1: **11**), with all employees striving to attain the same corporate goal, need to be encouraged in these circumstances.

(e) *Frustration*. This occurs when a person feels he or she is being prevented from achieving a goal by an outside influence. The sense of frustration is greater the more important to the person is the unachieved objective. Paradoxically, therefore, the highly motivated, hard working, enthusiastic and ambitious worker is sometimes more likely to become frustrated and raise a serious grievance. This type of problem should be dealt with via counselling, two-way communications, and joint manager/worker objective setting. If frustration is 'bottled up' within the person then he or she might fly off the handle following the most trivial incident, possibly an event totally unrelated to the issue causing the frustration.

2. Control of grievances

The first step is to identify precisely the cause of the grievance: the agreement that has been broken, the rule that has not been observed, the custom that has (allegedly) been violated, etc. Hopefully, written and detailed guidelines will exist; otherwise there is scope for argument over the *interpretation* of agreements and procedures, especially where 'custom and practice' is concerned. Examples of customary practices in work situations abound. They can relate to job gradings, methods for calculating bonuses, working hours, interpersonal relations between grades, demarcation of tasks, holiday arrangements, frequency of absenteeism, etc. Similar difficulties arise in interpreting the meaning of the words of a written agreement. For example, does 'part-time' staff mean people who work less than a certain number of weekly hours, or staff who come to work less than five days a week, or who work continuously for a few weeks at a time and are then laid off only to be redeployed a few weeks later, or employees who work five days a week but only in the afternoons, or what? The rule here is to apply the meaning *intended* by those who made the agreement in the first instance. What did those people want to happen as a result of the agreement – how would they have behaved in this situation?

Employees do not normally raise grievances they do not believe to be important. Therefore, management must be *seen* to be taking complaints seriously. (Indeed, in cases of alleged sexual or racial harassment there is a legal requirement to do so.) No organisation is so well managed that its employees never need to complain. Well-constructed grievance procedures enable firms to resolve complaints quickly, fairly, and without resort to industrial action on the part of employees. Formal procedures minimise the risk of inconsistent decisions: the employer is *seen* to be trying to be fair.

3. Grievance procedures

Most grievance procedures require the aggrieved worker to approach his or her immediate supervisor in the first place. Then, if the matter is not resolved, the worker might nominate a representative (often a trade union representative) who takes up the case. The union representative will discuss the matter with the supervisor and, if settlement is still not forthcoming, with higher levels of management. The problem then enters the firm's normal collective bargaining and/or arbitration system.

Normally the union must agree as a condition of its involvement not to initiate any form of industrial action until all stages of the procedure have been completed. It is important for the agreed procedure to set out any matters that management is not prepared to discuss, such as matters not related to the immediate workplace or questions involving wages and terms and conditions of employment, plus any restrictions on the right to use the procedure (for instance, if the employee must have worked for the organisation for some minimum period).

4. Formality versus informality

Formal procedures establish an agreed set of rules for settling complaints. A number of *advantages* accrue to having a formal procedure:

(a) Important matters are clarified in relation to the timescale for lodging a complaint, who is to hear the grievance, appeals procedures, etc.

(b) Both sides have a common understanding of how the grievance will be processed.

(c) The drafting of procedures requires management and employee representatives to discuss important issues including the *nature* and possible causes of grievances likely to arise.

(d) There is continuity in procedures. Note how promotions, resignations, transfers and retirements of staff mean that the managers and union officials who deal with grievances change periodically.

(e) Misunderstandings about what was discussed and agreed during the hearing of a grievance will be minimised if the hearing is recorded and follows a set of formal rules.

(f) Workers have the security of knowing that whenever major problems arise they can air their concerns to the highest levels of authority within the organisation. Management is compelled to consider the consequences of its actions in the context of their possibly resulting in invocations of the grievance procedure.

The main *disadvantage* to the formalisation of procedures is perhaps that it reduces flexibility, since precedents established through following formal rules must be adhered to in future cases. A mini legal system will build up around the policies, with its own protocol, norms, case law and rules of interpretation. It becomes impossible to 'turn a blind eye' to certain practices regardless of the circumstances in which they occur.

Further problems with formal procedures are:

(a) Their existence necessarily affects managerial prerogative (*see* 8: **14**) since departmental managers and supervisors, who occupy 'front-line' positions in management's contact with the workforce, are liable to have their decisions challenged.

(b) Unscrupulous unions might use grievance procedures vexatiously as part of a wider industrial relations offensive. (A union might, for example, instruct its members to invoke the procedure whenever possible in order to inconvenience the management and hence pressurise it into conceding a pay claim.)

(c) Formalisation does not remove the underlying causes of grievances, it merely changes the forum in which grievances are discussed. Grievances might be dealt with faster and more equitably if they are settled on the spot.

5. Union involvement

Although formal grievance procedures invariably provide for union involvement at some stage, this may not always improve the situation. Indeed, some
systems exclude union representation from the first stage of the procedure on
the grounds that complaints can often be settled more quickly and effectively
through relatively informal discussions between complainant and supervisor
without any outside interference. Other procedures allow for representatives to
present the complainant's case from the outset, arguing that representatives are
more objective, unemotional and thus better able to articulate a case in a lucid
and coherent (and hence more efficient) way.

Particular problems with union involvement occur in the following
circumstances:

(a) The cause of the grievance is itself attributable to the union, e.g. if management and the union have negotiated an agreement whereby certain groups will
be made worse off as part of a wider terms and conditions deal. A member of
the disadvantaged group might then complain, yet be denied union representation.

(b) Union representatives support some workers' grievances more vigorously
than others depending on the representative's attitudes and experience and
the difficulty of the case. A racially prejudiced union representative, for
example, might not wholeheartedly support a member belonging to an ethnic
minority group. Cases which are difficult, complex and/or emotionally harrowing might not attract the same degree of union support as other, easier
cases.

(c) Certain workplace representatives have friendly relations with management generally, and do not wish to prejudice this relationship through becoming
involved in contentious, confrontational issues.

6. Grievance interviews

These differ from disciplinary interviews (*see* 11:**12**) in that there is no presumption of anyone's 'guilt'. Rather the task is to establish facts and then either:

- remedy the grievance, or
- convince the aggrieved worker that the complaint is unfounded.

Another important characteristic of a grievance interview is that it is not possible
for a person hearing the grievance to predetermine a response, as he or she will
probably have little prior knowledge of the nature of the grievance until it has
been explained. Thus, grievance management requires good listening skills and
a flexible approach.

Grievance interviews normally proceed as follows:

(a) The complainant states the background to the case and is asked to outline
what he or she would like done. Interviewers then seek clarification of ambiguities or seeming contradictions in the complainant's case.

(b) Witnesses are interviewed, facts investigated.

(c) The company rule, policy, procedure or custom that must have been broken for a complaint to be valid is identified.

(d) Remedial action is implemented or an explanation given of why the complaint cannot be accepted.

It is important that interviews be conducted by managers empowered to take and implement decisions that will clear up the matter. Otherwise confidence in the system is undermined and much time is wasted in explaining problems to people unable to do anything about them.

Progress test 10

1. Give six examples of possible causes of employee grievances.

2. Define 'frustration' in the context of work and explain its consequences.

3. What is the commonest procedure for dealing with employee grievances?

4. List the arguments in favour of formal grievance procedures.

5. How does a grievance interview differ from a disciplinary interview?

11

TERMINATION

An employment relationship may be terminated because the employer no longer has any work for the worker to do ('redundancy') or in consequence of **(a)** the employee's incapacity to complete his or her duties, **(b)** misbehaviour, or **(c)** some other substantial reason. Additionally, contracts of employment can end through retirement or resignation, although these do not normally have employee relations implications.

COMPANY RESTRUCTURING

1. Downsizing

Changes in technology and economic recession have led to large numbers of workers in western countries losing their jobs. Even in Japan – where security of employment is an integral feature of the economic system – redundancy increasingly occurs. The dismissal of employees is an extremely serious matter for which careful planning is required. Procedures must be fair and seen to be fair: otherwise great disruption can ensue, followed perhaps by legal action. Allegations of unfair dismissal (including unfair selection for redundancy) are a major source of conflict and industrial disputes.

Delayering

This is a technique of downsizing and efficiency improvement that consciously seeks to increase senior managers' spans of control (*see* 8:**5**). It has been applied most commonly in tall managerial hierarchies containing several levels of middle management, each individual executive controlling the work of just a few immediate subordinates. A major justification for delayering an administrative system is the advent of computer-assisted management which sometimes enables managers simultaneously to oversee the work of up to 30–35 subordinates. This saves money and speeds up the flow of communications within the firm. Conditions for successful delayering are:

(a) It needs to be completed as part of an overall strategy for restructuring an organisation; not as a panic measure during a financial crisis.

(b) Paperwork and administrative bureaucracy must be reduced and simplified so as to enable the remaining executives to perform effectively.

(c) The company's most talented people should not be delayered just because they happen to occupy a certain position in the management hierarchy.

(d) Delayering should be done in a single 'big bang'; otherwise uncertainties concerning the possibility of further delayering exercises can greatly demotivate the surviving workforce.

Divestment

This involves the sale or closure of operating units (usually subsidiaries or divisions) in order to rationalise activities, concentrate resources in particular areas, or downsize the organisation (though note how downsizing can occur via reductions in the size of the labour force rather than shutting down whole units). Reasons for divestment include:

- financial losses attributable to specific operations
- the decision to focus all the firm's attention on its core businesses, at the expense of peripheral activities. This might result from perceptions that resources will be better used if they are concentrated in particular areas and/or that management is not able to control a widely diversified enterprise.
- the need to raise large amounts of cash at short notice
- government insistence that a firm be broken up in order not to contravene state monopoly legislation
- predicted technological changes that will cause products to become outdated
- collapse of a market
- failure of a merger or acquisition
- a division absorbing more of the firm's resources than management is willing to provide.

Note how the selection of a unit for divestment offers management a convenient scapegoat that can be blamed for all the company's past problems.

REDUNDANCY

The term 'redundancy' is frequently misused, although it does have a precise legal meaning (see below). Sometimes a management will declare an individual to be redundant when what they should really be saying is that the person concerned is being dismissed for incompetence, misconduct (see 7), or some other reason.

2. Meaning of redundancy

Redundancy is a dismissal situation in which the firm's requirements for the employee to carry out work of a particular kind have ceased or diminished or are expected to do so. Many countries have laws intended to help workers who face redundancy. In Britain, for example, anyone given notice of redundancy is entitled to (a) paid time off work to look for another job, and (b) a redundancy payment.

A redundancy can result from the firm's human resources plan, or unexpectedly through alterations in market forces or government policies. Note how it is a worker's *job* that becomes redundant, not a particular worker. Redundancy can sometimes be avoided through work-sharing or early retirement schemes. If not, criteria for selecting redundant personnel must be determined. These criteria should be fair and objective. Among the criteria commonly applied are length of service, age, capabilities, qualifications, experience, past conduct, and suitability for alternative employment within the organisation. Naturally, trade unions and governments are concerned that redundancy procedures be impartial, and many laws and codes of practice have been introduced including (usually) the following requirements:

(a) Workers' representatives must be informed immediately redundancies are proposed. Selection criteria should be disclosed and timetables for layoffs clearly stated.

(b) Management should provide reasons for the redundancies, and be prepared to negotiate on union proposals for their avoidance. In particular, management should seek alternative work for workers threatened with the sack.

(c) Before contemplating redundancies, management should stop recruitment, ban overtime, introduce short-time working, and insist that all employees over normal retirement age retire. Volunteers for redundancy should be sought. As far as possible, the workforce should be cut via natural wastage rather than compulsion.

The commonest criteria adopted when selecting workers for redundancy is perhaps that of 'last in first out', which minimises the value of redundancy payments but results in the firm losing its most recent (and possibly most able) recruits, usually young workers. Note also that any system of 'voluntary' redundancy is likely to mean that better qualified employees will leave, since these are the people who can find alternative work most easily. The cost to the firm of offering voluntary redundancy (severance pay, enhanced pension benefits, etc.) will be high, and could create skills shortages.

No sensible business deliberately wants to declare its employees redundant, since such a policy would lower morale among the remaining workforce and create unfavourable outside impressions of the firm. Indeed, current production might actually fall through employees reacting to threatened redundancies by working to rule, withdrawing co-operation, or even going on strike.

3. Role of human resources planning (HRP)

Forward planning can help a firm make the best use of its human resources, and is extremely valuable for avoiding redundancies. A human resources plan needs to compare the firm's existing labour resources with forecast labour demand and then schedule a series of activities for acquiring, training and perhaps redeploying workers. HRP activities include:

- the analysis of labour turnover rates for various occupational groupings and grades of labour

- prediction of the consequences of intended changes in working hours, holiday entitlements, production methods, etc.
- identification of potential labour deficits or surpluses and hence the preparation of recruitment, training and redeployment plans.

Effective redeployment requires that the firm's management know exactly what each employee is able to do. This information might be assembled via the preparation of a 'skills inventory' that lists all the attributes, qualifications and experience possessed by each worker. The problem is that employees may resent being questioned about aspects of their backgrounds not strictly relevant to their current jobs. On the other hand, the collection of such information enables management to assess each person's suitability for alternative work.

4. Outplacement

The process whereby management actively helps workers who face redundancy to cope with the situation is known as outplacement. Examples of outplacement include:

- assistance with financial planning (how best to invest a redundancy payment for example) and with procedures for applying for state financial support
- provision of information on pension rights and benefits for employees taking early retirement
- giving workers time off to look for other jobs over and above minimum statutory requirements
- helping employees draft and word-process their CVs
- counselling to assist affected employees cope with the psychological effects of being declared redundant
- psychometric testing to discover employees' aptitudes for alternative types of work
- providing retraining facilities within the firm
- contacting supplying and client companies to ascertain whether they have any vacancies
- circularising local firms advising on the availability of labour in the company in question and inviting them to conduct recruitment interviews on its premises.

5. Redundancy policies

Some firms negotiate redundancy procedure agreements with trade unions, stating:

- management's commitment to avoiding redundancies wherever possible
- specific measures to be taken to prevent redundancies (banning overtime for example)
- periods of notice and settlement terms to be applied when redundancies are inevitable

- the extent of the management information to be disclosed to unions
- criteria to be used when selecting workers for redundancy
- procedures for appeal against selection for redundancy.

Although some trade unions will not enter into redundancy procedure agreements on the grounds that they regard it as improper to negotiate away their members' jobs, others welcome the opportunity to help determine how redundancy matters are handled. Also, union involvement enables union representatives to negotiate the best settlement packages.

In Britain, managements are legally obliged to consult with *recognised* trade unions (*see* 2: 2) regarding planned redundancies not later than:

- at least 30 days before the first dismissal if 10–99 employees are to be dismissed over a period of 30 days or less at one establishment
- at least 90 days before the first dismissal if 100 or more employees are to be dismissed over a period of 90 days or less.

The unions must be informed in writing of the reasons for redundancy, the numbers and descriptions of the employees affected, the present number of employees of those descriptions, the proposed method of selection for redundancy and the proposed method of carrying out dismissals. An employer must reply to any representations made by the unions, giving reasons if any of them are rejected. This UK legislation incorporates the 1975 EU Directive on Mass Redundancies, which imposes similar requirements on all EU member states.

Redundancy payments

In Britain and many other countries, employers who declare workers redundant must pay them a limited amount of compensation. Sometimes the state itself will establish a 'redundancy fund' to finance such payments. British workers become entitled to a redundancy payment on completion of two years' continuous employment. The purposes of redundancy payments are:

- to help the individual worker financially during a difficult situation
- to encourage labour mobility through providing workers with a monetary incentive to move out of declining industries
- to minimise the extent of industrial conflict associated with redundancy
- to discourage overmanning.

OTHER FORMS OF DISMISSAL

6. Meaning of dismissal

Dismissal means the termination of employment by **(a)** the employer, with or without notice, or **(b)** the failure of the employer to renew a fixed-term contract, or **(c)** the employee's resignation, with or without notice, when the employer behaves in a manner that demonstrates refusal to be bound by the contract of employment. The latter is termed 'constructive dismissal'. It means the employer is behaving so unreasonably that the worker has no alternative but to quit.

Normally, an employer must give the employee notice of dismissal as stated in the worker's contract of employment. Occasionally, however, dismissal without notice is permissible. This is known as 'summary' dismissal and could occur when an employee's behaviour makes impossible the fulfilment of a contract of employment. Examples are theft, persistent drunkenness, violence, abusiveness to colleagues or customers, wilful disobedience, or incompetence that immediately causes damage to the employer's business.

Managements need coherent and consistent dismissal policies, including details of who may dismiss employees, and in what circumstances. Serious industrial disputes might follow a dismissal, so it is imperative that dismissals be fair and reasonable, having regard to all the circumstances, and be seen to be so.

7. Wrongful dismissal and unfair dismissal

Many countries have statutes that govern how employees may be fairly dismissed. In Britain, for example, there is the Employment Protection (Consolidation) Act 1978, under which employees covered by the Act (i.e. those with at least two years' continuous service) may only be fairly dismissed for genuine redundancy or for:

(a) *Gross misconduct*, e.g. refusal to obey reasonable instructions, dishonesty, persistent absenteeism, neglect of duties, etc.

(b) *Incapacity* to do the job, caused by such things as incompetence, illness (once the workers' contractual sick pay entitlement has expired), or the person not having the skills or aptitude for the work

(c) *Some other substantial reason*, e.g. going on strike, disruption of staff relations, or a temporary job coming to an end provided the impermanent nature of the work was fully explained to the worker when the employment started.

Wrongful dismissal

This occurs when insufficient notice is given. It gives rise to a civil action for damages equivalent to the actual loss incurred. Wrongful dismissal may be claimed by any dismissed worker, regardless of length of service – a worker who has been with the firm for only a few days may be 'wrongfully' sacked.

Allegations of wrongful dismissal are heard by normal county courts; cases concerning unfair dismissal in industrial tribunals. Note that whereas costs in the latter are intended to be minimal (and in normal circumstances are never awarded to the other side) costs in the county court can be huge.

8. Dismissal procedures

Key elements of a satisfactory dismissal procedure are:

- Precise specification of who is entitled to dismiss employees (heads of division, a personnel department, the chief executive, etc.).
- A clear set of rules (e.g. on timekeeping or not smoking in certain areas) that have been communicated to workers, preferably in writing.

- A formal system for recording disciplinary events and for issuing warnings. Note that an unrecorded 'informal' warning *cannot* be used to justify disciplinary action following a repetition of the offence. Informal warnings are precisely that, i.e. off-the-cuff reminders not to behave in a certain way. Vindication of disciplinary sanctions requires cataloguing of misdemeanours as they occur, and the issue of formal *written* warnings outlining the likely consequences of continuing errant behaviour.
- A right of appeal.

Need for reasonable behaviour

Any court or tribunal will expect the employer to have acted *reasonably* at all times. Employers must prove that misconduct vindicating dismissal actually occurred, and specify where and when the misconduct took place and how it affected the worker's job. The worker's past record must be considered, and actual damage to the organisation demonstrated. Then the firm will be required to show that the dismissed person was not selected unfairly from others who were equally guilty, that dismissal rather than some lesser action was required, that formal warnings were issued, proper investigations carried out and that a fair dismissal procedure was followed.

Natural justice

In addition to the above, courts and tribunals expect employers to apply the 'rules of natural justice' to all disciplinary matters. Natural justice requires that:

- the accused person be allowed to state a case and to hear the evidence given against that person
- accusations be supported by evidence
- the worker have access to all relevant information and documents
- the employer act in good faith and without bias.

9. The ACAS code

Disciplinary procedures should be in writing, easy to understand and made known to employees and their representatives. The UK Advisory, Conciliation and Arbitration Service (ACAS – *see* 3: 4) has issued an important code of practice on these matters. This code recognises that the maintenance of discipline is a management responsibility, but emphasises the desirability of involving workers' representatives when drafting procedures. In addition to the points outlined in 8, the main recommendations of the ACAS code are as follows:

(a) Employers should indicate the forms of conduct that are considered unacceptable, and in what circumstances. Rules should be particular rather than universal and justified in terms of the objective requirements of a job.

(b) All workers should be given a copy of company rules and have them explained orally as part of an induction programme. Employees should be informed of the consequences of breaking rules, particularly those rules which if broken may result in summary dismissal.

(c) Only senior management should have the power to dismiss.

(d) The accused person should have the right to be accompanied at disciplinary hearings by a trade union representative or by a fellow employee of his or her own choice.

(e) Employees should not be dismissed for a first offence (except for gross misconduct). The code distinguishes between informal oral warnings for minor infringements of rules, and formal written warnings issued following serious offences. Formal warnings should set out the nature of the breach of discipline, the likely consequences of further offences, and should state that the warning constitutes stage one of the formal procedure. If misconduct is repeated, a second and final written warning should be issued containing an unambiguous statement that a further recurrence of the offence will lead to whatever action (suspension, dismissal, or some other sanction) has been determined. Assuming the errant worker's behaviour does not improve the next step is suspension or dismissal, accompanied by a written statement of reasons for the action taken and details of the right of appeal.

(f) The employer should take into account the employee's age, position, length of service and general performance, and whether domestic problems etc. make it appropriate to reduce the severity of the disciplinary action taken.

Appeals

These should be considered quickly and be heard by a higher level of authority than took the original disciplinary action. Wherever possible the appeal should be considered by independent people who are not the immediate superiors of the manager who decided to dismiss the worker. The procedure should spell out the actions that may be taken by those hearing the appeal, and enable any new evidence to be made known to the employee.

10. Criticisms of disciplinary procedures

Criticisms of the concept of firms being required to operate formal disciplinary procedures are:

(a) They prolong unpleasant situations usually without affecting the outcome. If a worker is to be sacked it is perhaps better to have the matter dealt with quickly. Processing dismissals through lengthy procedures rarely affects the eventual outcome, yet involves the employer in significant expense and inconvenience.

(b) The need for clearly defined rules can lead to a proliferation of bureaucratic company regulations and directives.

(c) Availability of a procedure might itself cause certain employees to treat disciplinary matters light-heartedly.

(d) If management can discipline workers who misbehave, why should there not be a procedure for the workforce to discipline managers who act badly? This might be effected through having worker directors (*see* 6: **17**) with executive authority.

(e) They allow outside interference (via industrial tribunals) with the operation of the enterprise.

11. Management action

Motivated employees usually exercise effective self-discipline, though control is often improved if workers receive clear, precise and comprehensive instructions about what they are expected to do. Also careful records of workers' performances, attendance, timekeeping, etc., need to be maintained. 'Custom and practice' should be clarified, and expected standards fully explained. There is a minefield of legislation in the disciplinary area. Mistakes can be costly, and the entire process is harrowing for all involved.

Management should seek to pre-empt disciplinary problems by minimising the risk of poor performance and by creating conditions which allow employees to work satisfactorily. Probationary employees should be told what is expected of them. Employees should be regularly appraised so that when people do not come up to standard the cause is likely to be their own carelessness, negligence, idleness or misconduct, rather than incompetence.

Actions short of dismissal

These are disciplinary sanctions other than the sack (e.g. demotion, denial of pay increases, loss of fringe benefits or refusal of requests for time off). Actions short of dismissal can be an extremely useful means for offering an errant worker the chance to reform. The ACAS code (*see* **9**) suggests that formal oral warnings are appropriate for minor offences – formal in the sense that they are recorded on the employee's personal file, with the employee being advised that the warning has been recorded.

According to the code, an employee's substandard work should be dealt with initially by merely mentioning the inadequacy and reminding the person that he or she has a responsibility to achieve the required standard. Management should offer extra training, and give the employee adequate time for improvement, especially if he or she has recently been promoted and is having difficulty coping with higher level duties.

12. Disciplinary interviewing

Disciplinary interviews are inevitably more formal than other types of interview, and need to cover the following points:

- The rule or convention violated and why the breach was serious enough to justify disciplinary action.
- Whether the alleged offence was committed for the first time or is a repetition and, in the latter case, why the worker ignored previous warnings.
- Possible consequences of the employee's actions.

- Evidence relating to the supposed breach of discipline.
- Any extenuating circumstances to explain the employee's behaviour.
- An analysis of the facts of the case, a decision, and an explanation of the decision.

Interviews should be conducted soon after the event in question, otherwise memories of the details of what actually happened will fade. The interview needs to take place in private and without interruption. Workers should be allowed to be accompanied by a representative, and to ask questions of witnesses. The ACAS code recommends that whenever action beyond an informal warning is likely, the employee should be given a written statement of the allegations as well as being told about them orally.

PROCEDURE IN INDUSTRIAL TRIBUNALS

An industrial tribunal is a three-person court, with a qualified solicitor or barrister in the chair plus two lay members, that hears cases relating to alleged unfair dismissal, health and safety at work, equal opportunities, and certain other employment matters. Each of the lay members represents one of the two sides of industry (unions and employers' associations, which supply the UK legal authorities with lists of persons they wish to sit on tribunals). The background to industrial tribunals is explained in 3: 5. This section outlines the documentation and procedures to be followed in tribunal cases involving alleged unfair dismissal.

13. Initiating a case

To initiate a case the aggrieved person (referred to as the 'applicant') completes form IT1 (called an 'originating application') which he or she obtains from a post office, Job Centre, Citizen's Advice Bureau or the DSS. Only brief particulars of the case need be stated (no more than a paragraph or so) and the form is designed to be easy to complete. The IT1 must then be sent to the local office of the industrial tribunal (the address is provided with the form) where it is photocopied. One copy is sent to ACAS and another to the employer (called the 'respondent') who must complete and return form IT3. The latter is known as a 'notice of appearance', and is sent to the employer with the copy of the originating application. Like the originating application, form IT3 is very straightforward and only requires a brief outline of the employer's defence. Copies of the IT3 go to the applicant and to ACAS.

14. Role of ACAS

On receipt of copies of the IT1 and IT3, the local office of ACAS will charge one of its officials with the task of helping the parties settle the matter out of court. The ACAS official will offer to visit the complainant at home to discuss the case and will offer to speak to the employer. ACAS officers act only as intermediaries and are not allowed to take sides.

15. Further particulars

If the ACAS officer's attempts to obtain a mutually agreeable out-of-court settlement are unsuccessful a date is fixed for the hearing of the case. By this time each side will have seen an outline of the other party's case and, if it wishes, may request 'further and better' particulars of its substance. For example, if an employer states that a worker who alleges that he or she was unfairly dismissed was actually sacked for incompetence, the worker may demand precise details of the supposed incompetence. An employee accused of being persistently late can ask for the dates of his or her supposed latecoming.

Should a demand for further particulars be refused, the other party can ask the tribunal to order their provision. Refusal to obey such an order results in that party not being allowed to present a case when the tribunal convenes. This means that only one side of the story is heard so, normally, the party presenting the case will win. Similarly, both sides may request copies of documents that are relevant to the proceedings, e.g. contracts of employment, internal memoranda concerning disciplinary action, letters to outside persons (excluding legal advisers), work rotas, and so on. As with 'further particulars', a party can apply for a tribunal order that such documents be produced, with similar consequences if the order is not obeyed. Copies of all the documents to which either party intends to refer during the hearing must be sent to the other side a 'reasonable' time before the hearing takes place. Usually, the tribunal itself will want to receive copies of relevant documents prior to the hearing.

16. Preliminary hearings

These are held when there is doubt concerning a tribunal's legal capacity to hear a case, e.g. if the employer claims that the complainant has not completed the necessary amount of continuous employment to claim unfair dismissal. This preliminary hearing will investigate the tribunal's powers to deal with the case.

Pre-hearing assessments

On receipt of the documents relating to a case the tribunal will quickly examine the relevant facts and, if it seems that one party's case is sure to fail (e.g. because a dismissal was obviously unfair, or because a disgruntled worker has initiated a case frivolously or vexatiously simply to annoy the employer knowing full well that it cannot succeed), then the tribunal will order a 'pre-hearing' assessment to establish agreed facts and, if appropriate, warn one of the parties that its case will probably fail. If the party receiving the warning wishes to proceed with the case, it may do so (before a different tribunal, so that the eventual outcome is not prejudiced) but may if it loses be ordered to pay the costs. Also the tribunal may require that a small financial deposit be made – returnable only if the party paying it wins the case. In normal circumstances each side must bear its own costs, and tribunals are extremely reluctant to award costs to one of the parties even if the other party has been warned of this possibility at a pre-hearing assessment.

17. The hearing

Procedure in a tribunal is meant to be informal relative to other courts (members wear ordinary clothes, not wigs and gowns), although a substantial body of case law has arisen around the statutes interpreted by tribunals, precedents have been established and much legal jargon unfamiliar to the lay person is used. This is particularly noticeable where one party to a dispute is represented by a solicitor or barrister (or both) while the other is not. The three members sit facing the court behind a long table on a dais about a foot higher than the rest of the room. There is a witness box at right angles to the court. Witnesses must swear or affirm to tell the truth as in any other courtroom. Witnesses can be called to give evidence (on oath) and may be subpoenaed by the tribunal if they are reluctant to attend.

It is normal for the employer (or the employer's representative) to speak first at a tribunal hearing, though in sex and race discrimination cases it is the applicant who begins the proceedings. The first speaker makes an opening statement, witnesses are called and are examined, cross-examined by the other party and then questioned by members of the tribunal. Then the other side makes an opening statement and calls witnesses and then both sides sum up. This order may be altered at the tribunal's discretion.

Finally, the tribunal retires to consider its decision, which is announced either on the spot or, if complex legal issues are involved, within a couple of days. Reasons for the decision are later confirmed in writing. Appeals are allowed and are heard first by the employment appeals tribunals and then by the higher courts.

18. Presenting the case

A manager called to give evidence to a tribunal will be expected to recount events, give dates and times, confirm the existence of documents, etc. An important difference between an industrial tribunal and other courts is that hearsay evidence and leading questions can be allowed in a tribunal. It is very common for managers to be asked the extent to which the ACAS code on discipline (*see* 9) was applied to the case in question. Witnesses need to speak slowly (the tribunal members will be taking notes by hand), clearly and take care not to repeat points.

The best means to prove a case is by documentary evidence. Thus, in a dismissal case the firm should have comprehensive records of written warnings, memoranda to the personnel and other departments, written evidence of having actively tried to avoid the dismissal (say through offering extra training, a change of department, detoxification help for an alcoholic, etc.) and of being reasonable at all times.

Witnesses should not make unpleasant remarks about the complainant, or express opinions. They *must*, however, be able to explain company documents and administrative procedures to people without prior knowledge of these matters.

19. Remedies

A tribunal may order the reinstatement of a worker in his or her previous job or, if that particular job is no longer available, the person's re-engagement to undertake a different job with comparable terms and conditions in the same company. More commonly, however, successful applicants to industrial tribunals receive financial compensation, comprising:

(a) A *basic* award, equal in value to the statutory compensation the worker would have received were he or she to have been declared redundant.

(b) A *compensatory* award to cover the person's financial losses resulting from the dismissal (loss of earnings or pension rights, expenses incurred, etc.); and possibly:

(c) An *additional* award which is a further amount given to the worker if the tribunal has ordered the reinstatement or re-engagement of the person but the employer has refused to take back the worker.

Upper limits are imposed on the maximum values of these payments (subject to periodic review). Additionally, tribunals are empowered to make *special* awards that have no upper limits in certain cases, e.g. unfair dismissal on the grounds of union membership or non-membership or sacking a pregnant woman just because she is pregnant.

20. Criticisms of the industrial tribunal system

Opponents of the tribunal system argue that:

- It interferes with managerial prerogative (*see* 8: **25**).
- The levels of compensation awarded to aggrieved employees is very low compared to the payouts sometimes obtained in civil actions in other areas (libel for instance).
- The existence of tribunals encourages workers to complain needlessly.
- The costs to the taxpayer are enormous.
- It creates the *impression* that workers may obtain redress for employers' misbehaviour towards them, while in fact affording very little protection.
- Tribunals have become bureaucratic and legalistic, with much technical jargon and highly formal atmospheres that discourage individual workers from pursuing tribunal actions.
- Even when the employer has behaved properly and is extremely likely to win a case, the cost of contesting an allegation of unfair dismissal (time, documentation, research costs, engaging a solicitor, meetings, etc.) might be so high that the employer prefers to settle out of court – implying that the claim was justified. This could attract bad publicity for the employing company.
- Workers who take a case to an industrial tribunal are liable to be blacklisted by employers' associations and hence experience great difficulty in obtaining future employment.
- Arguably, tribunals are adjudicating cases which really should be handled

by the normal courts using full judicial procedures and the expertise of judges, barristers, etc.

Progress test 11

1. Define redundancy.

2. How can human resource planning help a firm avoid redundancies?

3. Give five examples of outplacement procedures.

4. Define dismissal.

5. Explain the difference between wrongful dismissal and unfair dismissal.

6. What is meant by 'natural justice' in the context of dismissal procedures?

7. List five criticisms of the practice of having formal disciplinary procedures within enterprises.

8. What is meant by 'action short of dismissal'?

9. List the main points that need to be covered during a disciplinary interview.

12

INDUSTRIAL ACTION

1. Forms of industrial action

Industrial actions are sanctions imposed by employees (normally acting through a trade union) against an employing firm in furtherance of an industrial dispute. Action normally begins with withdrawal of co-operation, meaning that workers will perform only those duties specified in their contracts of employment and will refuse to exercise initiative. Next, the union may instruct members deliberately to obstruct management by raising trivial grievances, declining to undertake demarcated tasks, and insisting on all contractual rights no matter how petty they might be. The workers may ban overtime, refuse to cover for sick colleagues, and ultimately, go on strike. Employers too can exert pressure: by withdrawing co-operation, insisting that procedural agreements be followed to the letter, refusing workers' requests for overtime, and so on.

2. Strikes

A strike is a concerted withdrawal of labour in breach of a contract of employment and involving one of the following:

- non-attendance at work
- refusal to continue work while remaining at the place of work (i.e. a 'sit-down' strike)
- leaving the place of work (i.e. a 'walk-out').

The purpose of a strike is usually to obtain an improvement in pay or working conditions or to resist a worsening in terms and conditions of employment. Other reasons might be to bring the employer to the negotiating table, or to register dissatisfaction with some action the management has already taken. Several forms of strike exist:

(a) *Official* strikes are those sanctioned by the trade union of the workers concerned (as opposed to 'unofficial' strikes called by local employee representatives without union backing).

(b) *Sympathy* strikes are those whereby workers in one firm demonstrate their solidarity with employees in another, even though their own employer is not involved in the dispute.

(c) *Secondary* strikes are those directed against firms not directly involved in an industrial dispute. In Britain, this type of strike (plus sympathy strikes) are only immune from civil legal liability when taken by (*i*) employees of suppliers or customers of the firm in dispute *and* when its primary purpose is to prevent or disrupt the supply of goods between the firm in dispute and its suppliers or customers, or (*ii*) employees of an associated company and aimed at preventing the latter from taking over the work of the firm in dispute.

(d) *Lightning* strikes are those which are called without notice and normally last for a short period.

(e) *Wildcat* strikes are unofficial lightning strikes.

(f) *Constitutional* strikes are those which only take place once all agreed management/union negotiating procedures have been exhausted. Unconstitutional strikes, conversely, occur in breach of agreed procedures.

(g) *Political* strikes are those intended to influence the government rather than employers. Note that these are not 'trade disputes' and thus do not enjoy civil immunity (*see* 3: 7).

(h) *General* strikes are those that involve a simultaneous withdrawal of labour by workers in all industries in all parts of the country.

Striking may or may not constitute grounds for fair dismissal, depending on the law of the country in which the strike takes place. In Britain, any worker who goes on strike is liable to be dismissed, provided the employer dismisses all strikers and not just some of them (except for unofficial strikes (*see* above) in which case strikers may be sacked on an individual basis).

Employers' responses to strikes

The worst strike-related scenario that an employer might face is to have a major stoppage occur suddenly and unexpectedly and hence not permit management to devise a plan for dealing with the situation. Normally, a management will wish to develop action plans before a strike takes place, to assess its likely extent and consequences, and to list the options available for resolving the dispute and the financial costs of various contingencies. Communications with the workforce will be extended in an effort to avert the strike, e.g. via leaflets attached to payslips, letters sent to employees' home addresses, etc. A publicity campaign involving local (and perhaps national) press and radio or television will be mounted. Further possible measures include:

- physical protection of the employer's property (keys, vehicles, computer terminals, etc.) during the period of the stoppage
- rescheduling of maintenance programmes so that plant and equipment can be serviced and repaired while employees are on strike
- in appropriate circumstances invocation of legal action against the union(s) calling the strike
- reallocation of tasks among workers not involved in strike action. Note the administrative difficulties associated with identifying which people are on

strike and which are still working. It is important only to stop the pay of strikers.
- establishment of a small team of senior managers to co-ordinate the firm's responses to the strike
- issue of formal warnings to strikers advising them that they are in breach of contract and of the consequences that might result from this fact.

Plans need to be flexible and to have a wide range of options available, as the situation could quickly improve or worsen. Also the management needs to be aware that the dispute will be settled sooner or later and that improvident behaviour today could have adverse effects on the firm's industrial relations for years to come, especially if legal action is taken against the union.

3. The right to strike in Europe

The right to strike is written into the constitutions of 12 of the 15 EU states (Ireland, Britain and Denmark being the exceptions). This means that strikers cannot be dismissed under any normal circumstances provided the legislative procedures prior to going on strike (e.g. giving certain periods of notice and/or exhausting all other processes – possibly including arbitration) have been strictly followed. Note, however, the steady long-term decline in the number of days lost through industrial action (although figures can fluctuate sharply from year to year) that has occurred in all EU nations, due partly no doubt to the higher levels of unemployment experienced throughout the EU over the last decade. In most years labour disputes account for (considerably) less than 1 per cent of all time lost to European industry. Sickness and accidents are responsible for a quarter of all time off; maternity leave and bad weather account for 3½ per cent each. Germany has had the lowest number of days lost per 1,000 through strikes on average over the last quarter century. Ireland has been the EU's most strike-prone country in recent years.

Examples of procedures which must, by law, be followed prior to a strike in certain EU countries are as follows:

Denmark

A three-quarters majority vote of the relevant group of workers is needed, and employers must be given seven days' notice of the workers' intention to strike. Unofficial strikers can be fined.

Greece

Workers must give employers 24 hours' notice of a strike and a secret ballot is necessary.

Portugal

Strikes can only be called by trade unions or workers representing at least 20 per cent of a firm's employees. Two days' notice of the strike must be given.

Spain

Five days' notice of intention to strike must be given. Workplace occupations are illegal.

4. Criticisms of strike action

Strikes and those who participate in them are sometimes criticised on philosophical grounds, as follows:

(a) Strikes represent an abuse of economic freedom and a return to 'the law of the jungle' in employee relations matters.

(b) They encourage retaliation and the harmful exercise of power.

(c) A successful strike (from workers' points of view) may have to be paid for by other groups less privileged than those organising the disruptive action.

(d) Strikes are a direct challenge to economic and social stability and as such inappropriate in democratic countries. Anarchy will prevail in a country bedevilled by constant industrial actions.

Against these points it has been argued that:

- Strikes are the only language that some managements understand.
- Collective bargaining is meaningless unless employee representatives have the ultimate sanction of calling a strike.
- The possibility of strike action keeps management on its toes and is a healthy antidote to managerial complacency and paternalism.
- Strikes are an *expression* of individual freedom rather than a violation of it.
- As management possesses and controls physical and financial resources, the strike weapon is necessary in order to restore the balance of power in industry.

5. Causes of strikes

Many factors lead to feelings of dissatisfaction in work situations: inadequate wages, poor physical working environments, denial of promotion, speed-ups in production lines, threats of redundancy, and so on. Human relations difficulties can also cause industrial disputes. Some problems, unfortunately, arise from intractable financial difficulties (low profits preventing payment of higher wages for example) which simply cannot be resolved through negotiation. Many disputes, however, arise more from breakdowns in communications than from objective considerations.

Factors affecting the propensity to strike include:

(a) How closely a trade union controls its members (especially workplace representatives).

(b) Workers' basic attitudes towards their jobs, e.g. whether they feel they 'own' their jobs and have 'rights' over how work is performed. In the latter case, workers will be more likely to react in a hostile manner if they perceive that their 'rights' have been violated.

(c) Media coverage of industrial disputes. To the extent that newspapers, television, etc., portray strikes in a negative manner the working public will be less inclined to respond to union calls for strike action.

(d) The quality and effectiveness of firms' grievance control and collective bargaining machinery.

(e) Lack of consensus within an organisation, caused by divergent opinions regarding the company's basic goals and / or conflicts of interest between various sections.

(f) Labour market conditions. Strike levels normally fall to low levels during periods of high unemployment.

(g) The proportions of (largely non-unionised) casual and part-time workers in a company's labour force.

(h) Labour intensity within an industry. If labour costs represent a high proportion of a firm's total costs then its management will do anything in its power to avoid strike action.

(i) The average size of establishments. In most countries it is the case that fewer strikes occur, on average, in small firms than in large companies, due perhaps to closer personal contacts between management and workers and the absence of union organisation in small enterprises.

(j) The extent of 'collective consciousness' among particular groups of workers, i.e. whether they perceive common interests, have homogeneous characteristics and constitute a cohesive occupational / industry group, and then translate these factors into the solidarity needed to initiate and sustain industrial action.

(k) The nature of the work undertaken. Employees who work in comfortable, pleasant surroundings and who complete interesting tasks may be less inclined to strike than (say) unskilled workers performing boring and repetitive jobs in dirty and noisy environments.

(l) The rate of technological development. Fast-changing technologies create unemployment and (critically) fears of redundancy which may induce workers to strike.

(m) Historical relationships between firms and the unions which operate within them, e.g. whether union recognition was granted only after a long and bitter recognition dispute. The number of unions operating within a company and the relations between them might also be a factor.

The political environment can affect the incidence of strike action. If unions have close links with a political party they might seek to obtain their objectives through political rather than industrial action. And when the party sponsored by the unions is in power the latter may actively dissuade their members from engaging in strikes. Equally, a fragmented and disorganised union movement might, other things being equal, be relatively strike prone in consequence of not being able to exert political influence.

6. Strike statistics

Care is needed when interpreting data on the number of days lost through strikes. In most countries there is no legal obligation on employers to report strikes so that some under-reporting is to be expected. Also it is not always clear as to whether a stoppage is a 'strike' or some other form of work interruption. Further problems are that:

- Stoppages lasting less than one day might be excluded. In Britain, for example, any stoppage involving fewer than ten workers for less than one eight-hour working day is not counted, unless the total number of days lost through short stoppages in the establishment exceeds 100 per year.
- Aggregate figures for industry sectors, geographical areas, etc., do not indicate which *particular* businesses are the most strike prone and *why* this is the case.
- Public sector reporting of strikes is likely to be extremely accurate whereas private sector firms might report strikes in a haphazard manner, leading to difficulties of comparison of strike activity in the private and public sectors.
- Typically the number of days lost to strikes in any one year mainly reflects the extent of stoppages in a small number of large industries. It is not unusual for more than half the annual total of days lost through strikes to be attributable to disputes in one or two major industries.

Characteristics of strikes

What does emerge from the strike statistics of all nations, however, is that strikes normally take one of two different forms:

(a) Long stoppages involving large numbers of employees, usually following protracted management/union negotiations concerning a wage agreement.

(b) Very short strikes only lasting for one or two days and representing more of a demonstration of employee dissatisfaction than a well thought-out strategy for attaining objectives.

Strike figures also reveal that over certain periods there are large variations in strike-proneness between various industry sectors, although the sectors that are the most strike prone alter over time.

7. Costs and benefits of strikes

Although strikes always impose financial costs on both the employer and the striking workers, benefits might also be forthcoming. For example:

- A strike might 'clear the air' in relation to a conflict that has been simmering over a long period.

- The outcome to a strike may establish an important point of principle (e.g. management's right to manage – *see* 8: **25**).
- The experience of the soul-searching connected with a strike could encourage both parties to the dispute to work harder towards seeking compromise solutions in future conflicts.
- Institutional rules and procedures for settling disputes might be drastically overhauled and improved following strike action.

Costs of strikes

Strikes impose many costs on workers, employers and the general public. The main costs are as follows.

(a) *Lost wages*. Employees must balance the long-term financial benefits of higher pay if the strike is successful against the loss of wages during the withdrawal of labour. Two factors that might influence this decision are:

(*i*) possibilities for overtime working at high bonus rates to make up for lost production once the strike is over

(*ii*) the likelihood that a short strike may cause management to be more generous with its offers in future negotiations. Note how unions sometimes call strikes simply to exert pressure on employers to induce them to improve 'final' offers, the eventual settlement being subject to compromise and negotiation. The extra pay emerging from the strike might be far lower than the cost of lost wages.

(b) *Lost production*. Firms usually are unable to produce while their workers are striking. However, the cost of lost production has to be set against the higher wage bill resulting from a settlement. Some firms try to schedule equipment maintenance and stock-keeping activities to coincide with annual wage negotiations so that if there is a strike the firm can at least be getting on with these duties. In prosperous times the use of the strike weapon is more likely to lead to significant concessions from employing firms, which are earning the profits needed to pay wage increases.

(c) *Disruption of third-party activities*. Suppliers and customers of a strike-bound company also suffer. The former will not receive orders for inputs (leading perhaps to severe cashflow shortages) while the latter are not able to obtain goods or services. Certain strikes have knock-on effects throughout the economy, especially strikes affecting public services.

8. Limitations of strike action

The basic problem with a strike (or indeed any other form of industrial action) is perhaps that, although they can alter an employer's *behaviour*, they rarely succeed in changing the fundamental *attitudes* that give rise to the employer's behaviour in the first place. Also, of course, the collapse of a strike can greatly weaken a union's credibility in the eyes of its members. In order to persuade workers to go on strike a union needs to convince them that withdrawal of labour is the right thing to do (many people have moral reservations about striking), that the strike will be conducted efficiently (with a beginning, a middle and an end), that strike action is justified, and that there is a high probability of success. Management is presented as unreasonable, intransigent and unwilling to honour its obligations. If after all this a strike is called and it crumbles, workers will not be inclined to repeat the (costly) experience ever again.

9. Strikes in essential services

Almost every country in the world has laws that prohibit certain groups from taking industrial action. Typically, a nation's police force and armed services are covered by such legislation, though in some countries a number of other groups are also included. Additionally, special restrictions on or disincentives to strike might be imposed on workers in 'essential' services (health workers, firefighters, electricity supply workers, etc.). Measures for restricting the rights of workers in essential services to take industrial action include:

- requiring a certain proportion of the workers involved in the dispute to remain in post to ensure a minimum service
- insistence that a substantial period of notice be given prior to a withdrawal of labour
- assumption by the government of the ability to impose legally binding cooling-off periods
- governmental assumption of emergency powers that circumvent the normal democratic process
- imposition of compulsory ballots on striking members in order to determine whether they wish to return to work
- the use of troops to replace striking workers.

Additional disincentives could involve legal prohibitions on trade union membership for members of certain establishments or occupations and the removal of immunity for civil legal action (*see* 3: 7) in respect of workers involved in a dispute.

10. The case for restriction

Arguments in favour of such curbs are that:

- Disruptions of essential services can endanger life, health and public order.
- The economic welfare of the nation is protected.
- Fair and impartial arbitration procedures can be used to settle disputes.
- Society as a whole has a vested interest in the maintenance of essential services, so that it is only right and proper for the government to take action to defend the social interest.

The case against restriction

A major argument against restriction is that the very concept of an 'essential service' is itself extremely ambiguous, since what is 'essential' in one society might not be considered as essential elsewhere (as in the case of health services, for example, which are run entirely by market-led private enterprise organisations in certain countries). Terms such as 'protecting the public interest' or 'damage to the national economy' can be meaningless in many situations. Another problem is that legal constraints on particular groups of workers reduce their bargaining power, leading perhaps to artificially low wages within certain sectors and hence to labour shortages. Also, once precedents for curbing the right to take industrial action have been established, the practice might spread, perniciously, to cover more and more employee categories. Further problems are that:

- Formal restrictions cannot prevent covert industrial action (sabotage, undeclared withdrawals of co-operation, etc.).
- Legal curbs could create bitterness among employees that greatly damage relationships with management and day-to-day performances in the long run.
- Troops might not be technically competent to replace striking workers.
- Employees can effectively withdraw their labour by resigning en masse.

Progress test 12

1. Define 'industrial action'.

2. Explain the terms (*i*) sympathy strike and (*ii*) wildcat strike.

3. What are the main philosophical arguments against strikes?

4. List five factors that might encourage strike action.

5. What are the main problems attached to the interpretation of strike statistics?

6. From a trade union point of view, what are the limitations on the effectiveness of strike action?

Part Three

THE FUTURE OF EMPLOYEE RELATIONS

13

CURRENT DEVELOPMENTS IN EMPLOYEE RELATIONS MANAGEMENT

EMPLOYEE RELATIONS AND THE MANAGEMENT OF CHANGE

1. Nature of change

More than ever before, organisations function in an environment of change. New products are introduced, new materials discovered, new markets and competitors constantly emerge. The cultural, political, economic and legal frameworks within which firms operate are today liable to rapid and far-reaching alteration. Enormous technological advances have occurred during this century, and particularly during the last thirty years. New economic alliances have developed; there has been an explosion in world trade. Economically and politically the world is now a much smaller place.

Change is inevitable. The problem from a managerial point of view is how best to harness change and use its forces for the benefit of the organisation. Some change can be initiated by management itself. Otherwise the organisation must learn how to respond to externally induced change; and adapt quickly and effectively to the requirements of completely new circumstances. Change can be smooth, uneven or discontinuous. 'Smooth' change is that which is predictable and the result of slow and systematic developments in the business's environments. Examples are the effects on consumer markets of rising living standards or changes in the calibres of fresh recruits to firms due to improvements (or deteriorations) in a nation's education system. Uneven change is predictable, but its timing erratic. Management knows that a new development is likely, yet cannot say when it will happen or how extensive its consequences will be. Discontinuous change results from trend breaks and/or major shocks in technical, legal, social or other environments.

2. Technological change

New technologies affect materials, processes, work locations, and organisational forms. Change might result from new inventions, discoveries or the accessibility of resources not previously available. Technical change is necessary for progress, though acceptance of change among those who will be affected by it may be extremely difficult to achieve. If possible therefore, the organisation should itself seek to initiate technical change, since then its economic and human relations consequences can be partly controlled. Technological change can alter the shape of an entire industry, and have far-reaching effects on everyday life. Otherwise, change might involve modifications to existing products or methods, or the need to replace entirely those items that have been rendered obsolete. Increasingly, technical change implies organisational change. Recognition of the inevitability of change should therefore be incorporated into an enterprise's long-term organisational development and overall corporate plans. If a firm fails to update its products, production methods and choice of markets its competitors will quickly take advantage of the fact. A major implication of the rapid product obsolescence characteristic of so many contemporary markets is the need either for individual firms to spend more on research and development (of markets as well as products) than previously has been the norm, or to imitate quickly the activities of successful competitors.

3. Technology and the nature of work

In modern times the dominant cause of changes in working environments and experiences has been technological advance. Working methods have evolved in parallel with new technologies, and organisational structures have developed around the needs of specific technical demands. Technology often determines the sizes of production units and hence working groups. It defines the nature of individual experience at work – the tools and equipment used, communications patterns, production methods, and the characteristics of the working environment. The organisation created around a particular technology will involve specific forms of supervision, control, management style and working arrangements.

Unlike machines, people respond to technological environments in sentient, reflective ways. People will seek to satisfy their social and emotional needs within the given technology. Such responses might be hostile and disruptive, as people fight against adversely perceived consequences of social change, or they could develop and reinforce new trends initiated by technical advance. Technical systems need people to operate them. New groupings of resources and employees emerge, and new methods of supervision, co-ordination and inspection of work become necessary. Sometimes, work can be reorganised to make it more varied and interesting within a particular technological framework.

4. Planning for change

Recognition of the inevitability of change naturally leads to desires to plan the business reorganisations and alterations in activities that change might necessitate. There are five steps in the process of planning and implementing change:

1. Precise definition of the operational changes that are needed.

2. Specification of how new working methods will affect particular people and groups.

3. Identification of attitudes and perspectives currently held by employees and how these support current working practices.

4. Statement of the attitudes and perspectives necessary to enable people to adapt successfully to new environments and working methods.

5. Implementation of measures designed to change existing attitudes.

Four strategic alternatives are available:

1. Altering technologies by introducing new equipment, methods, materials and systems. Existing staff may need to be retrained to handle a new technology, or different staff might be required.

2. Altering structures. This can involve organisation design: centralisation or decentralisation of functions, respecification of authority and accountability systems, etc.

3. Altering tasks, i.e. changing the content of employees' jobs, increasing or decreasing the extent of the division of labour within the organisation, and so on.

4. Altering the people who do the work. Here management focuses on solving the human problems created by change.

5. Resistance to change

As an organisation matures it becomes, typically, more formal and bureaucratic, set in its ways and generally resistant to outside pressures. Employees resist change for many reasons, including the following:

- feelings of insecurity generated by an intended change
- disruption of existing relations and patterns of behaviour
- threats to individual status and financial reward
- the influence of group norms and values that oppose change
- doubts regarding the technical feasibility of proposed changes
- the threat of having to retrain and acquire new skills in order to cope with altered working methods
- feeling of personal inadequacy *vis-à-vis* new technologies, e.g. fear of not being able to understand a recently installed computer system
- resentment over not having been consulted about a change
- the realisation that skills and experience acquired at great effort over many years are no longer of value to the organisation.

6. Management systems and resistance to change

R.M. Kanter completed a celebrated study of 115 examples of successful innovation occurring within American companies, concluding that certain management attitudes and practices invariably inhibited the introduction of change. Examples of these attitudes and practices were:

- suspicion of new ideas or of suggestions emanating from the base of the organisation
- management through committees
- allowing one department to criticise and interfere with another's proposals
- assuming that high-ranking employees know more about the organisation than low-ranking employees
- assigning unpleasant tasks (dismissal of employees for example) to subordinates
- not involving subordinates in decisions to restructure the organisation
- exercising tight supervision and control
- perceiving subordinates' problems as indications of their failure, and treating a subordinate's discussion of a problem as an admission of his or her incompetence
- telling subordinates that they are not indispensable
- regularly criticising subordinates but only rarely praising them.

7. Overcoming resistance to change

K. Lewin suggested three steps for overcoming resistance to change:

1. *Unfreezing* – getting rid of existing practices and ideas that stand in the way of change. Unfreezing can occur through dramatic events (a number of a company's employees being declared redundant for example), or by gradually making people aware of the need for and benefits of change. The latter might be achieved via training, team briefing sessions, videos or other communication devices. Workshops are a common device for unfreezing existing perceptions of issues. A workshop will highlight the nature and extent of the problems confronting the organisation, devise action plans, identify barriers to the implementation of change and suggest means for overcoming them. Often the participants in the workshop will divide into groups to discuss specific issues.

2. *Changing* – teaching employees to think and perform differently.

3. *Refreezing* – establishing new norms and standard practices. Refreezing involves the consolidation and stabilisation of the new situation.

Implementing change can involve the reshaping of strategies, organisational restructuring, measures to alter the culture of a business, or the introduction of new working methods. Specific techniques for introducing and overcoming resistance to change include the following:

(a) Maintaining existing work groups intact wherever possible.

(b) Employee participation in decisions concerning the practical implementation of change.

(c) Improved communication with workers, regularly informing them of intended alterations.

(d) Human resource planning, i.e. predicting the consequences of changes to working practices and redeploying workers to alternative functions.

(e) Creation of financial reserves specifically earmarked to pay for the retraining of employees adversely affected by new methods. The reserve could also be used to encourage natural wastage, e.g. through the early retirement of older workers.

(f) Careful explanation to employees of the benefits of change and of the technical superiority of new systems.

(g) Preparation of detailed records on each employee's qualifications, attributes and experiences, thus enabling management to assess a worker's suitability for alternative duties.

(h) Encouraging flexible attitudes in employees through training programmes and through arranging work in such a manner that the skills and experience acquired in one job can be quickly and easily transferred to others.

(i) Application of wage payment systems that encourage the adoption of new and better working methods.

(j) Ensuring (as far as possible) employees' security of tenure and informing workers of the measures that have been implemented to achieve this.

(k) Instructing employees in how to cope with change, emphasising the need for transferable rather than purely job-specific skills.

8. Organisation development and the role of the change agent

The term 'organisational development' (OD) is sometimes used to describe the process whereby management periodically and systematically audits the adequacy of its existing organisation structure for meeting current operational requirements. OD examines the effectiveness of internal communications, employees' awareness of company goals and procedures, the efficiency of decision taking, and the organisation's ability to respond to change.

Individuals responsible for implementing OD exercises are often referred to as 'change agents'. A change agent could be a member of the existing management, or an outside consultant hired specifically for the task. He or she might suggest:

- training and management development for employees
- creation of new departments and/or working groups
- restructuring departmental or individual responsibilities
- rearranging communication patterns.

It is important that senior management be quite clear about its expectations of an OD exercise, and be willing to finance and implement its recommendations. There is little point in commissioning an OD survey if its findings are largely ignored!

9. In-house change agents

Current employees are familiar with the existing organisation structure and (importantly) know exactly where to look for information. Internal staff are fully accountable for their actions; indeed, their future careers might depend on the success of OD assignments. They are, moreover, constantly and immediately available and subject to senior management's direct control. On the other hand, in-house staff:

(a) are not exposed to penetrating expert criticism from independent outsiders

(b) usually have limited experience of other industries and organisations

(c) may lack insight and creativity

(d) might not possess the management skills necessary to complete the work satisfactorily.

10. Role of the external consultant

Frequently, external rather than in-house change agents are better equipped to deal with organisational problems. Outsiders will take a more objective view of the organisation's activities and structural requirements, and will bring to the firm their experience of OD exercises implemented elsewhere. Outside consultants have no vested interests in the welfare of particular departments and are not involved in internal departmental politics. External advice is especially valuable when unusual organisational difficulties are experienced for the first time and an outside expert can explain their causes, consequences, and how they have been overcome in other organisations. The consultant might conduct research, test employee attitudes and opinions, suggest solutions to particular problems, discover new methods for organising work, and may be involved in the mundane implementation of his or her recommendations.

Further *advantages* of using an outsider include:

(a) They need not be afraid to ask embarrassing questions of anyone in the organisation, including top management.

(b) Few overhead costs are incurred.

(c) Expert consultants have up-to-the-minute knowledge of specialist techniques.

(d) The need to earn a profit will motivate a consultancy firm to provide an excellent service.

(e) An external consultant will have a wide range of contacts with other experts in the field.

(f) Internal staff will benefit simply by observing how an expert consultant tackles the job. This can be extremely useful for training and developing managerial employees.

In effect, using a consultant enables the organisation to benefit from other organisations' mistakes, since work undertaken for other clients will have enabled the consultant to acquire wide-ranging experience and skills.

The *disadvantages* of using external consultants include:

(a) If the consultant's work is unsatisfactory the effects of his or her bad recommendations might not be felt for several months, by which time the consultant will have disappeared.

(b) Outsiders' long-term careers will not suffer if a particular organisation development project fails, so that consultants might not possess the same level of motivation as in-house staff.

(c) A consultant will not possess detailed knowledge of the day-to-day operations of the firm.

(d) An outsider's actual competence and qualifications might not be as good as he or she initially claimed.

(e) Use of a consultant will probably be more expensive than using an existing member of staff.

11. Re-engineering

This means the radical redesign of business processes, normally via the use of the latest information technology, in order to enhance their performance. Conventional approaches to efficiency improvement sometimes fail because they focus on automating and speeding up existing systems and processes, merely perpetuating old ways of performing operations rather than addressing fundamental deficiencies and replacing out-of-date systems as a whole. Often, moreover, firms seeking efficiency gains do little more than tinker with the prevailing organisation structure in the naive belief that this alone will lead to the desired result. Problems with simple organisation restructuring are:

(a) The revised structure is likely to become out-of-date very soon after it is implemented.

(b) Frequent alterations in company structure destabilises the organisation and demoralises workers.

(c) Existing employees are likely to be thrust into new and unfamiliar roles for which they lack experience and/or training.

(d) Significant time periods are needed for people to adjust to each restructuring.

Re-engineering, conversely, involves challenging underlying assumptions and changing the basic rules and philosophies concerning the ways a business is managed. Examples of re-engineering include:

- abolition of job descriptions and departmental boundaries
- widespread use of empowerment (*see* 14:**18**)
- integration of a large number of operations

- finding new ways of achieving specific outcomes
- creating organisation structures based on desired results rather than on the functional duties needed to attain them, e.g. by having one person overseeing several types of task and assuming full responsibility for reaching a specific objective
- involving users of the outputs to processes in the design and execution of those processes. For example, departments that work on raw materials could be made partially responsible for selecting and controlling suppliers of the raw materials.
- centralisation of control procedures using computers
- having decisions taken on the spot, where work is performed. Note how this implies the removal of some layers in the management hierarchy and hence a 'flattening' of the organisation.

Typically, business process re-engineering attempts to simplify radically the basic low-level operations of a company (e.g. all the operations that go into satisfying a customer order). This could involve collapsing departmental boundaries, integrating computerised management systems, shortening lines of communication and removing marginally useful procedures.

12. The learning organisation

The term 'learning organisation' is sometimes applied to companies operating in turbulent environments that require transformations in working methods and which – in order to facilitate the introduction of new systems – train and develop their employees on a continuous basis. Hence the very essence of the business – its products, markets, processes and orientations – is likely to alter totally from period to period. Learning organisations discover the key characteristics of their environments and are thus better able to plan ahead. The learning organisation will attempt to identify interactions between the firm's sub-systems that facilitate or inhibit the management of change and is better able to cope with environmental and other change because it can accommodate unpredictability. It is not encumbered with rigid and out-of-date plans and procedures. Clearly, traditional organisation structures are not appropriate for firms that have to work in these circumstances. Instead the organisation needs to empower its staff; apply extensive teamwork; and have flatter organisation systems based on cross-functional co-operation among employees.

Nature of organisational learning

To learn means to absorb knowledge, acquire skills and/or assume fresh attitudes. Learning results in permanent changes in ability or behaviour, as opposed to short-term changes which are soon reversed. Organisational learning means all the processes whereby freshly discovered solutions to administrative problems pass into the firm's 'managerial memory', hence becoming integral parts of the organisation's mechanism for reacting to future events. A consequence is that decision-making procedures are continuously modified and adapted in the light of experience.

13. Single loop and double loop learning

According to Chris Argyris, organisations can be extremely bad at learning, unless the learning is simple and routine. Hence an organisation quickly loses the benefits of experience and reverts to its old bad habits. 'Single loop' learning, according to Argyris, is the learning necessary for an employee to be able to apply existing methods to the completion of a job. This is contrasted with 'double loop' learning that challenges and redefines the basic requirements of the job and how it should be undertaken. Single loop learning typically involves the setting of standards and the investigation of deviations from targets. Double loop learning means questioning whether the standards and objectives are appropriate in the first instance.

Implementing DLL

DLL inevitably occurs within organisations as they experience crises, fail to attain targets, and experience environmental change. Learning about mistakes in these situations however is costly and inefficient: decisions are taken too late to be effective, and all the benefits of forward planning are lost. Rather the organisation needs to:

(a) educate its managers in the methods of learning by doing

(b) formulate its objectives and standards in such a way that they can be evaluated on a continuous basis and the basic assumptions that underlie them can be empirically tested

(c) seek to learn in advance of environmental turbulence or, if this is not possible, adapt its behaviour systematically through trial and error as situations develop.

The first loop in the double loop system is the discovery of facts, acting upon them and evaluating the consequences. Knowledge gained is formal, systematic and explicit. The second loop involves the development of skills and 'know-how' resulting from the first loop and hence a change in fundamental perspectives on the matter under consideration. This feeds back into the interpretation of the facts embodied in the first loop and the actions taken thereafter. Hence, both behaviour and understanding of events and environments will change.

Training, employee relations and staff development

Companies operating in fast-changing environments require regular transformations in working methods and (in order to facilitate the introduction of new systems) must train and develop their employees on a continuous basis. Note however that a learning organisation is far more than a firm which spends large amounts on training. Rather, it requires the unqualified acceptance of change at all levels within the business, including basic grade operatives. Implications of the learning organisation for training, employee relations and staff development are as follows:

(a) Current policies should be open to question and challenged by all grades of employee. Indeed, management should welcome and actively support such questioning.

189

(b) Individuals should not necessarily be penalised for experimenting on their own initiative and making mistakes.

(c) There is a need for heavy emphasis on employee communication, with management diffusing information on current environmental trends throughout the organisation.

(d) Employee appraisal and reward systems need not be linked to the attainment of existing goals but rather to finding new and profitable fields of activity.

(e) Workers must possess an understanding of customer requirements.

(f) Employees need to 'learn how to learn', taking their example from top management.

(g) Managers should encourage workers to manage themselves in relatively autonomous work groups.

(h) Two-way communication between bosses and their subordinates is essential.

(i) Managers (especially supervisors) need to develop coaching skills, and to see their role as being that of facilitator rather than simply issuing instructions.

Note how an organisation is, at base, a group of individuals, so that the manner whereby groups within it learn is affected by social, interpersonal and other intangible factors as well as information systems and other formal learning facilities.

Problems of implementation

Creating a learning organisation is difficult, for a number of reasons:

(a) Employees at all levels within the organisation must want to learn. Thus, the establishment of a learning organisation is a bottom-up process that may not fit in with the culture of a pre-existing bureaucratic and hierarchical system.

(b) Inadequate information gathering and internal communication systems.

(c) Organisational politics that might impede widespread acceptance of the idea.

(d) Top management might not be genuinely committed to the idea.

(e) Certain employees may be unable to learn. Replacement of such people can be troublesome and expensive.

(f) Implementation requires careful planning.

14. Consequences of change for employee relations

It is obvious that JIT, TQM, flexible manufacturing and other advanced methods can only succeed if there are good relations between management and organised labour, if only for two reasons:

(a) *Every* aspect of these modern techniques will affect employee interests relative to managerial and ownership interests in some way or other.

(b) If a union operates within the enterprise it will need to overhaul drastically its fundamental approaches to management/employee relations and how best to protect the interests of its members.

The reality of the new situation is that firms which do not adopt the most up-to-date production methods will fail and be replaced by enterprises more in tune with the modern world. Technical change alters the occupational structure of the workforce: new products, materials and production processes are introduced which require fresh skills and training. The contents of the jobs undertaken within enterprises alter, and new pay relativities emerge.

New technologies have meant that people in organisations have had to adapt the ways in which they conduct numerous aspects of their working lives (though note how today's 'latest development' quickly becomes the norm and is soon taken for granted). Specific consequences of technical change for employee relations include:

(a) Trade unions with members engaged in redundant technologies lose revenue and influence.

(b) Countries with firms not taking up new technologies pay for this through increased unemployment, with consequent effects on employee relations.

(c) Skills shortages might be created in certain regions.

(d) New management structures and attitudes are required.

To succeed in today's business environment firms must maximise customer satisfaction through providing top quality products that are fit for use and available when needed. Computers and new technology furnish the *physical* capacity to satisfy these requirements, but it is the firm's *human* resources that ultimately determine the excellence of the goods and services it can supply. Inevitably, therefore, employee relations play a crucial role in the effective implementation of the new high-tech production and administrative techniques.

The dark side of the development of new technology, perhaps, is the potential for the emergence within companies of two levels of worker – trained and untrained – with trained employees commanding high pay and a satisfactory quality of working life while their untrained colleagues experience periodic bouts of unemployment, undertake casual and part-time jobs and, when they are at work, are subject to extremely close supervision.

THE CHANGING NATURE OF EMPLOYEE RELATIONS

15. Current influences on employee relations

The second half of the twentieth century has witnessed tremendous changes in how work is performed, where it is undertaken, and the terms and conditions of employment of workers. A number of factors are altering fundamentally the basic *nature* of employee relations. The following trends are especially important.

(a) High long-term unemployment in western countries, especially among unskilled workers. Also, employees who do possess a skill often find that it is no longer in demand and hence must seek employment in other areas. Industry or occupation based unions are increasingly irrelevant in this situation.

(b) The blurring of boundaries between occupations caused by new technologies (especially computer-assisted manufacture and IT-driven company administration).

(c) Decreases in the average size of commercial establishment. Larger enterprises have always been more prone to unionisation than small firms.

(d) Greater use by firms of (non-unionised) casual and part-time workers.

(e) Changes in public opinion away from collectivist and towards individualist values (*see* 2: **1**).

Customer care and employee relations

Empowerment (*see* 14: **18**), total quality management and related management techniques increasingly focus on customer service, thus generating the need for personnel policies which underscore and support a firm's customer care requirements. Such policies can have serious consequences for employee relations. For example, management may feel it appropriate to introduce covert surveillance of customer contact staff (e.g. other employees pretending to be customers and reporting to management on how they were treated), and this might severely damage the morale of the workers being assessed. Equally, customers may wish to be served at evenings and weekends, so that employees have to be prepared to work during these periods. Formal personnel policies associated with customer care include:

- minimum requirements concerning employees' standards of dress and general appearance
- restructuring working time arrangements, e.g., through the use of key-time employees (*see* 15: **9**) in order to satisfy customer demand during peak periods
- setting customer care related performance targets (such as having telephones answered within so many rings, or requiring that (say) 90 per cent of customer orders be processed within 48 hours)
- regular reports to staff (via company newsletters, team briefings, etc.) on the results of customer care initiatives.

Note however that it is unreasonable to expect staff to smile at and be courteous and friendly to customers when employees themselves are poorly paid, operate in substandard working conditions, are employed part time and/or on casual contracts, have minimal support from management, and so on.

16. New approaches to employee relations

Conventionally, the subject of employee relations has centred on bargaining (especially collective bargaining – *see* Chapter 9) between management and employees, on the establishment of procedures for handling grievances, disputes and disciplinary matters, and on the introduction of new working arrangements and techniques. Such matters have often been associated with *conflict* between management and workers. However, it is increasingly recognised that in the modern world, employee relations need to focus on *harmony* and co-operation among all the firm's interest groups, and on the common pursuit of a business's goals. Nowadays, employee relations need to be based on shared understanding of a company's objectives and on mutual trust between management and labour.

Manifestations of the new approach include:

- Improved employee communications plus extensive consultation and employee participation in workplace management decisions.
- Stronger links between individual pay and organisational performance.
- Provision of incentives and training to encourage flexible attitudes and working practices. Employees need to have inculcated within them attitudes and perspectives which make them willing to assume personal responsibility for quality control and problem-solving at their places of work.
- Recognition of just a single trade union covering all occupations and grades of employee (*see* 9: **19**).
- Single status (*see* 9: **17**).
- New techniques of collective bargaining, such as pendulum arbitration (*see* 9: **21**) and/or single-table negotiation (*see* 9: **14**).
- The creation of company environments wherein *all* issues and problems can be discussed and analysed at every level of the organisation. Adoption by managements of the view that *productivity lies in people*, not merely in the introduction of new machines.
- Regarding trade unions as *insiders* of the firm.

A disturbing trend in many western countries is that the gap between the ability levels of skilled and unskilled workers is greater today than ever before, creating new potential for conflict between the two categories. Also, managements may feel a need to treat skilled and unskilled employees entirely differently with regard to wage bargaining, participation in management decisions, etc.

17. The future of trade unions

In most countries, trade unions have been among the big losers of the last quarter of the twentieth century. Union density (*see* 2: **23**) has declined in nearly every nation outside Scandinavia, and the trend is towards continuing decline (high union density in Scandinavia is partly attributable to the fact that trade unions in the Scandinavian countries are involved in the payment of unemployment insurance). A number of explanations for falling union membership have been suggested, as follows:

(a) Recession, high unemployment and major reductions in the manufacturing bases of a number of countries which in the past were highly trade-union orientated.

(b) Increases in the use by employers of (non-unionised) casual, temporary and part-time labour, especially in service industries.

(c) New types of working environment which encourage loyalty and commitment to a team rather than a trade union.

(d) Changing lifestyles that emphasise individualistic rather than collectivist values (*see* 2: **1**).

(e) Intensification of legal control over trade union activity.

(f) Privatisation of previously state-owned enterprises and the contracting-out of public sector services once provided by state employees. Private employers are often less inclined to encourage trade union membership than are nationalised firms, especially considering that pay rises in private businesses have to be financed by the enterprises concerned and not by the government.

The main danger currently confronting the international trade union movement is perhaps that it will find itself representing predominantly the unskilled, low-paid and less well educated employee – precisely the sorts of worker prone to periodic bouts of unemployment and hence withdrawal from union membership. Also the representational and bargaining problems attached to servicing low-paid low-skill workers are onerous, placing heavy demands on union resources. And the workers themselves may be looking for union organisations that offer help with training, competence development and job seeking rather than the pursuit of traditional trade union objectives.

Another sad fact that trade unions have to contend with in the closing years of the twentieth century is, quite simply, that managements are having to present their proposals concerning changes in working practices, pay arrangements, etc., as conditions for the survival of their enterprises, not as a basis for discussion or negotiation.

18. Possibilities for future expansion

Financial problems and declines in the membership base of many unions have caused them to merge with others and / or to establish common support services. Union amalgamations reduce administrative costs and enable the resulting conglomeration to offer additional benefits to members. Note, moreover, that a small number of very large unions may be able to exert enormous influence on government and on individual employers.

The overall trend in industrialised economies has been for trade unions to adopt a less 'oppositional' role than in the past and instead encourage employers to provide skills training, better security of employment, single status (*see* 9: **17**) and fringe benefits to employees. In exchange unions are increasingly willing to forego the strike weapon and other disruptive tactics. Also, some (but by no means all) unions have launched major recruitment drives in traditionally non-unionised sectors of the economy, especially among female workers, ethnic minorities, the casually employed and part-time workers.

19. Member services

Of critical importance to union recruitment in the modern world is a union's ability to offer fringe benefits to its members. The commonest fringe benefit that unions provide is the 'discount package' whereby the union negotiates a deal with suppliers of products to offer a percentage reduction on the sale price of an item on production of evidence of union membership. In return the union advertises the availability of the discount in its communications with members. Other important union services increasingly offered are as follows:

(a) Sickness insurance schemes at preferential rates agreed between unions and insurance companies.

(b) Legal advice for domestic as well as work-related matters.

(c) Discounted financial services, including mortgages, household and motor insurance and personal loans.

(d) Assistance with planning for retirement, especially financial planning.

(e) Discretionary hardship grants.

(f) Job finding facilities, e.g. distribution to branches of news on vacancies in firms in which the union has a presence.

Many of these services have become available via unions' computerisation of their membership records and administrative procedures, which has enabled them to target and maildrop members likely to be interested in specific benefits.
    Problems with the provision of member services are that:

- They often cost the union money and require resources to be devoted to their administration.
- Arguably, they divert the union's attention away from fundamental industrial relations issues.
- Providers of benefits might not be properly vetted.
- Workers might join a union in order to obtain the fringe benefits, but be extremely hostile towards unions and the whole concept of collective action.

Check-off agreements

Under a 'check-off agreement', the employer deducts trade union members' subscriptions 'at source' direct from workers' wages, thus saving the union the expense and trouble of collecting union dues. Since 1993, UK union members have had to give their explicit individual written permission for this to occur and to review the mandate every three years. This had a serious adverse effect on the financial situations of many British trade unions, as check-off arrangements greatly facilitate the collection of subscriptions. Also there is some wastage of membership at every round of mandate renewal. Not surprisingly, therefore, unions increasingly encourage members to pay their dues by direct debit, possibly offering sizeable discounts for doing so. Employers agree to implement check-off systems in the interests of good industrial relations, and because the threat of withdrawal can be used as a weapon during collective bargaining. The extent of trade union membership can be monitored, and contacts between union members and workplace union representatives may be reduced (as there is no need for the latter to approach the former to request payment).

INTERNATIONAL MANAGEMENT OF EMPLOYEE RELATIONS

20. Human resources in the multinational company (MNC)

An international or multinational business's success or failure depends to a large extent on its ability to select, train, motivate, develop and manage its human resources. Specific reasons for an MNC having a human resources strategy include:

(a) Firms with the most productive workforces possess an international competitive advantage over rivals.

(b) Expenditures on personnel typically represent a very large proportion of an MNC's total spending.

(c) An MNC's capacity to adopt new technologies, enter fresh markets and/or undertake different lines of work frequently depend more on the capabilities of its people than on capital investment.

(d) Computerisation of manufacturing and administrative processes has greatly influenced the nature of work and the structure of employment within enterprises. Communication and control systems have altered; there is less demand for unskilled employees completing routine duties. Strategic human resources planning is necessary to cope with the resistance to change that new technologies might engender and the possible displacement of labour that might result.

(e) Increasing organisational complexity requires a suitable mix of specialist skills which cannot be obtained overnight.

(f) Extensive employment protection legislation in many countries imposes constraints on how managements may treat their workforces.

Problems with human resources (HR) strategies include:

(a) Strategies are sometimes formulated ritualistically, without genuine commitment to their implementation. Management might be as much concerned with *being seen* to possess an HR strategy as actually having one *per se*.

(b) Major differences of opinion over what constitutes an effective HR strategy may emerge between head office personnel specialists on the one hand and subsidiary managers on the other.

(c) There is little point in having an HR strategy if it is not properly communicated to *everyone* working for the firm throughout the world. Lack of management/

worker communication and employee involvement in HR management issues can make the implementation of HR strategies extremely problematic.

(d) Although a company may have an HR strategy 'on paper' and under the overall supervision of a head office personnel department, line managers might simply ignore the strategy at the subsidiary level.

(e) Difficulties caused by failures in an MNC's human resources strategy might not be as obvious as, say, the consequences of a collapse in financial strategy – at least not in the short term.

Note how immediate crises in human resources management can often be overcome by short-term measures such as compulsory early retirement for everyone above a certain age, extensive overtime working to meet staff shortages, emergency recruitment etc., but only at a heavy long-term cost to the firm.

21. Standardisation versus local control

The advantages to applying standardised HRM practices in all subsidiaries in all parts of the world include the integration of all HRM activities into a coherent whole, the creation of shared values and a common work culture, establishment of targets that are understood through the organisation, and the implementation of straightforward procedures for setting individual targets, appraisal and monitoring work. Nevertheless, many MNCs devolve responsibility for HRM to their foreign subsidiaries. Reasons for delegating HRM to local units include:

(a) The desire to relate employee remuneration to performance levels achieved in *local* operations.

(b) Increasing competence in the human resources management field of the line managers employed in the foreign subsidiaries of large MNCs, consequent to more extensive training and better staff development than in the past.

(c) The trend towards overall decentralisation and diversification of activities in large MNCs, with quasi-autonomous profit centres, budgetary control by local managers, decisions on industrial relations management being taken at the establishment level, etc.

(d) Effective teamwork within a local unit can be accompanied by team-based bonus systems.

(e) Local circumstances can be taken into account during collective bargaining.

(f) The possible strengthening of managerial authority at the local level.

(g) Unit-level communications between management and employee representatives are facilitated.

(h) The suitability of local control of HRM for international companies with foreign subsidiaries that undertake differing types of work and hence employ disparate categories of employee, each with its own special problems and set of terms and conditions of employment.

Disadvantages to local control include duplication of activity among subsidiaries, fragmentation of procedures, heavy dependence on *ad hoc* unwritten rules, and the formulation of policies by subsidiary managers with little expertise in HRM. Changes in working methods and terms and conditions of employment might be introduced to local units in an uncoordinated and haphazard manner. Also the issues discussed during decentralised negotiations are likely to become parochial, ignoring matters relating to global corporate strategy, planning and investment. A major problem with devolution of personnel and/or HRM work to non-specialists in subsidiaries is that non-specialists may be neither competent nor interested in personnel or HRM issues, and might not be motivated to complete HRM duties properly so that critically important personnel tasks are neglected. Bad HRM decisions lead to a poor corporate image, higher long-run costs and loss of output due to industrial conflict. Also subsidiary managers might focus all their attention on immediately pressing personnel problems, at the expense of long-term HRM planning, and it could result in HRM considerations not influencing strategic management decisions. Effective devolution requires:

- the provision of back-up services in relation to technical problems arising from contracts of employment, legal aspects of redundancy and dismissal, union recognition, etc.
- acceptance by everyone that subsidiary managers' workloads will have to increase following their assumption of personnel responsibilities
- training of line managers in HRM techniques and concepts.

Decentralisation of the HRM function to foreign subsidiaries is more likely where:

(a) There is little integration between the production systems of decentralised units (as sometimes happens when a business has expanded via mergers and acquisitions of other firms).

(b) The company has many products and operates in multiple markets.

(c) The impact of technical change is felt predominantly at the local workplace rather than at the company level.

(d) There is no overall corporate identity to which workers in subsidiary units can relate.

(e) The skills and competencies needed to undertake a subsidiary's work are found in local rather than national labour markets.

(f) There are big regional disparities in wage levels.

(g) A company's activities are spread over many nations.

Sometimes MNCs introduce two-tier devoluted HRM systems with basic policies being determined centrally, leaving incentive schemes, working hours, holiday entitlement, etc., to be decided locally. Note how the decentralisation of HRM requires a more active personnel department than otherwise might be the case. In particular, the personnel department needs to:

- provide expert help and advice to decentralised units
- develop schemes for training local managers in the skills of personnel management
- implement disciplinary, grievance and disputes settlements procedures at the local level.

22. Influences on international HRM strategy

HR strategies are necessarily affected by a variety of environmental factors. *External* influences include the following:

(a) *The legal framework.* Laws on collective bargaining in various countries, the right to strike, employment protection, employee participation in management decisions, minimum wage levels, etc., in each of the nations in which the company does or intends to do business.

(b) *Political factors.* Host country government attitudes, guidelines and Codes of Practice on employment matters. The general ambiences of host nation governments towards industrial relations and employment matters.

(c) *Economic factors.* Unemployment and inflation rates in host nations (both these variables affect employee demands for wage increases), competition within industries (intense competition implies the poaching of rival firms' staff), growth prospects, and so on.

(d) *Social trends.* Extents of female participation in national labour forces, amounts of part-time working, attitudes towards work and working hours, demands for improvements in the quality of working life, changes in living standards, educational opportunities, etc.

(e) *The technological environment.* Changes in working methods, needs for reskilling and greater flexibility of labour, and the implications of various technologies for management style.

Internal factors affecting international HR strategy are the degree of decentralisation of the organisation; the present state of morale; whether jobs can be completed by unskilled people; the natures of host country workforces in terms of background, education, perspectives, etc., the degree of trade union activity within subsidiaries; the attitudes of the company's principal shareholders towards employee relations; and the perspectives of individual senior managers.

23. International employee relations strategies

Few multinational companies even attempt to impose standardised employee relations policies on subsidiaries in different countries because of the wide variations in national labour law, norms and labour relations practices among nations. Nonetheless, the parent company is necessarily concerned with the state of employee relations in its subsidiaries, in order to control labour costs and ensure the continuity of operations. Accordingly headquarters staff are likely to fulfil an advisory and/or mediating role whenever employee relations problems arise. Hence, HQ will advise on:

- the company's overall philosophy on management-worker relations, the role of trade unions, and so on
- alternative solutions to employee relations problems that might be pursued
- cost constraints necessitated by overall company strategy
- the employee relations policies of subsidiaries in other countries and whether they have been successful
- wage rates and employment conditions in various nations (bearing in mind an MNC's ability to shift its operations across national boundaries)
- productivity improvement measures introduced in other countries.

The aim is to apply consistent (though not necessarily identical) policies in subsidiaries throughout the world. Managers within particular subsidiaries should know precisely where they stand in respect of employee relations matters, and policies affecting employees should be dovetailed into an overall company plan.

24. MNC relations with trade unions

An MNC's ability to shift production between countries gives it an important advantage in negotiations with local trade unions in host nations. Further problems for unions that have to deal with MNCs include the difficulties of obtaining information, of interpreting financial data and of identifying key decision makers within the parent firm. And there seems to be little enthusiasm on the part of workers in MNC subsidiaries in one country for taking strike action in support of workers in dispute with the same MNCs in other parts of the world. Nevertheless, trade unions are themselves increasingly internationally-minded and willing to co-operate across national frontiers (especially in the European Single Market). Also unions in one country may look at precedents relating to pay and working conditions set in other nations when formulating demands, thus forcing an MNC to co-ordinate its employee relations strategies centrally in order to present a consistent front. Little transnational employer/union collective bargaining has (to date) occurred, however, mainly because trade unions are quintessentially *national* organisations, with minimal experience of international affairs.

References

Argyris, C. (1957), *Personality and Organisation*, Harper and Row.

Argyris, C. and Schon, D. (1978), *Organisational Learning: A Theory of Action Perspective*, Addison-Wesley.

Kanter, R.M. (1983), *The Change Masters*, Simon and Schuster.

Lewin, K. (1948), *Resolving Social Conflicts*, Harper.

Progress test 13

1. What is a learning organisation?

2. List six practical manifestations of new approaches to employee relations.

3. What are the main problems likely to be experienced by trade unions in the early years of the next century?

4. Give six examples of fringe benefits that a trade union might offer to its members.

14

EMPLOYEE RELATIONS IN THE HIGH-TECHNOLOGY FIRM

1. Lean production

The introduction to business of advanced manufacturing and other technologies has many implications for employee relations. The term 'lean production' is used to describe manufacturing processes that minimise waste while maximising the quality of output. Lean production normally involves:

- just-in-time methods (*see* **19**)
- teamworking with teams themselves taking decisions and solving problems
- quality circles (*see* **25**) or productivity improvement groups fulfilling much the same function
- empowerment (*see* **18**) and on-the-spot decision-taking by employees rather than their having to refer matters to higher levels
- flexibility in working methods (*see* 2: **5**)
- extensive use of robotics and flexible manufacturing (*see* **6** and **7**).

Employee relations requirements

Lean production requires from management an approach to employee relations that encourages:

- commitment to high quality production and co-operation by *everyone* in the enterprise
- willingness to accept change
- employees' reluctance to enter into conflict with management or with fellow workers
- mutual acceptance by management and labour of the propriety of the interests of the other side, while continuing to strive towards common goals
- group cohesiveness combined with individual initiative.

Introduction of lean production often leads to substantial increases in company profitability. Its acceptance by the workforce might be facilitated if a certain predetermined percentage of all surpluses resulting from the new methods is specifically allocated to a financial reserve to be used only to help workers made worse off by the adoption of new methods.

Implications for management

For lean production to succeed, the firm needs to lay great emphasis on recruiting well qualified managers. It requires clear chains of command, well-publicised rules and procedures and the constant pursuit of increased efficiency. Critically, management's relations with its workforce must be *predictable*, with employees turning up for work on time and not engaging in voluntary absenteeism (*see* **20**). Lunch and other breaks should not be extended and the working day not finish early. A major advantage to single status (*see* 9: **17**) and management by walking around (*see* 5: **16**) is that company executives are (or should be) *seen* to be setting a good example in these respects.

FLEXIBLE WORKING PRACTICES

2. Fixed and flexible automation

Many of the new technologies and working practices depend on workers being willing and able to undertake a wide range of disparate tasks, utilising different skills and completing jobs in different sections of the enterprise. Often the need for this approach results from the introduction of flexible (rather than fixed) automation. Fixed automation involves processing and/or assembly via predetermined sequences of operations that cannot be altered by virtue of the nature of the equipment. Flexible automation allows for changes in the order and character of operations, thus enabling outputs to be varied periodically. When installing a flexible automation system the aim is to minimise the set-up periods required to alter equipment, goods transit arrangements, and so on.

The characteristic of fixed automation was that the division of labour was extensively applied and workers given repetitive tasks. With flexible automation, however, employees need to be able to undertake a wide variety of tasks and (importantly) to exercise discretion.

3. Advantages and disadvantages of flexible working practices

Flexibility has many *advantages*, as follows:

(a) It ensures the fullest possible use of plant, equipment, people and machines.

(b) Workers 'learn by doing' and hence improve their overall levels of skill.

(c) New equipment and working methods can be introduced quickly.

(d) Individuals are able to contribute to the firm's work to their fullest potential. Consider, for example, the conventional 'unskilled' worker who, at home, undertakes highly skilled work on a motor car or a building renovation.

Problems with multi-skill flexible working include:

(a) It involves heavy training costs.

(b) Some workers will have an aptitude for certain kinds of task, so why force them to undertake jobs at which they will be less efficient?

(c) To the extent that flexible working helps workers develop their levels of skill it becomes easier for workers to find jobs in other companies.

(d) Labour shortages in one work group can require their being covered by workers from another, thus detracting from teamworking.

(e) In principle, total flexibility should apply to management as well as operatives. However, managers may use their authority to avoid performing anything other than a narrowly defined range of tasks.

(f) According to some critics, flexible working undermines union solidarity and is intended to worsen rather than improve pay and working conditions in the longer period.

4. Trade union responses to flexible working

Confronted with the realities of recent developments in operations management and working methods, some unions have sought to negotiate 'flexibility agreements' with employing organisations. Under a flexibility agreement, employees consent to do anything within their capabilities at the behest of management, in return for union involvement in decisions concerning how flexible practices are to be applied. The employer thus retains 'managerial prerogative', but makes a quid pro quo in exchange for the workers' acceptance of the new approach.

Specific flexibility requirements may be incorporated into employees' contracts of employment. The Nissan Motor Company operating in the North East of England, for example, has just two grades of manual worker: manufacturing staff and manufacturing technicians. Applicants for jobs at Nissan must formally acknowledge that if appointed they might be moved to new operations or transferred to different departments at very short notice, and that the pace of work will be determined entirely by the speed of a moving production line. There is compulsory overtime at management's discretion, and a 'neighbour check system' whereby workers are required to inspect the quality of each other's outputs.

A flexibility agreement will typically provide for:

- abolition of all traditional job demarcations
- acceptance by employees that *all* decisions concerning labour deployment shall be made by management
- employee involvement in the implementation of production processes and work practices
- complete occupational mobility, with workers performing whatever duties are currently required by the company
- workers being prepared to help train other workers and being willing themselves to be retrained.

5. Flexibility and job evaluation

Job evaluation is the process of placing jobs in order of their relative worth so that employees may be paid fairly. It is a complex and difficult process and many carefully researched job evaluation methods have been applied to the task. Effective job evaluation should remove inequitable job structures, apply common criteria when rewarding various jobs, and establish a logical promotion system within the business.

Arguably, however, job evaluation discourages labour flexibility because the process of rigid job definition necessarily leads to demarcation of tasks and functions. Further criticisms are:

(a) Since it necessarily involves value judgements it can never be truly scientific, hence causing many disagreements and conflicts within the firm.

(b) Its outcomes can quickly become irrelevant in consequence of changes in job content and in the balance of supply and demand in the labour market.

(c) It ignores traditions that for many years may have helped set wage differentials within companies, quite independent of job content. These traditional disparities may not be objectively justified, but their removal can cause cultural shock waves that actually damage the company.

(d) Unscrupulous managements can use job evaluation to undermine collective bargaining.

(e) Job evaluation might mystify and deliberately confuse simple issues. Market forces (arguably) are the best means for determining the rate for the job.

Such problems have caused some high-tech companies to do away with job evaluation, or at least downgrade its role. Indeed, a number of important (mainly Japanese) companies have also abolished job descriptions on the grounds that to have them encourages attitudes that are not conducive to flexible working. Thus, operatives are responsible for keeping their work areas clean and tidy (rather than employing cleaning staff), for the maintenance of equipment where this is technically possible, for routine record-keeping, and so on.

FLEXIBLE MANUFACTURING

6. Nature of flexible manufacturing

A flexible manufacturing system (FMS) comprises a collection of computer-controlled machine tools and transport and handling systems, all integrated via the use of a master computer. This enables the manufacture of small batches of output each modified to suit the requirements of particular market segments, while continuing to obtain manufacturing economies of scale. New production specifications can be implemented instantly, thus allowing frequent modifications to the firm's product.

7. Employee relations implications of flexible manufacturing

With flexible manufacturing there is less need for control by (highly paid) managers and increased possibilities for tight central administration. The major employee relations implications of the introduction of an FMS relate, however, to their heavy reliance on the use of robots for routine production. In particular:

(a) Shiftwork creates fewer problems because not many people are needed to operate unpopular shifts (10 p.m. to 6 a.m. for instance).

(b) The ratio of managers to human operatives rises dramatically, so that each manager has fewer operatives to control.

(c) Robots do not demand higher bonuses for more intensive working.

(d) Training and other staff development costs fall.

(e) Use of robots means (importantly) that workplaces do not have to be designed to suit human needs: they can be as dirty, dangerous and noisy as is necessary, and there is no need for rest areas, toilets, or facilities for workers to interact socially and communicate. Hence, humans do not have to work in these conditions, or to lift heavy weights or undertake dangerous duties. Increasingly jobs will be moved from the factory floor and into the office.

(f) Because the employment of robots is obviously labour saving, the rewards of the enterprise can be shared out among fewer people. Deciding *who* exactly is to receive additional rewards might itself generate conflicts within the organisation.

Effects on workers' skill levels

The use of robots (or 'steel collar workers' as they are sometimes referred to) facilitates changes in production, making it possible to implement dozens (even hundreds) of alterations in product specification simply through reprogramming factory robots – as opposed to having to retrain manual workers. Robots, moreover, can work to a degree of precision not physically possible when the work is done by humans.

The question of whether robotics leads to loss of skills within the workforce or whether it actually *increases* skill levels (through multi-tasking, giving employees a wider range of duties, opportunities for greater workplace autonomy, etc.) is much disputed, and there exists empirical evidence to support either proposition. In general, however, the operative's role becomes one of *monitoring* assembly, watching to see that nothing goes wrong. This removes the human drudgery associated with assembly line work and the division of labour, but itself can create boredom and a stressful environment.

COMPUTERISATION

Working methods have been revolutionised by computerisation, which enables the rapid transmission of new ideas and systems between countries and firms and the application of fresh approaches to administrative control and quality management. Those who operate computerised production systems typically require a higher level of education and training than the traditional manufacturing worker. At the same time, however, the need for conventional craft skills has diminished. Labour flexibility within a computerised working situation requires *technologies* rather than craftspeople.

8. Implications of computerisation for employee relations

Computerisation of the workplace creates possibilities for the automation of production. Importantly, computerisation vastly increases the range and quality of the information potentially available to *everyone* in the organisation. Hence, traditional dividing lines between occupational categories break down, and the demarcation of jobs can become irrelevant: vertically as well as horizontally. Other important possible consequences of computerisation that have implications for employee relations include:

(a) Deskilling of tasks in certain parts of the enterprise, while new types of skill are required elsewhere, leading perhaps to resentments and conflicts between various categories of worker.

(b) Total integration of all phases of production, office administration and internal communications, causing more frequent and perhaps closer interactions among employees in different sections of the firm and between various levels in the managerial hierarchy.

The competencies needed to succeed within a computerised work environment are general in nature and not necessarily related to particular occupations. Hence there is much scope for job rotation, undermining thereby workers' specific control over what were previously highly specialised jobs that could not easily be given to other categories of employee.

Note how computer staff frequently occupy key positions in organisations whereby they can cause great disruption through taking industrial action. This could induce management to treat computing personnel more favourably than other categories, and to try and arrange the division and pattern of work so as to ensure that not too much disruptive potential lies in a few pairs of hands.

To the extent that computer staff are treated differently to other types of worker, a number of sources of conflict may arise, as follows:

(a) Sometimes, computer literate staff with specialist qualifications have the same status, earn similar salaries, and occupy the same grades as line managers who – although they contribute a great deal to the organisation's work – are not as well certificated academically and have not had to spend several years studying for professional examinations. Accordingly, those who operate the computerised system might treat with disdain the work of line managers and resent the fact that computing staff and line managers are graded and paid equally. Conversely, line managers may begrudge the computer worker's self-assumed intellectual status.

(b) Those who manage the computerised system might expect to be able to exercise discretion and judgement in the course of their work, but at the same time must comply with the bureaucratic rules and demands of the wider organisation. They are subject to the authority of senior administrators, yet

207

usually are not fully involved in the formulation of the administrative processes that determine the rules.

(c) Other categories of employee (including line managers) might form a coalition against computing staff whose level of education and social status they resent and whom they do not feel should be taking significant decisions on behalf of the firm.

9. Information technology

Information technology (IT), i.e. the acquisition, processing, storage and dissemination of information using computers, has revolutionised office work, and is about to revolutionise telecommunications (i.e. the transmission of information via radio waves or electric cables). Integration is the core concept in the application of IT to administrative duties. Computers may be linked and networks created. A network shares common information, each of its components having direct access to the processing capacities of other users.

Information technology presents the employee with:

- new alternatives regarding how work can be completed
- more interesting tasks, challenges and responsibilities
- a wider range of duties to be completed
- the need to take an increased number of decisions
- fresh possibilities for structuring the working day.

End-user computing

End-user computing means the imaginative manipulation of computer packages and systems by employees who have no special qualifications or expertise in computing or IT, so that non-specialist package users have maximum discretion in determining the outputs of the system. The implications of end-user computing for business organisation and employee relations include:

(a) There is a levelling out of the performances of the firm's best and worst employees, since the computer will do a lot of the employee's basic work. This makes it difficult to appraise workers' performances accurately and to determine a fair system for rewarding employees.

(b) Staff require a flexible approach to their work, must undertake tasks relating to a wider variety of business functions, and need to be able to assess the reliability of outputs from systems that contain information on topics with which they are not familiar.

(c) Workers' capacities to choose *how* they complete IT-related tasks should make their jobs more interesting and provide numerous possibilities for acquiring experience of higher level work.

(d) There is less need for middle managers.

(e) Employees have open access to a wide range of the firm's databases. Note how this can create data security problems and possibilities for the deliberate disruption of systems.

TEAMWORKING

A team is a working group that exhibits a high degree of cohesion, common attitudes and perspectives among members, who stand ready and willing to help each other out and have a genuine commitment to attaining group objectives. Team formation and the development of team spirit are discussed in 1: **11**.

10.   Why have work teams?

Reasons for teamworking include the introduction of modern management methods such as just-in-time production (*see* 14: **19**), total quality management, etc., and/or the consequences of delayering (*see* 11: **1**), empowerment (*see* 14: **18**), business process re-engineering (*see* 13: **11**), downsizing and the use of flexible working practices. Most of these techniques involve a slimming down of the organisation and the need, therefore, to concentrate the expertise of the remaining people into distinct units rather than their being scattered around the firm. Also the majority of the methods previously mentioned demand *cross-functional* working that only multi-disciplinary teams can provide (*via* the pooling of skills, ideas and experience).

Use of teams to complete manufacturing (and other) tasks rests on a number of assumptions concerning employee motivation, namely that:

- Human relations approaches to management (*see* 8: **11**) are basically sound in that people feel a need to belong to a working group.
- Individuals enjoy having their contributions to group activities recognised.
- Working groups themselves develop a collective identity, want to succeed, and seek to compete with other groups.
- Team members of well-functioning and well-constructed groups naturally become proud of their membership and of the group's high level of performance.

The existence of well-constructed smoothly functioning teams within an organisation can greatly improve its productivity and the harmony of management/worker relations.

Sometimes, tasks can be tailored so that they can be carried out *either* by teams *or* by individuals. In such cases the decision should depend on **(a)** how accurately and easily the successful completion of the task can be measured under either option, **(b)** the effect on the morale of the workforce, and **(c)** whether the task fits in with group rather than individual objectives. Efficient teamworking is facilitated if:

- there are regular interactions among group members
- group tasks combine to form coherent outputs to which all members visibly contribute
- the group controls how work is done
- group members monitor and provide feedback on each other's work
- tasks are varied and interesting and all participants learn how to complete them

- the group is set clear, attainable yet challenging targets.

Teams go through natural lifecycles. Initially there is unease and uncertainty regarding each person's role and what is expected from the team's efforts. Conflicts emerge as the team develops, and are resolved as team members recognise each others' strengths and weaknesses. Eventually the team works together harmoniously (or breaks up) and becomes largely self-managing.

Working groups can fail to develop into teams for a number of reasons, including:

- inappropriate company-wide organisation structures (e.g. trying to fit teamwork into tall and highly formal hierarchies)
- clashes of personality and/or interest within the group
- lack of communication between the group and middle management
- outside interference with the group's activities.

Note, moreover, that lack of confidence in workers' abilities to co-operate and control team activities can become a self-fulfilling prophesy: if workers are assumed to be inept, indifferent and individualistic then the management policies which are adopted to deal with workers might *themselves* cause workers to behave in these ways.

Members of teams have a dual role: to find better ways of doing their own jobs and to try and improve the entire system. Continuous improvement implies a unitarist perspective (*see* 1: **3**), without 'them and us' attitudes. Teams may be cross-functional and convened to complete a specific project, or sectional and with a long-term existence (although individual group members will change periodically).

Implementation of teamworking

Simply setting up teams to complete particular tasks will not improve organisational effectiveness *of itself*: supportive management structures and personnel practices (*vis-à-vis* recruitment, training, reward systems, etc.) are also required. Indeed, a major cultural shift among employees might be needed.

If it is to succeed, teamworking must be accompanied by a shift in the focus of the firm's management style away from individuals and towards teams. Also the company will need to revise its human resource management policies in order to facilitate teamworking.

Specific problems that could be experienced during implementation include:

- lack of clear definition of team roles
- bad selection and/or inadequate training of team leaders
- failure to modify the firm's reward system to accommodate teamworking
- absence of proper procedures for evaluating team performances
- constructing teams from existing employees who are not suitable for teamworking
- allocation to individuals of personal as well as team duties, so that they do not have enough time to complete either (bearing in mind the extra meetings and communications that teamwork involves)
- certain team members not pulling their weight, leading to resentments

among other participants who feel they are 'carrying' the people concerned. Appraisal of team performance needs to identify individual contributions to a team's failure or success.

Rewards

The main options available for rewarding team members are:

- A flat rate wage paid to each member of the team.
- Group payment-by-results systems.
- Individual wage rates paid to team participants plus team bonuses.
- Flat rate wages accompanied by individual bonuses for exceptional contributions to team performance (though note how individual performance-related pay might create internal competition that disrupts the work of a team).

11. Implications of team working for employee relations

Contemporary approaches to the development of group working within businesses typically involve an elevation of the status of the group (as opposed to departments or divisions) as the major unit of organisations, plus an increase in work group autonomy with groups exercising considerable discretion and themselves taking important decisions. Responsibility for completing tasks rests with the *group* rather than with individuals or a head of department. The group might itself set its own target, and will almost certainly determine the division of work among its members. These factors have the following implications for employee relations within the firm:

(a) Workers may feel great loyalty to the group to which they are attached. Multi-union situations might not be appropriate because union and/or industrial actions undertaken by some but not all members of a group could damage group cohesion and identity.

(b) The role of the first-line manager becomes more important and that of middle management less important where employee relations are concerned. First-line (supervisory) managers constantly interact with work groups, transmit and receive information and have their 'fingers on the pulse' of employee relations issues.

(c) Arguably, managerial prerogative (*see* 8: **25**) is undermined in certain areas, e.g. work scheduling, allocating of tasks to specific employees, the pace of working, aspects of quality control, etc.

(d) Training requirements are extensive, both for management and for individual group members. Provision of training can improve the morale of the workforce dramatically and help bond workers to their employing firm.

(e) Employee participation (*see* Chapter 6) in broader management decision-making is encouraged.

(f) Unitary rather than pluralistic approaches to employee relations (*see* 10: **3**) are likely to develop.

(g) Trade unions have to rethink fundamentally their aims and roles in the new situation, especially with regard to:

(*i*) group performance-related pay

(*ii*) the possible reduction of union influence resulting from *individual* employee involvement in workplace decision-making rather than involvement through union representatives

(*iii*) the consequences of flexible working without occupational demarcation for unions organised on occupational lines.

Unions are left perhaps at a 'loose end' in a high-tech team-based work situation, in that if on the one hand they oppose (or simply ignore) change and the use of flexible methods they are likely to be ignored both by the management and the workforce, while on the other their close involvement in the planning of new systems could lead to their abandoning the vital interests of some of their members.

(h) Union workplace representatives may become more influential than in other situations, because group-related problems, interpersonal conflicts, grievances arising from the allocation of tasks to individuals and so on are conveniently channelled through the workplace representative. Indeed, workplace representatives and first-line managers may themselves come to form an important problem-solving group.

12. Role of the team leader

The team leader occupies a critically important role in modern employee relations, being expected to undertake a variety of duties formerly completed by specialist managers and/or more senior staff. A typical team leader's responsibilities include:

- motivating team members
- facilitating and co-ordinating activities
- providing direction for the group
- defining problems and objectives
- offering ideas and opinions and encouraging others to do the same
- representing the group to outside bodies.

Team leaders need to command the respect of team members via their visible possession of qualifications for the job (technical or in terms of experience), should be good listeners, receptive to team members' suggestions and ideas, and enthusiastic and generally helpful.

Difficulties that could adversely affect a team leader's performance include:

- being expected to assume responsibilities for decisions at the team level while being excluded from decision-making at higher levels of management
- workplace union representatives bypassing the team leader and taking problems direct to middle management
- having his or her decisions overturned by higher management
- senior management communicating direct with the workforce without involving the team leader.

In some Japanese companies the team leader is intimately concerned with employee recruitment and induction. Hence the person participates in interviews and it is he or she rather than the personnel department who contacts successful candidates with job offers. Thereafter the team leader is the first to see recruits on their first day at work, and is closely involved with the recruit's subsequent training and development.

13. Team building

In the 1970s, R. Meredith Belbin and colleagues developed a theory of teambuilding which suggested that certain types of individual do not perform well when working together in the same team. Belbin argued that people have different psychological characteristics which cause them to adopt particular roles at work, and that an appropriate combination of persons assuming various roles is essential for the creation of a well-balanced team. Nine team roles were identified, each of which needed to be fulfilled within a successful team (although they did not have to be present in equal measure). Team members would instinctively adopt specific roles according to their psychological make-ups, defined in terms of their intelligence, extroversion/introversion, dominance, and degree of stability or anxiety. The nine team roles were as follows:

1 *Co-ordinator*. The co-ordinator is a mentally stable individual, extrovert and dominant, and makes an ideal chairperson. He or she is self-confident, mature, a good speaker and listener, and adept at clarifying issues and facilitating group decisions. Unfortunately, other team members may perceive the person as manipulative and as someone who personally avoids completing tasks.

2 *Team worker*. This person is also mentally stable and extrovert, but low in dominance. The team worker is perceptive, able to identify problems, and promotes harmony within the group. However, he or she will avoid confrontation and tends to be indecisive.

3 *Specialist*. The specialist is a dedicated professional who provides technical skills and knowledge. He or she may fall into any personality category.

4 *Plant*. A 'plant' is a major source of a team's ideas and creativity, although the person might not be a good communicator. Plants are imaginative problem solvers: intelligent, introvert and dominant.

5 *Shaper*. This personality type is dynamic, outgoing, extrovert, dominant and highly strung. The shaper is task-oriented, argumentative, and thrives on pressure. He or she will overcome obstacles, albeit at the expense of other team members' feelings.

6 *Completer-finisher*. The completer-finisher is an unassertive introvert who is reluctant to delegate, and inclined to worry unduly. Strengths of this personality type are that such people are painstaking, conscientious and have a permanent sense of urgency.

213

7 *Implementer*. An implementer is practical, stable and controlled, and capable of turning ideas into action. He or she is disciplined and reliable, but prone to inflexibility and rigid attitudes.

8 *Monitor-evaluator*. This person is a critic rather than a creator: stable, intelligent, introvert, and capable of deep analysis of issues. Such individuals lack warmth, are rarely able to inspire others, yet are usually correct in their assessments.

9 *Resource investigator*. The resource investigator is a relaxed, positive and enthusiastic person who goes outside the group to discover new ideas and information. He or she is a dominant extrovert who inclines towards over-optimism and tends to lose interest in projects once his or her initial enthusiasm has passed.

Problems with the Belbin approach include its subjectivity (there is little empirical evidence concerning the personal characteristics of members of highly successful teams) and the difficulty of appraising *team* as opposed to individual performance. There is little hard evidence that any one mix of team types is any more effective than others (Furnham 1990).

A somewhat similar categorisation of team roles was developed in the 1980s by C. Margerison and D. McCann (see IRRR 1994). According to these authors there are three aspects of team performance:

1 The extent of the functions that need to be carried out by the team. Margerison and McCann measured this by a 'types of work index' (TWI).

2 Individual preferences concerning the way each person works. Typically, people concentrate on things they enjoy doing and neglect or perform badly tasks they dislike. A team management index (TMI) was constructed to analyse personal preferences.

3 Communications and interactions within the team, as measured by a linking skills index (LSI).

Eight major team roles were identified:

1 The *creator-innovator* who obtains and experiments with new ideas.
2 The *explorer-promoter* who looks for and informs others of fresh opportunities.
3 The *assessor-developer* who tests the applicability of various ideas.
4 The *thruster-organiser* who devises and implements new ways of making things work.
5 The *concluder-producer* who is best at operating existing systems and practices.
6 The *controller-inspector* who checks and audits systems.
7 The *upholder-maintainer* who ensures that standards are upheld.
8 The *reporter-adviser* who gathers and disseminates information.

Additionally all team roles must perform linking activities, in order to co-ordinate and integrate the work of the other eight roles.

Relative needs for the fulfilment of the various roles within a particular team were assessed using the TWI, a 64-item questionnaire. The personal preferences

214

of the individuals who would undertake particular jobs were evaluated via the TMI, which categorises people under four headings:

1 Extrovert/introvert

2 Practical/creative

3 Analytical/believing. An analytical person uses objective criteria when taking decisions, whereas the other personality type pays more attention to personal beliefs and principles.

4 Structured/flexible. Someone who is 'structured' is well-organised, neat and tidy, and likes to take decisions quickly. A 'flexible' individual prefers to spend time thinking over a problem and will not reach conclusions until all relevant information has been considered.

Comparison of the TWI and TMI supposedly indicates overlaps between job demands and personal preferences. Differences between the two indices might suggest needs for job redesign, training, reallocation of duties or changes in team membership. The LSI diagnoses team members' individual strengths and weaknesses in terms of eleven key linking skills: listening; communicating with others; team development; work allocation; respecting, trusting and understanding colleagues; delegation; maintenance of quality standards; target setting; representing the team to outsiders; problem solving and counselling; and participation in team activities. Note the questionable reliability of the three indices used in the analysis, as they are largely based on self-reporting.

Teambuilding in practice

Teambuilding in practice involves a structured attempt to improve the effectiveness of a group in terms of its outputs and/or the quality of internal relations (co-operation, enthusiasm, etc.). This might require encouraging people to become team-centred rather than individualistic; open and communicative rather than reticent; to assume rather than avoid responsibility; and to be creative, trusting and co-operative (Clark 1994).

14. Autonomous teamworking

The Volvo motor company developed this method in its truck assembly unit in Sweden. Each team:

- established its own targets (subject to constraints imposed by higher management)
- assumed full responsibility for quality control
- selected its own leader
- allocated work among team members
- set its own pace of work.

With autonomous teamworking each group has a complete and self-contained task to perform, and group members themselves choose the methods whereby work is completed and then monitor and appraise their own performances.

Group members are given the authority needed to implement their own decisions.

Volvo found that productivity increased sharply following the introduction of autonomous group working. Employee relations improved while the amount of defective output diminished. However, the benefits of specialisation were lost and labour cost per unit remained (by international standards) substantial. Volvo allege that the method was most successful when applied to self-contained, clearly defined activities.

Self-managed teams

Arguably there is little need for formal leadership in the modern workplace situation, which is increasingly likely to involve working in a team. According to this view, employees are quite capable of motivating themselves to perform unattractive as well as appealing tasks (Manz and Sims 1987) and to determine which group members are best qualified to complete particular duties. Advantages to self-managed teams include lower supervision costs, higher levels of employee interest in the work of the organisation as a whole, and hopefully the optimum use of human resources.

According to S. Kerr and J.M. Jermier, the need for leadership can be mitigated in many workplace situations by a number of factors:

(a) *Organisational characteristics* such as cohesive work groups that remove the need for supportive leadership, and the formalisation of working procedures (which results in group members not needing to ask a leader how to perform duties).

(b) *Job characteristics*, e.g. routine duties, feedback within a task and/or interesting and satisfying work.

(c) *Employee characteristics*. It is unlikely that workers who are experienced, trained, willing and able will need to be led. Professionally qualified employees are normally capable of looking after themselves.

To the extent that work groups do not need to be led, the particular style of leadership applied by the group's formal supervisor is largely irrelevant, explaining perhaps the very mixed results that have been obtained from many empirical studies in the leadership behaviour field.

FURTHER TECHNIQUES

15. Cell working

The cell work group system involves placing together all the machinery needed to produce the same type of item, rather than arranging machinery according to function (e.g. grouping together all cutting machines). Items are then produced on a U-shaped production line by operatives who are trained to use all the various machines within the cell. Hence workers are given a wider range of tasks to perform, plan their own work, and themselves undertake routine maintenance of equipment. There is no demarcation of employees' duties. The cell system has the following *advantages*:

(a) Items do not have to be shunted around a factory to receive different treatments.

(b) It is flexible in that work groups can easily increase or decrease outputs as demand fluctuates.

(c) The system is ideal for the implementation of quality circles (*see* 14: **25**) because quality and productivity improvement is possible within an individual cell.

Problems with the cell system are that much co-ordination of activity is necessary, and that workers need extensive training in the various machining tasks they have to perform (which makes them difficult to replace at short notice).

16. The quality of working life (QWL)

QWL means the totality of human satisfaction at work. Accordingly, attempts to enhance the quality of working life within an organisation need to encompass employee participation mechanisms; measures to reduce stress at work, improvements to environmental conditions, enhancement of employee communications (*see* Chapter 5), etc.

Hopefully, the introduction of a QWL programme will cause workers to feel that they can influence certain aspects of their environments, with consequent improvements in employee morale and efficiency. Note, however, that QWL programmes are *organisational* devices for improving productivity, motivation and management control over working environments, with contents ultimately determined by management and not through genuinely democratic processes. A further problem with QWL schemes is that they might encourage conformity to existing methods, rather than stimulating new thinking.

17. Employee involvement in objective setting

Joint determination of individual and team objectives by management and workers should (hopefully) encourage co-operation and employee motivation while establishing *sensible* targets against which workers can be appraised. Further *advantages* are:

(a) Logical criteria will be used to determine objectives. Workers have the opportunity to explain why unrealistically ambitious targets cannot be met.

(b) Resource requirements can be discussed when targets are agreed.

(c) Personal and team achievements are recognised and rewarded.

(d) Management and workers are *compelled* to communicate.

(e) Employee training requirements are identified.

(f) The causes of successes and failures in relation to the realisation of specific targets can be analysed.

Objectives must be clearly stated and understood by workers. *Difficulties* arise if teams or individuals are not given the resources or authority necessary for completion of tasks allocated to them, and where targets cannot be stated in numerical terms. Note, moreover, that:

(a) The consultation process can be extremely time consuming. A system whereby managers simply impose targets on subordinates without consultation might be more efficient.

(b) Targets might become out of date immediately following their determination.

(c) The achievement of short-term goals might be overemphasised at the expense of longer-term objectives.

18. Empowerment

The quality of an employee's working life may be greatly improved if he or she is given the power to complete tasks and attain objectives *independently*, without having to refer back to management for permission to take certain actions. This gives the individual a feeling of being in control and of significantly contributing to the organisation's work. It requires management to place their trust in employees' abilities to take sensible decisions, but also entitles management to expect employees to attain high levels of performance. Practical examples of empowerment include:

(a) 'Free flow' production lines whereby workers themselves are empowered to change the speed of a line. The worker completes a task to his or her personal satisfaction and then pushes a lever to advance the unit to the next stage. Operatives decide when to take rest breaks and for how long. This is made possible by installing a number of 'idle stations' at critical stages in the line where work can accumulate without disrupting the flow of production. Hence an operative can work quickly, pass a large number of units to the next idle station, and then take a break until they are cleared.

(b) Having work teams determine the extent and intensity of the use of robots within a section. Accordingly, workers decide which tasks to complete themselves and which are best done by robots.

(c) Authorising customer contact staff to negotiate with customers (e.g. by offering *ad hoc* discounts in order to secure a sale) or personally to take decisions on whether to give refunds.

Intelligent use of empowerment within an organisation should ensure that decisions are taken at the most suitable level. It can only succeed, however, if managers allow their subordinates to work independently and there are good communications at all levels (implying a flat managerial hierarchy within the firm). Further advantages of empowerment are that it can minimise employee frustration (resulting from their not being able to pursue their objectives with a free hand), it encourages initiative and creativity, it causes employees to feel personal responsibility for the welfare of the whole organisation, and it helps bond the worker to the firm.

JUST-IN-TIME METHODS

19. Nature of just-in-time (JIT) methods

In a JIT production control system, work is planned so that each production unit delivers to the next unit precisely the input it requires in order to proceed with the next stage of manufacture (or processing) and delivers the input just in time for the work to begin. In consequence, few if any stocks of inputs are carried, and there is no bunching of production lines or queues anywhere in the system.

To operate JIT systems, workers are put into teams which organise their own work and take responsibility for the repair and maintenance of the equipment they use, of quality control, and the timing of movements of work from one cell to another. Hence they acquire much experience of operational decision-making and routine production control. Just-in-time has been described as a guerilla method of production: cheap and flexible – seeking to eliminate *all* spare capacity while meeting customer demand. With JIT there is no question of employees standing idle waiting for work to arrive. Rather, they are obliged to move around undertaking whatever duties are necessary and helping to repair breakdowns wherever and whenever these happen. Workers deal with problems themselves wherever possible.

Implications of JIT for employers

JIT is doomed to failure unless *consistent* quality is maintained at each stage in the process; otherwise the occasional batch of substandard inputs will disrupt the entire system. Accordingly, the workers involved in JIT processes must be fully trained in quality control methods and (importantly) entirely committed to their successful implementation. The implications of JIT for employees include:

(a) Workers' tasks are simplified so as to facilitate waste elimination, but each employee must be capable of undertaking a wide range of functions and of moving very quickly from one type of work to another.

(b) Employees need to be trained and competent to undertake routine maintenance of equipment and to be proactive in identifying problems and rectifying faults. There can be no demarcations between operatives' work and maintenance or any refusal to complete tasks at (significantly) different levels of skill.

(c) Grading and payments systems must reflect the requirement of complete job flexibility.

(d) Workers should be empowered (*see* **18**) to stop the entire system in order to obtain expert assistance in appropriate circumstances. Note how in conventional systems this would be a junior management decision.

The need for sound management/employee relations is underscored, of course, by the vulnerability of JIT systems to industrial action. A lightning strike by just a handful of workers can cause the complete system to collapse. Also, JIT cannot succeed if workers are regularly absent from work. Hence the management of absenteeism becomes a major priority in firms using JIT systems.

20. Managing absenteeism

Companies operating lean production methods are necessarily compelled to adopt a tough line on absenteeism, since a single worker missing without due cause can disrupt an entire production process. Policies for dealing with absenteeism range from attempts to improve recalcitrant employees' attitudes towards this matter (via exhortations, counselling, etc., through to formal disciplinary proceedings – warnings, actions short of dismissal (*see* 11: **11**), and so on). Careful monitoring and record keeping is essential in order to identify sections and types of work with the highest absenteeism rates. Some firms also give special bonus payments to employees with good attendance records. Further measures for reducing absenteeism might include:

- redesigning jobs to make them more interesting and/or to give the people completing them a higher level of responsibility
- improved recruitment and selection procedures aimed at fitting individuals to jobs.

TOTAL QUALITY MANAGEMENT

21. Meaning of total quality management (TQM)

A firm's total quality management system comprises all the policies, tactics, operational methods (statistical quality control, inspection, quality assurance schemes, etc.) and organisational structures concerned with quality management and the continuous improvement of the quality of its outputs. TQM focuses on the totality of the system rather than its individual parts, seeking to identify the *causes* of failure rather than the simple fact that failures have happened. Causes of failure could involve communications breakdowns, poor teamwork, bad leadership, lack of individual commitment and motivation and other psycho-social problems, as well as technical operator and/or equipment inadequacies.

The modern approach is to regard production and inspection not as independent functions but rather as integral and interrelated components of the total quality system, with operatives *themselves* assuming responsibility for quality control. Excellence is taken for granted, so that independent inspections are seen not as a means for improving quality, but as an insult to the workers concerned.

22. Implications of TQM for employee relations

TQM has implications for employee relations because (along with JIT) it demands a far higher standard of management than previously and, critically, a style of management that evokes full and committed co-operation from labour.

It is conventional to distinguish two aspects of quality, namely:

(a) *Conformance quality,* which means the degree to which an item satisfies its technical specification; and

(b) *Design quality,* i.e. all the attributes that customers perceive as contributing to the worth of the product.

Conformance quality is maintained by constant cross-checking of each individual's output *within* the work group, so that operatives (rather than inspectors) monitor the quality of the group's work. Use of inspectors external to the group can encourage individuals mentally to abrogate responsibility for quality, on the assumption that defective output will be 'picked up' elsewhere in the organisation. Note how this reduced emphasis on inspection means that management needs to concentrate on setting an example rather than exerting strict control.

TQM requires from *management*:

- commitment to the provision of long-term security of employment for workers
- provision of training to enable employees to complete a multiplicity of tasks
- trust in workers' abilities to deal with quality issues
- day-to-day involvement and face-to-face communication with the workforce.

It requires from *employees*:

- acceptance of collective responsibility for the success of the business
- flexible attitudes and a willingness to undertake a wide range of duties
- willingness to contribute to problem-solving.

Further implications of TQM are that:

- Even the totally unskilled worker requires training, i.e. instruction in the need for quality and how the organisation is seeking to achieve it.
- Employees working in different departments need to know about each others' problems.
- Piece rate wage payment systems are to be avoided, as they encourage the production of substandard output.

23. Implementation of TQM

Typically the steps involved in implementing a total quality management system are:

(a) Senior management itself becomes fully aware of the concepts and techniques of quality management.

(b) Steering committees are formed and pilot projects identified.

(c) *All* employees are introduced to the basics of TQM and informed of top management's commitment.

(d) Training programmes are devised and effected.

(e) Suppliers are brought into the company's TQM planning.

(f) New methods relating to continuous improvement, prevention of defective output, reduction in variation, etc., are introduced.

(g) The system is monitored and audited.

Clearly, the above demand that employees be intimately involved in the implementation process and that their knowledge and capabilities be respected. In particular, employees need to be recognised as **(a)** problem-solvers, **(b)** the people who actually implement solutions, and **(c)** improvers of current working methods. TQM also requires first-class leadership, with managers who are able to instil a sense of purpose and commitment to TQM procedures. Employees simply *cannot* be passive bystanders in the TQM process.

Policy requirements for involving employees in TQM include:

- Management should consciously regard employees *as if* they were the firm's customers. Hence, management must attempt to discover employees' needs, perspectives and situations. Managers become mentors and facilitators rather than authority figures.
- Managers need to regard basic grade workers as having valuable contributions to make to the quality management process. This may require a sea-change in attitude in some enterprises.
- Workers have to be educated to believe that they *should* seek continuously to improve working practices. This means convincing the workforce that employee suggestions and contributions are highly valued.
- Each worker needs to be shown how his or her actions affect the attainment of the firm's quality objectives.

Quality champions

One way to inculcate a commitment to TQM among the existing workforce is to identify among supervisors and within the workforce a handful of highly influential individuals and enlist their support in championing the cause of quality management. People who are known, liked and trusted by current employees are far more likely to be believed than any amount of management exhortation. Recruitment of quality champions will not be possible if management is not **(a)** itself totally committed to the new methods, **(b)** seen to be attempting to protect employees' interests, or **(c)** making available the information and resources necessary to effect change. Quality champions might be invited to participate in planning the implementation of intended systems and in solving problems as they arise.

24. Employee training and education for TQM

Training and educating employees in TQM is a vital task, helping to bond the worker to the firm, instil appropriate attitudes and equip the worker with the basic competencies needed to operate effectively within a TQM environment. Instruction is necessary in the following fields:

- collection and analysis of the data needed to measure performance
- teamwork and group problem-solving
- relations between production, process improvement, product presentation and customer satisfaction
- the facts concerning the firm's commercial situation
- methods for detecting and eliminating waste.

Just-in-time training

TQM training can be conveniently delivered via a just-in-time programme, i.e. knowledge and competencies are imparted just in time for them to be used. Training occurs predominantly on the job. It does *not* involve giving instruction to large groups in lecture situations where workers cannot immediately apply what they are learning. Rather there is instant reinforcement of technical knowledge and no wasteful expenditures on training. Information overload is avoided, and workers become intimately involved in the training process. Also, the approach is suitable for the multi-skill training needed to cope with flexible working methods.

As many different instructors from as many sections of the organisation as possible are used to deliver the training. Fellow trainees as well as instructors are used to monitor trainees' performances.

QUALITY CIRCLES

Much has been written about quality circles (QCs) over recent years. The initial concept has been developed in several directions and the term 'quality circle' is nowadays rarely used. Rather, descriptions such as 'quality improvement task force' or 'productivity and quality enhancement team' are more common. For convenience, however, the single term 'quality circle' is used in the following pages.

25. Origins of quality circles

Initially an American idea, QCs were introduced to a large number of Japanese companies in the 1960s and 1970s. A quality circle is a workers' discussion group which meets regularly during working hours (though in Japan workers meet in their own time) to encourage the involvement of operatives in the solution of production and associated problems. Participants pool their ideas about how to solve current difficulties, and also about how productivity can be improved. What distinguishes a quality circle from conventional suggestion schemes is that the group itself is given training in managerial problem-solving and, importantly, is allocated resources for use in overcoming specific problems.

26. Circle leadership

Often departmental supervisors lead quality circles, but sometimes leaders are elected by the group. In Japan, participation is voluntary; in other countries membership of a circle might be contractually required, or management may provide significant inducements to workers who attend: time off, expenses, hints of possible promotion, open disapproval of those who do not participate, etc.

In Germany (*see* Chapter 16) management/union teamworking agreements are common, covering:

- the formation and functioning of quality circles
- time off work for team discussions
- workers' rights to elect team leaders
- the extents of *ad hoc* expenses payable to team members.

27. Nature of QC activities

Use of QCs is a bottom-up management technique, in that activities are initiated at the base of the organisation, though occasionally higher management will delegate problems to a quality circle for investigation and resolution. In all cases, however, it is the circle that devises appropriate methods of solution, and the circle will itself plan, implement and monitor the consequences of new methods. Quality circles have in practice a good record for improving productivity, quality of output, and general employee moral in the short term, although in western countries the longer-term benefits are less certain.

Advantages are that individuals are encouraged to take an active interest in departmental management and to become personally involved in management decision-taking. Managers and other workers are brought together; employees' feelings of loyalty towards and commitment to the organisation should increase. Workplace decisions taken jointly by supervisors and operatives are almost sure to be implemented, whereas decisions arbitrarily imposed by management, without any consultation with the workforce, might not actually be carried out.

28. Criticisms of quality circles

Critics of quality circles allege that such groups might quickly begin to involve workers in much extra work for which they are not properly paid. Production may increase, but there might not exist distinct connections between higher pay and improvements in productivity. Also, if the training given to circle participants is limited, they will not be equipped to handle serious problems, particularly if the sources of major problems are beyond the circle's immediate control. Apathy is not uncommon in quality circles, especially when their initial novelty has worn off and participants begin to wonder to whom the benefits will accrue.

Other problems are:

(a) Departmental managers who are not circle leaders might be subject to criticism by circle members. This will expose managerial inefficiencies, and could provoke hostile reactions from heads of departments.

(b) Pressures of work may prevent circles meeting regularly.

(c) As circles develop, extra resources and further access to management control information will be required. Also, experience of decision-making through quality circles might encourage workers to expect participation in higher level management. But management itself may oppose worker participation in other fields.

(d) Acrimonious conflicts could develop between circle members and higher managers over how particular problems should be resolved.

(e) Circles may wish to consider welfare and industrial relations matters which management is anxious not to have discussed.

Successful implementation of quality circles requires:

- genuine commitment on the part of middle and senior management, including a willingness to provide the training and resources required
- co-operation from a company's trade unions
- visible reinforcement of positive outcomes to circle activities via rewards, praise, recognition, etc.

References

Belbin, R.M. (1981), *Management Teams: Why they Succeed or Fail*, Butterworth-Heinemann.

Clark, N. (1994), *Team Building: A Practical Guide for Trainers*, McGraw-Hill.

Furnham, A. (1990), *Personality at Work: the Role of Individual Differences*, Routledge, Chapman and Hall.

IRRR (Industrial Relations Review and Report) (1994), 'Team building and development', *Employee Development Bulletin*, 55, July 1994, 2–11.

Kerr, S. and Jermier, J.M. (1978), 'Substitutes for leadership: their meaning and measurement', *Organisational Behaviour and Human Performance*, Dec. 1978, 375–403.

Manz, C. and Sims, H. (1987), 'Leading workers to lead themselves: the external leadership of self-managing work teams', *Administrative Science Quarterly*, Vol. 32, 106–107.

Progress test 14

1. Explain the implications of lean production for employee relations.

2. List the main advantages of flexible working methods.

3. What are the main criticisms of job evaluation?

4. Explain the employee relations implications of flexible manufacturing.

5. In what circumstances might a working group fail to develop into a team?

6. List six implications of teamworking for employee relations.

7. What is meant by the 'quality of working life'?

8. Define 'empowerment' and give three examples of its practical application.

9. What are the implications of just-in-time methods for employee relations?

10. List six techniques that can be used to reduce employee absenteeism.

11. List the main steps involved in the implementation of a TQM system.

Part Four

INTERNATIONAL COMPARISONS

15

EMPLOYEE RELATIONS IN CONTINENTAL EUROPE

1. Why study the employee relations systems of other countries?

To succeed in today's business world, firms (including many small to medium sized enterprises) increasingly require an international perspective. New ideas concerning production and marketing constantly cross national frontiers, and the same is becoming true of human resources management and approaches to employee relations. International comparison of the employee relations systems of various countries enables the manager:

- to cope with employees of differing cultural backgrounds and with different customs
- to relate personnel and employee relations policies to the needs of new technologies imported from other countries
- to observe how firms in various nations solve their people problems, develop their human resources and improve the performances of their workers.

Common technologies are used throughout the world. Yet management techniques differ enormously, leading it seems to large differences in the financial returns obtained from identical technologies in various nations. The examination of national cultures and working practices can reveal the basic factors which explain such productivity differences.

This chapter discusses EU employee relations in general. Three EU countries are looked at in some depth in Chapter 16. The employee relations systems of Japan, the US and certain Pacific Rim countries are examined in Chapters 17 and 18.

EMPLOYEE RELATIONS IN THE EUROPEAN UNION

2. Common elements in European systems

Although there is great diversity among the employee relations systems of various EU countries, a number of common elements may be discerned. The main commonalities (which apply in most but not all continental EU states) are that:

- Collective agreements are legally binding (*see* Chapter 9).
- There is compulsory employee representation in management decision-making within large (and sometimes not so large) firms via works councils (*see* 6: **14–16**) and/or worker directors on company boards (*see* 6: **19**).
- Working conditions, hours of work, employment of casual and part-time workers, night working, etc., are subject to extensive legislative control.
- Tripartism (*see* 2: **30**) is generally encouraged.
- All EU countries impose statutory notice periods that must be given to workers whose contracts of employment are being terminated. Appeals against dismissal via labour courts, industrial tribunals, etc., are possible in all EU nations, and compensation for unfair dismissal is available in all EU states.

Otherwise, major disparities occur in employee relations laws and practices, with each country's system resulting from a specific mix of political, cultural and religious factors.

Substantial differences in west European employee relations systems exist in relation to:

- Their degree of centralisation. Some countries (the UK and Switzerland for example) have extensive company-level bargaining; others operate centralised systems whereby unions, employers' associations and the government determine across-the-board wage and conditions of employment agreements on an annual basis.
- The extents to which the law is involved in employee relations.
- Whether unions actively co-operate with managements (as in the German co-determination system for instance – *see* 16: **15**), or adopt confrontational approaches.
- Employee participation in management decisions.

3. Recent trends

A number of common trends have occurred in most European nations during recent years, notably:

- shifts away from national collective bargaining towards enterprise-level collective bargaining
- large increases in the numbers of part-time and casually employed workers
- expansions in service sector employment accompanied by reductions in the numbers of manufacturing employees
- greater occupational mobility and the removal of traditional lines of demarcation between jobs.

Note how cross-border mergers and acquisitions could bring about *pan-European* collective bargaining in large EU conglomerates. Indeed, it is already the case that managements and workers in many EU businesses observe closely the deals negotiated in comparable firms in other EU nations. Also, of course, the possible creation of a common European currency in the EU's core economies will, if it happens, force a convergence of economic policies and performance among these nations, encouraging thereby the equalisation of wage settlements in various countries and the harmonisation of collective bargaining methods.

Increasingly, employers' associations and trade union confederations belong to pan-European bodies, notably:

- ETUC (the European Trade Union Confederation) which was created in the early 1970s to assist unions develop European cross-border contacts and operations
- UNICE (the Confederation of Industries in the European Community) – the central employers' associations for all EU and EFTA countries belong to this body.

Both these organisations seek to co-ordinate the views of their members and to act as spokespersons at the EU level.

4. Union density

Union density is highest in Belgium and Denmark (at 70–80 per cent), and lowest in Spain and France, where density is barely 10 per cent of the workforce. Denmark's high rate of unionisation is partly attributable to union involvement in the provision of social security benefits (which is true also of the EFTA nations such as Norway). Overall, unionisation is today far less important in West European countries than in the past due to some extent no doubt to the occurrence of recession and high unemployment throughout the European Union, but due also perhaps to a fundamental change in social attitudes towards individualism, collectivism (*see* 2: **1**) and the role of trade unions in employee relations.

Long-term reductions in union density have been matched by a steady long-term decline in the number of days lost through industrial action (although figures can fluctuate sharply from year to year). See Chapter 12 for further information on this matter.

5. Conditions of employment

These are tightly controlled by law in many EU nations. Examples are given below.

(a) Statutory limits on the maximum probationary periods that may be required of freshly recruited employees are imposed in Belgium, Denmark, Italy, the Netherlands, Portugal and Spain.

(b) A maximum number of hours that may legally be worked in any one week is specified in all EU nations apart from Denmark and the United Kingdom.

(c) Legal restrictions on the amount of overtime that can be worked apply in eleven of the 15 EU countries.

(d) Employers are legally required to give workers paid leave for compassionate purposes (bereavement, marriage, etc.) in most countries.

(e) Statutory career breaks (e.g. to undertake training or for parenting) are available in France, Belgium (for public sector workers), Germany, Greece and Spain.

Austria, Belgium, Denmark, Luxembourg and Greece draw an important statutory distinction between white collar (salaried) and blue collar (manual) employees. Under Belgium's 1978 Contracts of Employment Act, for example, a worker's status as white or blue collar affects (a) his or her probationary and notice periods, (b) when notice of termination begins to take effect (the Monday following notification of dismissal for manual workers, the *month* following notification for white collar staff), and (c) provisions regarding unfair dismissal, sick pay and wage systems. Denmark also has distinct legislation for specific employee groups which determines sick pay entitlements, notice periods, holiday entitlements, termination payments, and probationary periods. In Greece, blue collar workers cannot lawfully be instructed to undertake clerical work.

Notice periods and termination payments differ for blue and white collar employees. In Luxembourg white collar workers are subject to separate rules in relation to sick pay, working time and termination payments. Austrian white collar staff have different statutory probationary and notice periods, wage payment systems, sick pay, termination payments and rights to claim unfair dismissal compared to manual employees.

Some EU countries lay down minimum wage premiums for overtime working. French, Greek, German and Irish workers are entitled to at least time and a quarter for overtime; Portuguese employees have to be paid at least time and a half for the first hour of extra working and time and three-quarters from then on. In Spain *all* overtime attracts a 75 per cent statutory bonus.

6. Equal opportunities legislation

Equality of treatment at work for men and women is guaranteed under the Treaty of Rome. Moreover, Article 119 of the Treaty specifically requires all EU states to apply the principle of equal pay for men and women doing equal work. Article 119 encompasses wages, fringe benefits, payments in kind, access to pension schemes, etc. Equal work means work of equal value (not just people engaged in identical duties) and the onus is on the employer to prove that any discrepancy between male and female rates of pay is *not* due to sex discrimination.

Belgian victims of unfair sex discrimination can seek compensation (of up to six months' pay or the actual value of damages suffered) from a labour court. Criminal penalties ranging from small fines to one month's imprisonment are also available. The same applies to unfair race discrimination. Additionally, French firms employing more than 50 workers must prepare and submit to union representatives and the Labour Inspectorate an annual report on the degree of equality of men and women within the enterprise. Job applicants in Germany rejected on the grounds of sex may claim four months' pay for the work they would have done had their applications been successful. The same applies for internal promotion.

In Greece, a person who suffers from an act of sex discrimination must apply to the civil courts for damages, although small fines can also be imposed by the Ministry of Labour. Irish victims can claim up to 104 weeks' pay, and courts may impose daily fines for as long as discriminatory practices continue.

Race discrimination

Ten EU countries have laws that prohibit race discrimination in employment (Britain, Finland, France, Germany, Ireland, Italy, Netherlands, Portugal, Spain and Sweden). Finland and Spain restrict protection to persons *already* in employment, while Irish legislation only applies to dismissals. In the other countries the law extends to recruitment processes as well as treatment within employment. 'Race' can refer to ethnic origin, nationality or skin colour. Six of the nine have anti-race discrimination provisions written into their constitutions (France, Germany, Italy, Netherlands, Portugal and Spain); the other three rely on *ad hoc* legislation. Note however that all EU nations apart from Ireland have ratified the 1965 United Nations International Convention on the Elimination of all Forms of Racial Discrimination, which requires governments to undertake to prohibit and eliminate racial discrimination in all its forms and to guarantee the right to everybody to equality before the law in relation to conditions of employment, free choice of employment, fair treatment at work, equal pay for equal work, etc. EU countries other than Ireland, Luxembourg and the United Kingdom, moreover, have signed the 1958 International Labour Organisation Convention on Discrimination in Respect of Employment and Occupation, which imposes on governments the obligation to 'declare and pursue a national policy designed to promote equality of opportunity in respect of employment and occupation with a view to eliminating discrimination.' Acceptance of such Conventions puts pressures on national governments to legislate in order to meet agreed international standards, but does not guarantee that they will do so.

To date, EU institutions have expressed concern about racism, although no substantial legislation has emerged. At the time of writing however a proposed Draft Directive on the matter is under discussion, which if adopted would effectively outlaw all forms of racial discrimination. The United Kingdom government has announced its intention to veto the proposal. Presumably the intended Draft Directive could then be implemented under the Maastricht Protocol. At present the only protection available via EU law is on the grounds of *nationality* rather than race or colour, since discrimination related to nationality is prohibited by Article 7 of the Treaty of Rome. Thus, for example, a black or Asian UK citizen seeking a job in an EU country outside the UK is not protected against discrimination on the basis of colour (as opposed to nationality). This lack of concern with race discrimination is in sharp contrast with the comprehensive EU legislation against sex discrimination that has been in place since 1975.

7. Parental leave

The term 'parental leave' is used to describe leave taken by women *after* the expiry of maternity leave and which is unpaid (or paid at a very low rate) and carries the right to re-engagement in a similar position in the former employing firm. Statutory provision for parental leave varies widely across the European Union. In Ireland there is no statutory right to parental leave whatsoever. Thereafter there are large differences in conditions and benefits, ranging from:

- Zero length of service requirements in five EU countries, four weeks' service in Germany, six months in three nations, and one year in the remaining half dozen
- Leave durations of three months (in Greece) to three years (in France, Germany, Norway and Spain)
- No financial payment in four countries, a flat rate monthly sum in five others, through varying percentages of previous earnings elsewhere.

Nine EU nations give people returning from parental leave the legal right to insist that they be employed part time.

The issue of parental leave is important because of the huge increase in the number of working women in EU countries that has occurred over the last couple of decades, in combination with the rise of single person households.

Advantages claimed for the practice of granting employees parental leave are:

(a) Employment and family responsibilities may be reconciled.

(b) Equal opportunities for women are promoted (through enabling women to remain in the labour force).

(c) Women are encouraged to have more children. This is a critical factor in countries where the birth rate is in sharp decline.

(d) Unemployment is reduced as fresh workers are engaged to cover for people who are away on leave.

(e) Firms retain trained and competent staff for longer periods.

(f) Mothers have more time to spend with their families. Equal sharing of family responsibilities between men and women is facilitated, as women are relieved of the (stressful) burden of having to return quickly to a job while caring for an infant at the same time.

(g) The state formally recognises the social importance of parenting.

Criticisms of statutory parental leave are:

(a) It is more efficient to allow market forces to determine whether parental leave is necessary. If firms really require the long-term services of the women involved they will be prepared to pay the appropriate rate to retain them.

(b) Employers' wage bills are higher than otherwise would be the case, possibly helping to make European firms uncompetitive in world markets.

(c) The long-term absence of key employees can severely disrupt an organisation's work.

(d) Having to find replacements for people away on parental leave is troublesome and expensive. Replacements have to be inducted and trained, only to be dismissed on the return of the absent worker.

Paternity leave

Seven EU countries give fathers the statutory right to a few days' paid leave at the times their children are born. The period involved varies from two days in Spain to ten days in Sweden. Additionally eleven EU states allow fathers to take, by law, a longer period of unpaid leave for parenting purposes, provided the mother waives her entitlement to all or part of her statutory parental leave. The shortest duration of this kind of paternity leave applies in Denmark (ten weeks); the longest in France, Austria and Germany (two to three years): six months is the commonest period. In 1994 the UK government vetoed an EU Draft Directive on parental leave that would have given all employees the right to at least three months' unpaid leave (whether working full time or part time) following the birth or adoption of a child. At the time of writing the other 14 EU member states are devising plans for introducing a revised form of the Draft Directive under the Maastricht Protocol (*see* **16**).

Benefits resulting from the practice of granting paternity leave are:

(a) Employees are helped to reconcile their work and family responsibilities.

(b) Gender equal opportunities are facilitated; women are allowed greater flexibility in their working lives and hence can better pursue and develop their own careers.

(c) Beneficiaries are likely to be more loyal to the firm.

(d) Companies can plan ahead to avoid possible disruptions caused by men taking time off work (through formal leave or deliberate absenteeism) when a child is being born.

The disadvantages include:

- the final costs imposed on employers
- reductions in productivity caused by the use of inexperienced temporary replacement workers
- adverse effects on individual career development.

8. Part-time and temporary working

Part-time and temporary working has increased significantly in western Europe over the past decade, with almost 15 per cent of employees currently on part-time and 10 per cent on temporary contracts. Part-time work is concentrated among females, with nearly 30 per cent of EU women employees lying in this category (5 per cent for men). In the Netherlands about 60 per cent of women work part time; for Britain and Denmark the figure is around 43 per cent. The lowest percentages are in Italy, Portugal and Greece (10 per cent) and in Spain and Luxembourg (14 per cent).

Spain and Portugal have the highest proportions of their workforces on temporary contracts (22 and 19 per cent respectively). Luxembourg and Belgium have the lowest (4 per cent and 5 per cent). Women are more likely to be working on a temporary contract in all EU countries except Greece. More than half of all EU temporary workers are under 25 years of age, although temporary working among older age groups is common in certain countries (notably Britain, Greece and Italy).

A number of EU countries provide statutory protection to those who work part time and/or are on temporary contracts. Also there are (quite severe) statutory restrictions on the circumstances in which temporary labour may be used by firms in certain nations. Belgian part-timers, for example, must be provided with work lasting at least one third the hours of a full-time employee and have at least three consecutive hours of work at a stretch. Importantly, employers are legally obliged to pay part-time workers pro rata to full-time employees. French part-timers have exactly the same legal right as regards working conditions, protection against unfair dismissal, etc., as full-time employees. Also, French law strictly regulates the use of temporary contracts, which must specify details of the employee who is temporarily replaced (if appropriate) and the expected duration of the assignment (which may not exceed 18 months in normal circumstances). The law restricts temporary employment to seasonal work, *ad hoc* projects, unexpected increases in workload, and filling in for sick workers. Firms imposing redundancies cannot hire temporaries for six months after the redundancies have been implemented. A 15 per cent end-of-contract bonus must be paid to compensate a temporary worker for the eventual loss of his or her job. Essentially similar provisions apply in Germany and Portugal.

Comprehensive employment protection legislation in Germany has prevented the widespread use of casual labour that has happened in some other countries. The legislation inhibits management's ability to discard labour as demand reduces, but does compel businesses to devise long-term human resource plans – arguably to the benefit of the employing organisation. A 1987 court case (*Bilka Kaufhaus* v. *Weber von Hartz*) ruled that occupational pension schemes which exclude part-timers are unlawful because they discriminate indirectly against women (who form the bulk of the part-time labour force). This principle has been extended by other German court cases which have determined that *any* employment provisions that exclude part-timers are illegal unless they can be justified by objective factors. The same qualifying periods for access to benefits, legal protection, etc., must be applied to part-time and to full-time employees.

Italian part-timers and temporary workers must be given pay and benefits pro rata to those who work full time. In Spain a part-timer is not legally entitled to pro rata pay but does have the same statutory employment protection rights as a full-time employee.

9. Employee relations implications of the use of casual and part-time workers

Extensive use of part-time and/or casual workers creates a schism between, on the one hand, 'core' workers who are full-time permanent employees and, on the other hand, 'peripheral' workers who are hired as and when required on short-term and/or part-time contracts. Peripherals exercise little discretion over how they perform their duties. They might include job sharers, agency employees, homeworkers, and self-employed contractors as well as casuals and part-timers.

Special problems apply to the management of flexible workforces, possibly including:

- poor communications with and among peripherals
- deciding how to appraise the performances of casual and part-time workers
- securing adequate representation of peripheral employees in management/ union negotiations, on health and safety committees, etc.
- low morale among peripherals, who do not feel they really 'belong' to the organisation
- preventing permanent full-time workers resenting the presence of peripherals, whom they might regard as a threat to their jobs.

In countries where there is minimal legal protection for part-time and casual workers (*see* above), a small number of companies have attempted to address such problems through such measures as:

- incorporating grievance procedures, right of appeal against dismissal, etc., into peripherals' contracts of employment
- paying peripheral workers to attend training courses and general discussions about the firm's objectives
- offering guarantees of re-entry to a job after a break in continuity of service
- making peripherals responsible for the quality of their outputs, and generally broadening the variety of tasks they undertake
- offering working conditions comparable to those of permanent core workers, including full recognition to peripheral employees' contributions.

Key time working

Workers on 'key time' contracts are called in as required at the busiest times of the week, month or year. Such arrangements are convenient for firms with highly cyclical business characterised by large peaks and troughs, e.g. on Saturday mornings or during the New Year sales. Advantages to the employing company of hiring labour on key time working contracts include flexibility of staffing levels, the ability to cope with an increased volume of business during certain periods, reductions in customer waiting/queuing times, and greater customer satisfaction. Employees, however, receive lower incomes and are uncertain as to when and how intensively they will be working. Key time staff differ from part-timers in that they have no set working hours. Indeed, the employer has no commitment to employ them in any period; rather they are called in when needed, working alongside full-time staff and conventional part-timers. Key timers themselves are under no contractural obligation to accept work as it is offered.

This form of employment is said to be suitable for people taking early retirement and for those with variable family commitments. Key time contracts might be offered to workers made redundant from full-time jobs. Problems with using key time staff include:

- administrative difficulties associated with calling in the appropriate number of people at short notice
- possible resentments among full-timers at having to work alongside key time staff, whom they might perceive as a threat to their security of employment
- additional staff management problems (training, appraisal, etc.)
- erratic earnings for key time workers
- the need to pay key time employees on a weekly basis.

10. The EU Draft Directive on casual and part-time employees

Concern for the employment rights and terms and conditions of employment of part-time and casual workers has become a major issue to the European Commission, which has prepared a Draft Directive on employment protection for part-time workers. The proposal provides for:

- the right of part-timers to claim unfair dismissal on the same basis as full-time workers
- proportional entitlement to paid holidays, sick pay, redundancy and retirement benefits
- equal rights in relation to health and safety at work
- equal access to occupational pension schemes
- making it unlawful to discriminate unfairly against part-timers when selecting employees for promotion
- equal access to vocational training
- wages for part-timers that are strictly proportional to wage levels paid to full-time workers doing the same work.

The Draft Directive applies to all part-timers working at least eight hours a week. An employer intending to use part-time (or temporary) workers would have to inform employee representatives about this in good time. Employers would also be required to advise part-time (and temporary) workers of any permanent full-time vacancies that arose.

Fixed contract workers

Similar provisions apply to a Draft Directive on temporary and fixed contract workers, who would become entitled to social security benefits identical to those of permanent employees. Individuals engaged under temporary contracts would have to be informed of the reasons for their being on temporary rather than permanent contracts. Additionally, the client companies of employment agencies would be made liable for the pay and national insurance contributions of temporary agency workers following an employment agency's collapse. All EU health and safety legislation would apply equally to full-time, part-time and temporary workers.

Objections to the Draft Directives

Opponents of the Commission's proposals argue that they will:

(a) interfere with market forces and create unemployment through reducing the number of firms willing to engage part-time or casual employees

(b) reduce the international competitiveness of EU industry. Wage costs will increase dramatically in certain countries, including the UK. In particular, the Directive would oblige employers to pay national insurance for all workers employed more than eight hours a week, including those earning less than the current NI threshold. Up to two million UK workers could be affected by this change.

11. Age discrimination

Justifications sometimes given for age discrimination are that older workers are slow, have low productivity and are poor learners. However, older employees have lower-than-average absenteeism, lateness and labour turnover, and it has been demonstrated that older employees tend to be more satisfied with their jobs (possibly because their expectations are lower and because they are better adjusted to work routines than younger workers). Note, however, that companies which recruit large numbers of older employees might become unattractive to young people because of the consequential loss of immediate short-term promotion prospects for young workers. Also, since older employees are less likely to quit their jobs, reduction of the size of a firm's labour force through natural wastage can become extremely difficult. This is because a freeze on recruitment means that younger people (who tend to leave their employers more frequently) are not replaced, thus increasing the average age of remaining workers.

Age-related decreases in individual productivity are likely to be very marginal, and outweighed by the benefits of experience. Training difficulties might be due more to older people being out of practice than to lack of ability, and training programmes can be adapted to take this into account.

Specific problems confronted by older workers include:

- early loss of employment because of age
- difficulties in finding fresh employment
- targeting of older people in company downsizing exercises
- what are in effect compulsory early retirement schemes
- exclusion from government retraining programmes and, where such programmes exist, the training materials used to reskill older workers being based (unsuitably) on those applied to the training of very young people
- loss of statutory protection against unfair dismissal once an employee has reached a certain age.

No EU country has constitutional provisions barring age discrimination, although Belgium, Italy, the Netherlands, Portugal and Spain have constitutional clauses from which the impropriety of age discrimination may be inferred. Italy's constitution, for example, states that all citizens must be treated equally regardless of 'personal and social conditions'. France and Sweden ban the use of maximum age limits in job advertisements, while decisions of the Irish Labour

Court have held that specification of maximum ages can amount to indirect sex discrimination. Germany, Finland and Sweden have *ad hoc* laws that outlaw age discrimination *within* employment. In Ireland and Italy it is illegal to dismiss an employee on the grounds of age. Austria and France have laws that make it inconvenient and costly (though not illegal) to dismiss older workers, while in Sweden the minimum period of notice to be given to employees is age rather than service-related.

12. Works councils and worker directors

Statutory provision for employee participation in management decision-making exists in most EU countries, either through compulsory employee representation on company supervisory boards (*see* 6: **18**) or through 'works councils' (*see* 6: **14**). The advantages and disadvantages of employee representation in management decision-making are discussed in Chapter 6. Note, however, that the mere exist-ence of laws requiring employee participation does not mean that it actually occurs! In France, for example, every firm with at least 10 employees is legally obliged to have some sort of works committee, although (according to the French Ministry of Labour) about 20 per cent of such businesses in practice operate without one (due to insufficient workers volunteering to serve on the committee).

At the time of writing, the only EU countries that do not require some form of employee representation in management decision-making are the United Kingdom, Ireland and Italy. Both Ireland and Italy, however, are currently experimenting with various means for extending employee participation. The Irish government is seeking to apply the board room employee representation arrangements that already exist in the public sector to a wider range of enter-prises. In Italy there is a plan for introducing compulsory works councils into large firms, with members drawn from trade unions and/or individuals com-manding at least five per cent of the aggregate workplace vote.

Establishment of works councils

Within the EU there are large differences in the number of workers a firm needs to employ before it becomes necessary to set up a works council. Also there are wide disparities concerning the extents of **(a)** the issues on which the council must (by law) be consulted, and **(b)** the council's statutory decision-making powers. The latter vary from internal works rules (operation of grievance procedures for example) to recruitment methods and decisions on whether to engage temporary and/or part-time employees. Often, councils have a statutory right to receive and discuss large amounts of important management information regarding the work of the firm, including financial structures and plans, new investments, acquisi-tions, mergers and divestments, working practices, introduction of new technol-ogy and so on. The implications of this are examined in 6: **14, 15, 16**.

The Works Council Directive 1994

In 1991 the European Commission issued a Draft Directive that would require EU-wide companies with more than 1,000 European employees and at least two establishments in EU states, each with 100 or more workers, to establish cross-border group or company-wide works councils. Management would be legally obliged to inform and consult these councils on matters relating to job reductions, the introduction of new technology, and changes in working practices. The proposal was vetoed by the British government, but the (then) other eleven EU countries decided to go ahead with the Directive under the procedures established by the Maastricht Protocol agreed in December 1991. Accordingly the UK exercised its opt-out so that when the Directive was finally adopted in 1994 it did not apply within the UK. Note however that British transnational companies employing 100 or more workers in a subsidiary in any one of the other 14 EU states are bound by the Directive in respect of their operations in these states.

Under the Directive a cross-frontier group or company-wide works council must have up to 30 members and the right to at least one meeting with management each year. A second meeting can be called in exceptional circumstances. A group or company is not compelled to form such a works council if its employees do not want one, but if the workers express a wish to have a cross-border works council and management fails to respond to a written request for a council to be implemented then legal processes can be invoked to force management to comply with the demand. (See the M&E text *European Business* for further information on the Works Council Directive.)

THE SOCIAL DIMENSION

From its beginning the EU has sought to incorporate a social dimension to its decision-making procedures and its operations. Indeed, the raising of the living standards of EU citizens is a major requisite of the Rome Treaty. Thus the European Commission has initiated policies in relation to:

- equal opportunities for male and female workers
- job creation and employment training
- provision of information on job and training opportunities
- health and safety at work.

13. Social cohesion

Such policies reflect the Community's concern for 'social cohesion', i.e. the bringing together of management and labour and the implementation of measures intended to improve employment and social conditions. Specific measures introduced or proposed in order to promote social cohesion include:

(a) Several Directives on particular aspects of health and safety at work, plus a 'Framework Directive' imposing a general duty on employers to ensure the prevention of occupational risks, eliminate dangers, inform and consult with workers, and invite the 'balanced participation' of employee representatives when dealing with health and safety matters.

(b) The 1977 Transfer of Undertakings Directive that requires employers to consult with workers with a view to (*i*) avoiding dismissals and (*ii*) guaranteeing workers' accumulated employment rights on the transfer of ownership of enterprises.

(c) The employee representation provisions of the proposed European Company Statute (*see* 6: **21**).

(d) A 1992 Directive that compels employers to adapt a pregnant employee's hours, duties and/or working conditions, without loss of pay, in order to ensure her health and safety. Pregnant employees' minimum statutory maternity leave and pay entitlements are specified within the Directive.

(e) A Draft Directive on working hours. Contentiously, this proposal was tabled as a *health and safety* measure by the Commission in 1990 so that it could be passed by a qualifying majority (rather than unanimous) vote. At the time of writing this is being challenged by the UK government, and its status with regard to majority voting has yet to be resolved. Under the Draft Directive a maximum working week of 48 hours would be imposed, with a minimum eleven consecutive hour rest period in each 24 hour period.

(f) A Draft Directive on night working which would impose statutory daily and weekly rest periods on night workers plus controls on the amounts of overtime they are allowed to complete. Under the proposal, night workers would not normally be able to work more than eight hours in any 24-hour period, and overtime would not be permitted without special permission (if permission is granted, the overtime working must not last more than six months).

(g) A Draft Directive on the protection of part-time and casual employees (*see* **10**). If accepted, this proposal (which is embodied in the European Social Charter – *see* below) will have enormous consequences for employment conditions in certain countries, especially Britain which has nearly seven million 'atypical' (i.e. part-time and/or casual) workers.

The Social Action Programme 1995

Arguably the Social Action Programme announced in 1995 marked a retrenchment of EU social policy, necessitated perhaps by changes in economic conditions. The Programme itself outlined the European Commission's intended work in the social and employment field until 1998 and included the following provisions:

- Prioritisation of job creation as the number one goal.
- Linkage of social policy to the international competitiveness of EU industry and other economic dimensions.
- Extension of EU social policy beyond the world of work.
- An increase in the amount of research into social issues sponsored by the European Commission.
- Consideration of the possibility of enlarging the European Social Charter (*see* **17**) to cover a wider range of individual rights and responsibilities.
- Introduction of a Draft Directive on the portability of occupational pension rights within the EU.

In addition to the above, the Programme had a section headed 'potential legis-lative proposals' concerning matters about which consultations were to be initiated with a view to proposing further EU legislation. Subjects listed in this section included part-time work, individual dismissals, the right to payment on public holidays, and parental leave (*see* 7).

THE EUROPEAN SOCIAL CHARTER

The European Commission has always maintained that economic progress within the EU is impossible without social cohesion. Without doubt the Euro-pean Social Charter is the major consequence of these concerns.

14. Origins of the European Social Charter

The term 'Social Charter' is in fact an abbreviation of the document's official name, i.e. the *Community Charter of the Fundamental Social Rights of Workers*, which originated during the 1987 Belgian Presidency of the EU's Council of Ministers. This document was put forward as a suggested device for ensuring that basic employment rights would not be eroded following the intense business compe-tition expected to occur in consequence of the completion of the single internal market. Further objectives were to encourage EU governments to harmonise national employment laws and practices and to confirm the Union's commit-ment to an active social policy. The Social Charter was intended as a grand gesture towards the EU's labour force, representing an unequivocal statement that *people* matter as well as business competition and that the interests of employees are just as important as those of firms.

There was of course an element of political self-interest in the Commission's advocacy of the Social Charter, since to the extent that workers feel threatened by free trade and the intensification of business competition they might turn against the Single Market, with damaging political effects. The first draft of the Charter was published by the European Commission in May 1989 with the intention that each member state would implement its requirements at the national (rather than Community) level. Action would not be taken by the Union (via Directives, Regulations, etc.) provided the Charter's basic objectives could be effectively attained by member states or bodies within them. (This approach is known as the 'subsidiarity principle'.)

15. Contents of the Charter

The basic rights to be established by the Charter were:

(a) Fair remuneration. This would involve the specification of rules for estab-lishing a fair wage.

(b) Health, protection and safety at the workplace.

(c) Access to vocational training throughout a person's working life, including the right to retraining.

(d) Freedom of association and collective bargaining, i.e. to belong or not belong to a trade union and for unions to have the right to bargain with employing firms.

(e) Integration into working life of disabled people – the provision of training for the disabled, accessibility to work premises, availability of special transport, and explicit consideration of disabled people during the ergonomic design of equipment.

(f) Information, consultation and worker participation in company decision-making, especially in enterprises that operate in more than one EU country.

(g) Freedom of occupation, residence and movement of workers, including equal treatment as regards local taxes and social security entitlements.

(h) Improvement in living and working conditions. This embraces equality of treatment for part-time and temporary workers, controls on night working, and requirements for weekly rest periods and paid holidays.

(i) Social protection, including adequate unemployment and other social security benefits.

(j) Equal treatment of men and women.

(k) Protection of young people, with a minimum working age of 15 years (16 for full-time employment) and a ban on night work for those under 18.

(l) Reasonable living standards for senior citizens, with a specified minimum income underwritten by the state.

Discussions and bargaining followed publication of the May Draft and a number of points were clarified. For example, it was established that Irish trade unions would still be able to offer no-strike deals to foreign companies investing in the Irish Republic, while Portuguese subcontract workers would be exempt from local social security payments while working in other EU states. At the same time, however, negotiations resulted in some ambiguities creeping into the Charter, notably that:

(a) The requirement that an equitable wage (i.e. a wage sufficient to provide employees with a 'decent standard of living') be established 'by law' was replaced by the requirement that equitable wages be set 'in accordance with arrangements applying in each country'.

(b) The insistence that each country have laws guaranteeing a worker's right to strike (and hence not face dismissal) was superseded by a right to strike, subject to 'obligations arising under national regulations'.

(c) Certain issues were classified as 'health and safety' matters (and thus subject to majority rather than unanimous voting so that the UK cannot exercise a veto). But where do 'health and safety' questions end and employment protection issues begin?

The final version was completed in October 1989, was signed in October 1989 by all countries except the UK, and is supported by the European Parliament.

16. The Maastricht Protocol

It is important to note that under the Single European Act 1987 (which amended the Treaty of Rome so as to facilitate the rapid completion of the Single Market), any proposal regarding employee rights and interests and / or the free movement of people requires unanimous agreement among member nations before it becomes legally binding. Accordingly, acceptance of the Social Charter is *voluntary* and may not be imposed on an EU state against its wishes. Accordingly the UK exercised its veto against the implementation of the Social Charter at the 1991 Maastricht summit, thus preventing the Social Charter from passing into Community law. In response the (then) other eleven EU states resolved to adopt key elements of the Charter independently of the EU via a separate 'Maastricht Protocol' that did not involve Britain.

17. The case for the Social Charter

Advocates of the Social Charter claim that it will:

- create a social partnership between the two sides of industry and will improve social cohesion within the EU, hence raising living standards and the skill levels of workers and greatly contributing to increased productivity
- pull together into a unified whole a variety of currently fragmented employment and social policies
- have the force of law so that workers will be *guaranteed* certain minimum standards. Note that the Charter insists that signatories commit themselves to 'mobilise all resources necessary' to implement its provisions.
- ensure a 'level playing field' where employment standards are concerned, with all firms in all EU countries knowing precisely the minimum terms and conditions to be offered to workers. In the absence of harmonised minimum conditions, firms with permanent establishments both in countries applying the Charter and in countries not applying the Charter will need to operate two-tier personnel policies and procedures; leading perhaps to bitter resentments among their lower paid and otherwise disadvantaged employees.

It is important to realise, moreover, that many continental EU trade unions have political links with the centre right rather than (as in France and Britain) the left, notably with Christian Democratic parties. Hence, there is no political mileage to be had from Christian Democrats criticising trade unions, or even the basic principle of social cohesion. Another factor encouraging widespread acceptance of the idea of the Social Charter is the fear expressed by the richer, industrially efficient high-technology countries that without the *pan-EU* application of minimum social and employment conditions, 'social dumping' is likely.

18. Social dumping

Concerns have been expressed (especially by the German trade unions and the European Trade Union Confederation (ETUC)) that the current situation makes possible the unfair undercutting of the price of labour by low-wage countries. Absence of a minimum wage, lack of employment protection for part-time and casual labour, no maximum working week and the widespread denial of Social Charter benefits enables employers to reduce wage and other employment costs and hence charge lower prices for their outputs.

Social dumping allows firms in certain countries to compete not in terms of the quality of their products, customer care and after-service facilities, etc., but through lowering terms and conditions of employment – possibly including health and safety standards. Also, businesses might set up or relocate their operations in countries with the lowest standards of employment protection, hence creating unemployment, reducing economic growth, and exerting downward pressure on pay and conditions in other nations. This is seen as a violation of Single Market principles and has led to calls for retaliatory action, e.g. by having the European Commission critically examine the legality of domestic rules on business competition *as a whole* within these countries (merger, takeover and tied distribution arrangements for example).

The huge disparity in the treatment and employment conditions of part-time and casual workers in various EU states has attracted particular criticism. In some nations (e.g. France and Germany), part-timers must by law receive pay and benefits strictly pro rata to full-time workers. Elsewhere there is minimal legal protection, leading to allegations that employers in the latter nations enjoy a significant cost advantage (e.g. by not having to pay social security and occupational pension contributions and not having to provide access to training for part-time employees) compared to employers in other states.

Whether social dumping will in fact lead to the countries involved having a competitive advantage is questionable, since a low-wage low-productivity labour-intensive economy is only suitable for the production of certain items. In the long term it could lack the high technology skills, education and training systems and the dynamics needed for sustainable growth. Also, industrial relations problems may be more severe in low-wage countries.

19. Arguments against the Social Charter

The fundamental objection to the Social Charter is the proposition that unregulated labour markets allocate resources in the most efficient manner possible, boost the competitiveness of businesses, create jobs and attract international investment.

Note that the employee benefits envisaged by the Charter – pro rata pay and equal access to superannuation schemes for part-time workers, protections for the casually employed, a minimum wage, legal rights to vocational training, compulsory employee participation in management decisions, etc – have *already* been implemented in several industrially advanced continental states. Hence, no *additional* costs will be incurred when these provisions become law. Not surprisingly, therefore, the strongest supporters of the Charter are the EU countries with the most advanced employment protection and social protection legislation, as firms in these nations have nothing to lose through the Charter's introduction. At the same time, these countries have been the most economically successful. Introduction of the Social Charter in other states at high cost to businesses would give firms in the successful advanced nations a *further* competitive advantage since (unlike firms in rival countries) they will not have to raise their prices.

Further objections to the Social Charter have included:

(a) Matters pertaining to consultation, employee representation, etc., are perhaps best resolved through *voluntary* collective bargaining between employers and trade unions.

(b) Cost increases in certain EU businesses necessitated by the implementation of the Charter could cause them to be uncompetitive compared to companies in Pacific Rim countries and the USA.

(c) As laws on social protection are harmonised there could be a tendency to 'harmonise upwards' towards even higher (and more expensive) common standards thus imposing unbearable additional costs on poorer EU countries.

(d) Application of some of the Charter's provisions would necessitate the creation of large bureaucracies within government departments and much administrative inconvenience within firms.

20. The Action Programme

An Action Programme comprising ten Draft Directives on health and safety, seven Draft Directives on employment protection, five EU Recommendations, five statutory instruments, three Decisions of the European Court of Justice and three EU Regulations was proposed by the European Commission in order to implement the Charter. Moreover, the Commission has stated its desire to achieve the following:

(a) An extension of the social dialogue between management and labour at both the pan-EU and industry sector levels.

(b) Encouragement of tripartism (*see* 2: **30**) within EU member states. The eleven parties to the Maastricht Protocol agreed in 1991 that any proposal relating to social policy be referred to each nation's central trade union and employers' association for a consultation period of nine months. If consensus on this matter is not forthcoming among the Protocol eleven the European Commission will proceed to draft its own Directive.

(c) Initiation of research intended to identify the possibilities for and obstacles to EU (rather than national) level employee relations, including collective bargaining.

INTERNATIONAL LABOUR STANDARDS

21. Nature of international labour standards

Industrially developed nations have for many years attempted to establish internationally agreed norms and standards of behaviour for the conduct of employee relations. The primary motive for this was to ensure that no one country would compete unfairly against its rivals through reducing labour conditions within its industries to unacceptably low levels. Among the most important of the bodies that set recommendations for labour standards are the International Labour Organisation (ILO), the United Nations, the Council of Europe, the Organisation for Economic Co-operation and Development (OECD), and the EU. Standards themselves relate to minimum conditions for people at work and to social security for those who are unemployed. With the exception of EU Directives and Regulations, standards are voluntary unless formally incorporated into the laws of particular member countries. Often, governments prepare codes of practice based on the recommendations of international standards-setting bodies.

The argument against the existence of international standards is that they can distort free markets, inhibit competition among nations and create unemployment. Inevitably, some countries will fail to adhere to standards and hence the firms within them might be able to operate with lower costs for labour.

22. The International Labour Organisation

Founded in 1919 the ILO is the oldest and most influential body concerned with setting labour standards. The ILO's constitution (which was jointly drafted by the victorious powers at the end of the First World War) requires the organisation to:

- encourage the improvement of the conditions of workers
- discourage particular countries from failing to adopt humane conditions of labour
- promote the principle that labour not be regarded as a mere 'commodity or article of commerce'
- support the view that the price of labour be determined by human need and that workers are entitled to a reasonable standard of living.

Each ILO member nation sends two government representatives, one employer representative and one trade union representative to the ILO Conference which meets annually in Geneva. Conference debates and accepts or rejects recommendations put to it. Examples of recommendations accepted by the ILO Conference are that

- there be freedom of association in all member countries
- workers have the right to strike
- specific health and safety measures be obligatory in certain industries
- recognised trade unions (*see* 2: **21**) have the right to conduct activities on employers' premises

- employees be protected from dismissal for trade union membership.

The obvious problem facing the ILO is that national governments will only adopt an ILO recommendation if it corresponds with current government policy. Otherwise it will be ignored, or left to collective bargaining, or introduced in a greatly weakened form.

23. The Council of Europe

This is *not* an EU body; rather it was founded in 1949 to safeguard the ideals and principles of its members, which have to be parliamentary democracies. Currently there are 25 member nations. The most important of its outputs is the 'European Convention on Human Rights and Fundamental Freedoms' which is enforced by a European Court of Human Rights established for this purpose. Articles of the Convention guarantee political freedom plus the freedoms of assembly, association, expression and privacy. A special Commission on Human Rights oversees the operation of the Convention and may prosecute national governments before the Court, which can award damages to persons whose rights have been violated.

24. The OECD

The OECD was founded in 1961 and has 24 member countries. Its objective is to help members achieve full employment, rising living standards and economic growth. In 1984 the OECD, EC and ILO adopted an OECD drafted 'Declaration on International Investment and Multinational Enterprises' which recommended, *inter alia*:

- that the right of employees to join and be represented by trade unions be respected and that MNCs engage in collective bargaining with employee representatives
- the provision of facilities to employee representatives to help them conduct collective negotiations
- that MNCs give employee representatives meaningful information for the purpose of collective bargaining, including relevant financial information
- observe standards of employment not less favourable than local norms in the host country
- the training and, wherever possible, promotion of local workers
- that MNCs give adequate notice of intended closures and/or relocations of production and discuss with employee representatives measures for mitigating the adverse consequences of closures
- equality of treatment of all groups of employees in relation to recruitment, dismissal, pay, promotion and training
- that MNCs not use the threat of transfer of an operating unit to another country as a bargaining weapon when negotiating with unions.

These guidelines are voluntary, but the adverse publicity likely to accompany a complaint made to the OECD under them may persuade multinational corporations to observe their major elements.

25. The single European currency

The use of a single common currency by the European Union's core nations will alter fundamentally and forever the volume and characteristics of Continental European trade. A single European currency will require firms to quote prices in a common unit and enable consumers to compare easily the prices of similar items sold in various EU states. It means pan-European price labelling and packaging, and the absence of currency conversion costs for businesses in countries that are members of the scheme.

Wages, national insurance contributions and social security benefits will be payable in the same currency throughout the common currency area (CCA), enabling instant and meaningful comparison of reward packages in different CCA countries. The common currency should encourage pan-Union management/ union collective bargaining and a harmonisation of wages across national frontiers. For example, a bank clerk in London will clearly see a difference between his or her salary and that of a bank clerk in Dusseldorf or Amsterdam. Large disparities in wages for comparable work will usually be attributable to differences in productivity levels between countries. These differences will be brought into the open, and workers (through their unions) are sure to exert pressure on employers in low-wage countries to improve productivity in order to enable wages to increase. If, with a common currency in place, unions and managements in one Member State agree wage increases of around 15%, while deals in another Member State average 2%, then (other things being equal) firms in the former state will start going into liquidation – thus creating unemployment which itself will put downward pressure on wages. Pay settlements in high inflation countries with resultant high annual wage increases will have to adjust to the CCA norm.

Employees doing identical work in firms using the same level of technology in various EU regions will be able to compare their earnings and living costs against a standard and understandable yardstick. This could encourage the migration of labour from less prosperous to more affluent areas. Equally, the transparency of labour costs could lead to firms relocating in low-wage regions.

Progress test 15

1. List the major types of difference that occur in the employee relations systems of west European nations.

2. Which European countries have the highest union densities?

3. What are the main provisions of the Treaty of Rome in relation to equality of treatment for male and female employees?

4. Explain the difference between core and peripheral workers.

5. What objectives have been raised against the Draft EU Directive on the employment of part-time workers?

6. What is meant by 'social cohesion'?

7. List five objections to the European Social Charter.

8. What is the ILO and what does it do?

16

EMPLOYEE RELATIONS IN BELGIUM, FRANCE AND GERMANY

The employee relations systems of Belgium, France and Germany are representative examples of the practices applied in a number of west European states. All have clearly defined legal foundations. Thereafter, however, a number of significant differences emerge.

BELGIUM

Belgium is an interesting country to study where employee relations are concerned because the Belgian system involves an extremely high level of legal regulation and state intervention in employment affairs.

1. Unions and employers' associations

There are two major trade union confederations, the FGTB (Socialist) and the CSC (Christian Democrat) both of which are organised on industry lines, plus a smaller confederation (the CGSLB) which has a Liberal political orientation and does not recognise industry divisions. Although these confederations reflect differing political ideologies they do not have formal links with political parties, and do not make political contributions. Union density is high at an average of 75 per cent of the national workforce (up to 85 per cent in certain sectors). Trade unions cannot be sued for damages or served with injunctions.

Belgium has a single dominant confederation of employers' associations, the FEB. Tripartism (*see* below) is encouraged, and there is a National Labour Council comprising representatives of employers' associations and trade unions (plus an independent chair) which oversees national collective agreements and advises the Minister of Labour on industrial relations issues. Prior to legislating in the employee relations field the Belgian government is obliged to consult with the National Labour Council and, while the government is not legally required to take the Council's advice, it invariably does so.

2. Tripartism in Belgium

Tripartism has been an important characteristic of the Belgian industrial relations scene since the end of the Second World War, when a 'social compact' (formulated in 1943/44 when Belgium was still under German occupation) between major employees, unions and the government came into operation. This involved:

- a joint declaration on the need to improve the country's industrial productivity
- acceptance by all parties of the sanctity of agreements concluded via collective bargaining
- union recognition of the legitimacy of the market economy
- provision by firms of representation rights to any union commanding the support of the majority of a company's workers.
- establishment by the state of a comprehensive social security system.

The social compact in conjunction with high union density has given Belgian unions a high national profile, status and extensive involvement in state economic planning. Belgian unions have generally sought to co-operate with management rather than become involved in radicalism and confrontation.

3. The legal framework

The state imposes numerous (legally binding) controls on working conditions, including:

- a maximum legal working week of 40 hours, with no more than eight hours per day
- maximum probationary periods for newly engaged workers of between seven days for blue collar workers and one to 12 months for white collar employees (according to earnings)
- maximum overtime working of 65 hours per three-month period, *provided* equivalent time off is granted the following quarter
- compulsory availability of up to ten days per year paid leave for compassionate purposes
- statutory notice periods of at least seven to 56 days for blue collar workers and three to 15 months for white collar employees
- a minimum of four weeks annual paid holiday.

Statutory career breaks of six to 12 months are legally available to public (but not private) sector employees. Legal restrictions apply to the use of temporary workers, who may only be employed to cover for sick workers, for exceptional workloads, or to replace a dismissed employee for up to three months.

Collective agreements are legally binding and can be imposed on non-signatories at the government's discretion. Workers between age 60 and 65 may themselves choose when to retire. A legally binding national collective agreement between unions and employers' associations entitles Belgian job applicants to total privacy during the recruitment process. In particular, questions concerning marriage or family plans are unlawful. The collective agreement requires employers to return to unsuccessful candidates all documents accompanying an application. Recruits under the age of 21 *must* be given a medical examination. It is illegal to use press advertisements for job vacancies for implicit corporate image advertising (offering jobs that in reality do not exist).

There are negligible restrictions on the rights to strike, picket or take secondary action, except for essential national services. Strikers may be dismissed, provided they receive normal statutory notice or payment in lieu. Strike ballots are not legally necessary, but invariably occur in practice.

4. Employee representation in management decisions

All firms with at least 100 workers must establish works councils (*see* 6: **14–16**) comprising equal numbers of employees and management representatives. Workers' representatives are elected by secret ballot of all employees for four-year terms. Councils are required to meet on a monthly basis and *discuss* a wide range of topics, including:

- investment plans and financial data
- sales and levels of production
- wage costs, profits and prices
- intended takeovers and mergers
- the introduction of new technology
- personnel policies and practices
- working methods and organisation and any company plans likely to affect the workforce.

Councils are legally empowered to take *decisions* on internal works rules and on the criteria to be applied when hiring temporary employees and selecting workers for redundancy.

5. Threats to the system

Threats to the Belgian system include:

(a) Mounting pressure on the country's social security system resulting from high unemployment and inadequate public finances.

(b) Increasing demands by Belgian employers for the decentralisation of bargaining procedures (*see* 9: **8**).

(c) Industrial conflicts arising from technological change and an overall reduction in the profitability levels of some of Belgium's leading enterprises.

(d) Significant increases in part-time, white collar and female employment, leading to a slowing down of trade union recruitment.

(e) Through encouraging compromise, the system tends to generate settlements that do not fully satisfy any one of the parties.

FRANCE

6. Trade unions

Union density (at 10 per cent of the workforce) is the lowest in the European Union, and the French union scene is characterised by fragmentation and disunity. Often, French workers choose a union according to their political or religious inclinations rather than as a result of occupational considerations. A number of trade union organisations operate, notably:

- the CGT, a politically left-wing body (predominantly communist prior to the events in eastern Europe in the late 1980s and the break-up of the Soviet Union)
- the CGT-FO, a break-off from the CGT
- the CFDT, which initially was a Christian trade union organisation but now recruits on a general basis
- the CGC, a body representing professional workers.

This fragmentation of the French union movement has severely limited its ability to take effective joint action and/or to influence national institutions. Also, the managements of French companies are frequently able to choose the particular set of unions with which they negotiate. Low union density results, moreover, in unions not possessing the financial and organisational resources needed for effective collective action.

Low union density has been attributed to French unions':

- early commitment to militancy and the overthrow of the capitalist system rather than concentrating on building up a stable mass membership
- lack of bureaucratic organisation to ensure the continuity of policies and procedures
- tendency to rely on strikes as a means for securing objectives rather than compromise and collective bargaining. Militant action has generally failed to secure benefits for union members, causing many French workers to question the value of belonging to a union.

There is, moreover, a tradition of paternalism (*see* 8: **29**) in many French enterprises, causing perhaps a disinclination of French employees to become involved with unions – particularly in small companies. Also the French union movement has had difficulty in:

- establishing a common perspective on the role (even the concept) of trade unions
- defining its relationship with the French working class
- deciding how it wants to relate to its members (as the vanguard of a political movement or as the provider of mundane employee welfare services)
- determining its relationships with national governments, many of which have actively sought to promote the union cause.

7. Employers' organisations

As in Germany, French businesses are required by law to belong to a chamber of commerce, giving chambers of commerce the resources and influence necessary to promote employers' interests to local and national government. Additionally, France has about 80 well-organised industry-based employers' associations and around 140 multi-industry employers' groups. The overwhelming majority of French employer's associations belong to a single body, the CNPF, which covers three-quarters of all French businesses.

8. Collective bargaining

Collective agreements are legally enforceable, and can be declared legally binding on firms and workers not party to them at the government's discretion. The French government sought to encourage collective bargaining via a series of measures (the 'Auroux Laws') introduced in the early 1980s in order to facilitate bargaining within individual enterprises (rather than at national or regional level). Specific provisions of the Auroux Laws (named after the then French Minister of Labour) are that:

- Employers must open negotiations on pay and working hours on an annual basis with unions operating within the company, although there is no compulsion to reach a settlement (or even to negotiate in good faith).
- Unions operating within a company can veto an agreement concluded between management and one specific union, provided the unions opposed to the deal gain the backing of more than half the votes of employee representatives on the firm's works council. This measure was intended to prevent a single union dominating a firm's employee relations.
- Management and unions are obliged to meet at least once every five years to discuss job classifications.
- Unions have substantial rights to receive management information.

These laws have led to an increase in the number of plant-level collective agreements, mostly related to wages and working hours (and not to the introduction of new technology, flexibility and training as the government had hoped).

There are no general legal restrictions on the right to strike, although compulsory arbitration can be imposed at the government's discretion. Also the following specific constraints apply:

- sit-ins (*see* 12: 2) are illegal if they impede the running of the business
- public (but not private) sector employees must give five days' notice of strike action
- lock-outs in response to strikes are illegal unless the strike causes a complete breakdown in the company's operations.

Strikers may not be dismissed for the act of striking.

Plant-level agreements are not allowed to violate or contradict terms and conditions negotiated at the industry level. Rather they tend to involve rules for the *implementation* of higher-level agreements.

9. Works councils

These are compulsory in all firms employing more than 50 workers. Councils have between two and 20 members (with two extra for every 250 workers in excess of 1,000 employees) and meet once a month, or fortnightly if a majority of the firm's employees so decide. Membership of a works council consists of equal numbers of management and directly elected employee representatives (the latter including trade union representatives if the company has a trade union). Council members serve for two-year terms. Firms with more than ten workers are legally compelled to have 'works delegates' elected by the workforce. A works delegate may or may not be a union representative. The role of a works delegate (who is elected annually by a secret ballot) is to handle individual employee grievances and problems arising from the implementation of collective agreements.

Any employee with more than a year's service with the enterprise can become a delegate, who:

- is entitled to 15 hours per month paid time off work in order to complete his or her duties
- can insist on a meeting with management at least once a month
- cannot be dismissed for any reason other than gross misconduct
- may represent workers' interests to management on issues connected with labour law, health and safety and collective agreements. However, they cannot engage in collective bargaining over pay and conditions. Management is legally required to *consult* (but not negotiate) with delegates on proposed changes in holiday arrangements and intended redundancies.

Functions of the works council

Works councils must take *decisions* on the introduction of profit-sharing agreements, health and safety matters, and the reduction of paid working hours. They must be *consulted* about:

- planned redundancies and dismissals
- training
- the introduction of new technologies and working methods
- proposed changes in working conditions
- intended company mergers and takeovers.

Additionally a works council has to be *informed* of:

- the company's general economic prospects
- rates of pay of various groups of employees
- the employment of part-time and casual workers
- the extent of overtime working.

Employee representatives on works councils are entitled to 20 hours' paid time off work per month to attend to council duties. Like works delegates (*see* above) they cannot be dismissed except for gross personal misconduct.

Although the country has extensive legislation to guarantee employee representatives' involvement in management decision-making, there is a good deal of apathy among French workers in these respects. In 1990 a government investigation revealed that 64 per cent of firms employing between eleven and 49 workers did not have employee delegates; 60 per cent of enterprises with between 50 and 100 employees had no union representatives, and 30 per cent of firms in the latter size category could not muster enough volunteers to be able to form a works council.

Right of expression

A law of 1982 provides workers with the legal right formally to express to management their views on the firm's organisation. Expressions of opinion occur at meetings between management and employee representatives the frequency and conduct of which are subject to negotiation. Employers are not obliged to act on employees' expressed opinions, only to hear them.

10. Current trends

The dominant issue facing French unions is how to maintain their memberships and retain credibility in the modern era. Even the 'official' figure for union density of around 10 per cent is probably exaggerated as it includes many workers who are not regularly paying union dues. Financial difficulties for French unions will worsen, with consequent effects on their abilities to attract new members. An important result of the decline in union influence has been a reduction in the number of union representatives elected to works councils in French firms (*see* 9). Other trends in French employee relations include:

- a large increase in the number of (non-unionised and predominantly female) part-time and casual workers
- more direct communication between French managements and their work-forces and the use of modern techniques of employee participation in management decision-making (due in part to the widespread modernisation of French industry occurring in the 1980s and the introduction of flexible teamworking, quality improvement procedures, etc.)
- greater use of profit-sharing agreements and individual performance-related pay.

Criticisms of the French system are:

- Governments have insisted on treating unions as social partners despite extremely low union density (which presumably reflects French workers' dislike of trade unions). In particular, it is arguably unfair to impose the outcomes to collective bargaining involving a small minority of the French workforce on large numbers of employees not party to the negotiations.
- Legal interventions to protect individual employee rights have under-mined the role of collective bargaining.
- French unions have devoted too much attention to politics and religious differences, leaving important matters relating to working methods, job contents, introduction of new technology, etc., mostly to management's discretion.

GERMANY

11. Trade unions

Germany's major unions (of which there are less than 20) recruit on an industry basis, representing all occupations and grades of worker in the industry concerned. Unions co-ordinate their policies and tactics centrally through a national trade union organisation (the DGB) which employs a substantial staff of trained permanent officials available to supply member unions with expert help and advice. The DGB is essentially non-political and does not finance any political party. It has links with the Social Democratic Party, but maintains relations with the Christian Democrats as well. The country's entire trade union structure was reorganised (along industry lines) immediately following the Second World War at the insistence of the occupying powers. The aim was to create a system in which labour and business became social partners, and there is much (legally enforceable) co-operation between the two sides. Union density is about 40 per cent.

In practice, collective agreements apply to the overwhelming majority of employees and not just to union members. Both the national government and regional government authorities have the power to declare a collective agreement applicable to *all* workers in an industry.

12. Employers' organisations

German business has a long tradition of organising via chambers of commerce and employers' associations.

Chambers of commerce

All German companies over a certain size are legally obliged to join chambers of commerce, which **(a)** represent the general economic interest of members, **(b)** provide training and oversee apprenticeship programmes, **(c)** operate licensing systems on behalf of the government, and **(d)** provide advice.

Employers' associations

These negotiate multi-employer industry wage agreements with the relevant trade union, normally at the regional level. Industry sector employers' associations belong to the Confederation of German Employers' Associations (the BDA), which itself does not negotiate but rather has an advisory and mediation function. The BDA represents employers' interests to the federal government. About 80 per cent of all private sector German workers are employed in enterprises affiliated to the BDA.

13. Collective bargaining

Bargaining at the plant level occurs via works councils, otherwise between a company and a (single) trade union. There is much overlap between employee representatives on works councils and union representatives (about 80 per cent of the employee side of a works council typically consists of union people) so that management/union discussions implicitly occur at the works council level. A works council can put issues before a local labour court for arbitration, but cannot lawfully call strikes.

14. The legal framework

Collective agreements are legally binding for the duration of the deal. Thus, strikes seeking to overturn a collective agreement are unlawful while it is in force. Several other constraints apply to a German union's ability to take industrial action, as follows:

(a) Strikes are only legal if called as a last resort, following genuine attempts to resolve the dispute peacefully.

(b) Workers must be balloted prior to a union calling a strike and a substantial majority in favour of the action obtained. The exact majority required depends on the constitution of the union involved. Usually it is 75 per cent.

(c) Strikes not related to matters conventionally determined by collective bargaining are illegal, as is any strike called malevolently in order to 'damage social welfare'.

Other laws on strikes (statutes and laws determined by test cases) are that:

- Strikes (or lock-outs) are only legal if such action is 'proportional' (i.e. not excessive) in relation to the issue under dispute.
- Only trade unions may call strikes.
- Strikes suspend but do not terminate contracts of employment – strikers cannot be dismissed.
- Lock-outs in response to strikes may not exclude substantially more workers than the number on strike.
- Conflicts of right (as opposed to conflicts of interest) cannot lawfully be settled by strike action. Rather, such conflicts must be resolved by negotiation or, ultimately, the labour court. Note that since many conditions of employment in Germany are subject to extensive legislation (including maternity rights, occupational pension arrangements, maximum working hours, holiday entitlement and so on) then the *scope* for disputes of right is considerably lessened so that fewer industrial conflicts relating to these matters are likely.

There are no direct laws on union recognition or to regulate the internal affairs of trade unions.

15. Co-determination

The term 'co-determination' describes the system of worker participation in company management used in Germany. It provides for employee representation on supervisory boards (*see* 6: **18**), plus works councils and the provision of management information to workers. By law, all public companies (AGs) and any business employing more than 500 persons must have 33⅓ per cent worker representation on their supervisory boards. For companies with at least 2,000 employees the figure is 50 per cent, although the casting vote lies with the chairperson (who is elected either by a two-thirds vote of the board or by shareholders' representatives alone, depending on the rules of the company).

West Germany's first post-Second World War employee participation legislation occurred in 1952 via the country's Management Organisation Act, whereby large firms had to establish management labour consultation committees (works councils) which could operate without labour union representation. A 1972 update to the Act changed this, however, and unions active within a company were given considerable rights to management consultation.

16. Works councils

All German firms with at least five employees must have a works council comprising management and employee representatives (who need not be trade union members, although most are), the latter being directly elected by the labour force for four-year terms. Councils must meet at least once a month. Multi-plant enterprises must have a combined works council if employees so desire.

A works council is legally empowered to *take decisions* on the following matters:

- changes in working hours
- holiday arrangements
- training within the enterprise
- disciplinary procedures
- recruitment methods.

Additionally, works councils are obliged to *discuss* (but not necessarily take decisions) on:

- health and safety of employees
- wage systems and working methods
- company structures
- new investments and changes in plant or premises
- financial matters relating to the business
- redundancy and dismissals
- mergers and acquisitions
- the training and welfare of apprentices. In large organisations a special sub-committee ('Jugendvertretung') of the works council deals with apprenticeship matters.

A council cannot be mandated by the workforce, but must call a meeting of all employees at least once every three months and report its activities. Employee representatives are legally prohibited from disclosing confidential business information to the workforce.

Workplace union representatives

These operate alongside works councils. Normally, each union representative looks after 30 to 50 employees in a particular section or department of a firm. Their functions are largely administrative: distributing union information, recruitment of new members, etc.

Implications of the works council system

The existence of compulsory works councils in German enterprises has a number of implications:

(a) As intended mergers and takeovers must be discussed by works councils, employee representatives can (and invariably do) try and influence management against any proposed merger or takeover situation even remotely likely to harm workers' interests.

(b) Arguably, works councils have stabilised German employee relations and contributed a great deal to the nation's prosperity.

(c) Managements can force employee representatives to share responsibility for unpleasant decisions.

(d) A 'participation culture' has been diffused throughout German industry, leading perhaps to easier introduction of the latest production methods.

17. Advantages and disadvantages of the German system

The following *benefits* have been claimed for the German system:

(a) Co-determination and two-way communication between management and labour creates a stable framework for the conduct of employee relations, mutual trust and lasting collective agreements.

(b) Employers only have to deal with one union, thus facilitating collective bargaining.

(c) The legal rules surrounding German labour relations ensure that both sides to a dispute know what they may and may not do.

(d) Works councils, etc. provide effective mechanisms for settling disputes prior to industrial action.

Criticisms of the German approach are that:

- Its rigidity and bureaucratic procedures may encourage complacency and resistance to change.
- German unions (arguably) have 'sold out' to the bosses so that co-determination enables managements to sidestep and undermine trade unions by dealing with workers direct.
- The system has led to German employees receiving favours and benefits which could make German industry uncompetitive in the long run.
- The administrative costs of running works councils (which must be borne by the employer) can be extremely high.

Current trends

East German workers are more likely to join trade unions than in the west of the country, although unemployment is far higher in the east. Overall, German reunification seems to have strengthened union consciousness among the German workforce. Further important trends are:

(a) high union density in strategic sectors of the German economy

(b) a shift in the structure of union membership towards the service sector and white collar workers. Between 1950 and 1990 the percentage of white collar members of the DGB rose from 10 to 24 per cent

(c) higher numbers of non-unionised female workers in the German labour force.

Progress test 16

1. How does tripartism operate in Belgium?

2. List Belgium's legal rules on the recruitment of employees.

3. What is the level of union density in France?

4. Explain the consequences of the Auroux Laws for French collective bargaining.

5. How are Germany's major trade unions organised?

6. What is meant by 'co-determination'?

7. List the implications for employee relations of the German works council system.

17

EMPLOYEE RELATIONS IN THE UNITED STATES

1. Introduction

The United States is a large country both in terms of its geographical size (it covers twice the area of the EU countries combined) and its population (250 million). Parts of the US have a sub-tropical climate (Florida for example); parts of Alaska lie within the Arctic Circle. Twenty-five US conurbations have populations in excess of 1.5 million. New York (including northern New Jersey) has 18 million people and Los Angeles 14.5 million. Three-quarters of America's population live in cities. The country is ethnically diverse and religiously multi-denominational.

The US population can be roughly categorised as 20 per cent poor and 20 per cent affluent, with the rest in the middle. Unemployment is unevenly distributed. Black people, Hispanics and the poorly educated experience the highest rates of unemployment (around 30 per cent for black youths). The American Department of Labour predicted in 1991 that by the end of the decade less than 5 per cent of new jobs in the US labour force would be for unskilled people. As in other western countries, the proportion of the US labour force employed in manufacturing has declined, while the proportion engaged in services is continuously increasing. Since 1980, fewer people have been employed in US manufacturing than in wholesaling and retailing. This has greatly reduced the bargaining power of (unionised) manufacturing workers, whose wage levels relative to other employee categories have deteriorated. The new jobs created over the last 20 years have tended to be in office administration and catering, and are frequently low paid and part time. Jobs lost have been in well-paid skilled and semi-skilled manual occupations. In the 1970s only 20 per cent on average of the new jobs created each year fell within the Federal Department of Labour's lowest category of income. Through the 1980s the figure was 60 per cent, and one-third were part time.

Despite these problems, the USA retains an enormous manufacturing capacity, and in most years the country's GDP per head of population ranks the sixth or seventh highest in the world. Major US corporations are huge and exercise enormous economic power. Many of them have turnovers well in excess of the national incomes of most countries. Also the US possesses vast natural resources.

Further characteristics of the US relevant to the study of employee relations are:

(a) Size and ethnic diversity mean that employees in various regions may have widely different cultural traditions, attitudes and perspectives.

(b) The US continues to accept large numbers of immigrants from other countries, with the consequence that the skilled labour force has been supplemented even when birth rates were down. Also the US has a younger work force than either Europe or Japan.

(c) Despite the New Deal and Great Society programmes (*see* **6**) the American economy is and always has been based on private enterprise. Market forces determine the pattern of most economic activity (apart from the nation's extensive defence industries). Vigorous competition and the regular business shutdowns/start-ups that it implies have led perhaps to a greater willingness to accept change than in some other countries and to a workforce that is prepared, on the whole, to move to areas and industries where jobs are available.

THE POSITION OF TRADE UNIONS

2. Trade unions

The US trade union scene is characterised by its diversity. There are around 175 national unions (although only two of them have more than a million members) plus about 40 national non-union employee associations. Collective bargaining has traditionally taken place at the enterprise rather than industry or national level. Also, American unions negotiate on a far wider range of matters than their west European counterparts, especially regarding fringe benefits (health and welfare schemes, extended holidays, occupational pensions, etc.). US unions' successes in negotiating with managements in relation to fringe benefits derive in part from the Wagner Act (*see* **7**) which empowers the US National Labour Relations Board (NLRB) to compel employers to bargain with unions on a multitude of issues. Also the role of the state in providing welfare benefits is severely restricted in this country.

Union recognition

To gain recognition against a management's wishes a union must petition the NLRB which then organises a ballot to establish the wishes of the firm's workforce. If the ballot goes in favour of the union then management is legally obliged to negotiate with that union. Only one union is entitled to negotiating rights within a particular workplace. If another union gains a foothold in the firm it must approach the NLRB and ask for a fresh ballot to determine which union shall be recognised. There is no legislation compelling employee representation on company boards.

Certain US business sectors have a long history of 'union avoidance', and the practice has been pursued vigorously by some American companies. Measures intended to prevent union involvement with a firm have included:

- referring *all* labour relations matters to company lawyers, so that union members must discuss issues with a lawyer rather than a line executive

- identification and intimidation of potential union supporters
- unfair (and unlawful) sacking of union representatives knowing that the costs to the company in fines and compensation to the affected individuals will be lower than the possible effects on the wages bill if the firm is unionised
- encouraging non-union employees of unionised businesses to file derecognition petitions with the NLRB (*see* 7).

Because of the US tradition of unions negotiating with companies on an individual basis (encouraged by the Wagner Act) there is no single centralised US employers' association strictly comparable to those of European countries. The vast size and regional diversity of the country is also relevant in this connection.

3. Collective agreements

Two-thirds of US collective agreements are for three or more years' duration. (Compare this with Britain, where less than 10 per cent of agreements cover more than a 12-month period.) One consequence of this is that firms and unions can predict the timing of likely disputes well in advance of their occurrence.

Contracts of employment

A major reason for collective agreements generally lasting for longer periods in the US than in other western countries is that American employment law is based on the doctrine of 'employment at will', i.e. the freedom of employers to hire and fire as they please and to terminate an employee's job at any time and for any reason – subject to the person's contract of employment. Hence contracts of employment with terms and conditions determined by collective bargaining assume great importance within the system. They are legally binding and provide the basis for a worker's security of employment, with terms and conditions typically renegotiated every two or three years (via collective bargaining in unionised firms). Not surprisingly, therefore, industrial action occurs predominantly when collective agreements are being renegotiated.

As in other countries, the incidence of strike activity has fallen dramatically over the last quarter century. In the early 1970s around 65 million days per year were lost to strikes; by the 1990s the figure was about 20 million days annually.

4. Recent trends in US employee relations

Further trends in US employee relations practices are:

(a) The rise of 'concession' bargaining, i.e. unions recognising they have no chance of securing wage increases in certain situations and opting instead to negotiate improved performance-related pay systems and better security of employment for their members. Note how wage *cuts* are imposed in US firms more commonly than in European nations.

(b) Moves towards more plant-level bargaining (*see* 9: **5**) and flexible labour practices.

(c) Greater voluntary provision of management information to employees (*see* 7: **8**).

(d) The use of group working and the introduction of quality improvement circles (*see* Chapter 14), etc.

(e) More trade union co-operation with managements than has occurred in the past.

(f) A long-term decline in union density.

Union density

US union density (*see* 2: **23**) has been in decline for the last three decades, currently standing at around 18 per cent (though higher in manufacturing). Reasons for the decline may include:

(a) Shifts in employment away from traditionally unionised industries.

(b) Movements in population and employment from heavily unionised Northern (especially Northeastern) regions towards less unionised California and the south.

(c) Increased numbers of non-unionised female, Hispanic and ethnic minority workers.

(d) Changing perspectives among the US labour force causing individuals to be less inclined to join unions. Evidence for this is provided by the increasing propensity of US workers to vote in favour of a union in NLRB elections (*see* 7).

5. The AFL-CIO

America's main national union organisation is the AFL-CIO, which was formed in 1955 from a merger of the American Federation of Labour and the Congress of Industrial Organisations. The AFL emerged from the combination of a number of US craft and general unions in 1886. At the time of its foundation the AFL was nominally left wing and committed to 'the class struggle'. Thereafter, however, it became increasingly locked into the American political institutional establishment. This led to internal frictions and a split in the AFL, and hence to the formation in 1935 of the CIO from breakaway AFL unions. CIO was more militant than AFL and attracted many politically left-wing and militant activists. Leadership of the CIO, however, was politically moderate.

Corruption

One of the first problems experienced by the newly formed AFL-CIO was a corruption scandal said to involve an extensive part of the US labour movement. The allegations came from the McClennon Committee of the US Senate in 1957, and resulted in the expulsion from the AFL-CIO of several large unions (including the Teamsters, the Federation's biggest single affiliate) and the imposition of tight supervisory control over some other affiliated unions. Expulsion of the Teamsters (which covers workers engaged in transport and road haulage) was an extremely serious matter because the huge geographical size of the country and hence business's dependence on road hauliers for the effective distribution of products gives the Teamsters a special position in the nation's economic and social affairs. Numerous strikes by other unions succeeded or failed according to the level of support offered by the Teamsters (e.g. by refusing to cross picket lines).

GOVERNMENT INTERVENTION IN INDUSTRIAL RELATIONS

The US has a long history of government intervention in industrial relations. In particular there exist the following:

(a) Statutory procedures whereby unions and other employee representational groups can obtain bargaining rights within enterprises. Ballots of the workforce may be imposed, and a range of issues to which collective bargaining is to apply can be specified by the Federal authorities. Note that the statutory procedure can also be used by employers to derecognise unions (subject to the approval of a majority of the workforce).

(b) Provisions whereby the American President can intervene and order an 80 day cooling-off period in disputes which the President considers to endanger national health or safety. Again, compulsory balloting of workers is an integral part of the procedure. It is worth noting how cooling-off periods have sometimes been used in fact to 'hot up' disputes by canvassing support from outside parties, skilful manipulation of the media, delaying putting further offers on the table until just before the cooling-off period is due to expire (in order to engineer a last minute crisis situation), etc.

The historical circumstances leading to these situations are briefly outlined below.

6. The New Deal

The US depression of 1929–33 led to mass unemployment (a quarter of the workforce at times), a halving of US national income, and a 50 per cent rise in the annual rate of business failures. Wage cuts were imposed throughout the American economy: by 1933, 85 per cent of US businesses had lowered employees' wages by an average of 18 per cent of the 1929 level. The poverty, social tensions and potential for political upheaval caused by the situation led the then President F.D. Roosevelt (elected in 1932) to launch a 'National Recovery Plan' intended to restore full employment. This 'New Deal', as it became known, was based on the propositions that:

(a) The unemployed and poor were the *victims* of the depression, not its cause. (Arguably the unemployed had created the depression through not accepting further wage cuts – *see* Chapter 4.) Hence the poor were worthy of public support and subsidy.

(b) The provision of work to the unemployed was better than simply paying them unemployment benefit.

(c) The federal government could and should regulate market forces.

New Deal policies included:

- a public works programme to create new jobs
- federal assistance to private-sector job creation projects
- establishment of a 'Civilian Conservation Corps' and a 'National Youth Administration' to provide jobs in socially useful fields
- introduction of welfare benefits for the unemployed and public housing for those on low incomes.

Labour and the New Deal

New Deal legislation gave US workers the right to organise into trade unions of their own choice and the *legal* right to bargain collectively with employers. It also provided for minimum wages and maximum working hours. Two critical pieces of legislation were:

- The Norris-LaGuardia Act 1932 which **(a)** restricted employers' abilities to take out federal injunctions against strikers to compel them to return to work and **(b)** outlawed contracts of employment that forbade union membership.
- The National Labour Relations Act 1935, which continues to govern US industrial relations (*see* below).

Restriction on employers' use of injunctions was necessary because, under the Clayton Act 1914, an employer could obtain an injunction in any situation that threatened the employer's property or property rights and US courts had interpreted this to apply to a wide range of industrial actions.

7. The National Labour Relations Act 1935

This had its origins in a 1933 government recommendation that industry sectors draw up voluntary codes of practice that would provide workers with the rights **(a)** to organise, **(b)** to bargain collectively, and **(c)** not to be interfered with by employers while engaged in union activities. However, firms did not on the whole take these codes of practice seriously and there was no mechanism for their enforcement. Hence the government legislated in 1935 via the National Labour Relations Act (NLRA) – otherwise known as the 'Wagner Act' after the US Senator, Robert Wagner, who promoted it. The Act sought to equalise the balance of power between management and labour, giving workers the *legal* right to organise. All employer interference in union affairs was outlawed.

An important element of the Act was the creation of a National Labour Relations Board with legal authority to:

- determine appropriate bargaining units (*see* 7: 7)
- order and supervise elections for union representation

- hear and adjudicate on complaints of unfair labour practices and issue orders to cease unfair practices.

Hence the NLRB forces employers to recognise and deal with unions if a majority of a firm's employees vote for this to happen. Also it decides which unions shall have bargaining rights and the issues over which they can negotiate. Note how all this can make industrial relations highly legalistic, and both employers and unions rely heavily on the advice of their lawyers.

Another important element of the Act was that employers were put under a legal obligation to negotiate 'in good faith'. Unions alleging that employers are not negotiating in good faith can complain to the National Labour Relations Board, which is empowered to compel the employing firm to change its behaviour. The Taft-Hartley Act (*see* 9) imposed a parallel obligation on trade unions.

8. Fair standards and the minimum wage

The Fair Labour Standards Act 1938 required that all employees of firms engaged in inter-state trade be paid time and a half for every hour worked beyond 40 hours per week, and established a national minimum wage. An Act of Congress is needed to raise the level of the minimum wage. Prior to 1981 this occurred virtually automatically on an annual basis, but since 1981 (the year the Reagan Administration began), increments have been rare and of low value. Hence the earnings of workers paid the minimum wage fell to about one third of the national average (and far below the official poverty level) so that the existence of a legal minimum wage came to have little meaning. This has created a 'poverty trap' for many unemployed American workers, i.e. the situation that arises when an unemployed person becomes financially worse off through taking a low-paid job, losing in consequence a variety of state benefits only available to the unwaged. The problem is particularly acute for black families living in inner-city areas. Advantages and disadvantages of legal minimum wage rates generally are discussed in 4: **15**.

9. The Taft-Hartley Act 1947

New Dealism had greatly strengthened the hand of the US trade unions in the late 1930s. After the Second World War the government of the day sought to moderate (as they saw it) union power and privileges, especially following a wave of wildcat strikes (*see* 12: **2**) occurring in the immediate postwar period. Accordingly the Taft-Hartley Act contained the following provisions:

(a) The US President was given the right to obtain from the Congress an injunction banning for 80 days any strike which the President considered a threat to national health and safety. Intervention occurs when a stalemate in negotiations has been reached. A report on the dispute is commissioned and the two sides are instructed to co-operate with the Federal Mediation and Conciliation Service. The NLRB (*see* **7**) ballots the workers in the dispute to establish whether they wish to accept the employer's latest offer. If the answer is negative the dispute continues without further interference.

(b) Individual states were allowed to ban the closed shop (i.e. a situation in which a firm will only employ union members). Such prohibitions were called 'right to work' laws and inhibited union organisation, especially in Southern states.

(c) Secondary actions (*see* 12: **2**) were outlawed, as were strikes relating to inter-union disputes.

(d) Collective agreements became legally enforceable.

(e) Workers refusing to join a union were given legal protection.

Additionally the Act (the 'Labour-Management Relations Act' to give it its formal title) compelled unions to have internal ballots for union officers. This latter provision was extended by the Labour-Management Reporting and Disclosure Act 1959 (otherwise known as the Landrum-Griffin Act) which set down precise rules for union electoral procedures, specified the rights of trade union members, required that detailed financial reports on union operations be filed with a central authority, provided safeguards for the handling of union funds, and severely restricted the use of secondary action and picketing.

The provisions of the Taft-Hartley Act are intended as last-resort measures for use only in exceptional situations. In practice, the Act is rarely invoked and when it is it is normally the case that a voluntary settlement soon follows. Note than when NLRB ballots are taken in these circumstances they invariably result in workers rejecting the employer's latest offer.

POLITICAL ORIENTATION OF US UNIONS

10. Business unionism

The practice of American unions restricting their activities strictly to economic and industrial matters and not becoming involved in politics has been termed 'business unionism'. American unions generally accept the social and political status quo, focusing their efforts on the improvement of members' pay and welfare benefits. Note that a number of social benefits (sickness insurance for example) provided by the state in many West European countries were (and to some extent still are) supplied by employing organisations in the US, so that the betterment of members' welfare could be best achieved through influencing individual employers than by influencing the state. Note, moreover, that the large American unions developed independently and did not have a central co-ordinating body until the 1950s. Hence they could not speak with a single voice.

Paradoxically for the country that is the home of business unionism, a significant section of the American labour movement was heavily committed to left-wing socialism during the American union movement's formative years in the latter half of the nineteenth century.

11. Socialism and the AFL

The US Socialist Labour Party (SLP) was founded in 1877 and, prior to 1915, achieved considerable electoral success in local government elections. It advocated 'new trade unionism' that would seek to attain wide-ranging political objectives. However, there was a split between SLP members who wished to work *within* the AFL, converting it to the socialist cause, and those who wanted an independent and militant socialist trade union movement.

In 1893 the SLP managed to dominate the AFL's annual conference, delegates to which voted overwhelmingly for socialist resolutions, including one calling for collective ownership of the means of production. Thereafter, however, a number of frictions arose between the AFL leadership and its socialist wing, notably concerning whether craft unions (*see* 2: **4**) or industrial unions should lead the American labour movement. According to the SLP it was essential that the mass of industrial workers be organised in order to overthrow the capitalist system. AFL orthodoxy, conversely, favoured craft unionism as the basic model for union operations. By 1913 the socialist element in the SLP had been routed, and interest in socialist ideas began to decline in the union movement and in society at large.

12. The Wobblies

The SLP/AFL debate on industrial unionism became extremely acrimonious in the early 1890s. A critical event was the AFL's refusal to support a series of bitter strikes occurring in the metal mining industry in Colorado. These strikes were led by the Western Federation of Miners (WFM), formed in 1893 as an industrial union committed to organising *all* workers in the American metal mining and smelting industries, regardless of level of skill. The leaders of the WFM were socialists and attracted to the idea of militant industrial unionism. Hence, in 1905 they formed (together with a number of smaller unions) an organisation called the 'Industrial Workers of the World' (IWW) which was commonly referred to as 'the Wobblies'. This movement attracted a great deal of attention for a number of years and contested for leadership of the American labour movement, but it eventually failed.

Characteristics of IWW

The Wobblies advocated syndicalism, i.e. the doctrine that industries be nationalised and controlled by workers organised on industry lines. This aim was to be achieved by industrial action, including general strikes. The core aim was to form a single giant union of the US working class which would be so powerful that it could demand that industries be handed over to workers' control. If industries were not handed over to the workers, the IWW would call strikes that would paralyse the nation. Hence the IWW was committed to *industrial* rather than political action. It saw little point in having its members stand for election to political office. Further characteristics of IWW were that:

(a) It sought to organise (with some success) groups of workers that the conventional US trade union movement had largely ignored, especially agricultural workers, itinerant workers and immigrant labour.

271

(b) It was one of the first American labour organisations to be fully and genuinely committed to the recruitment of black workers on identical terms with whites and to integrate black people into the union without any form of racial discrimination. This enabled the Wobblies to recruit substantial numbers of black dock workers in the East of the country and agricultural workers in the South. Black membership of the IWW reached about 10 per cent of the total, an unprecedentedly high figure for any US labour organisation.

Influence of the Wobblies

Despite the IWW's failure, it has an historical significance in that it represented an alternative to mainstream US labour ideology at a critical time in the country's history. Importantly, moreover, the Wobblies used methods that were emulated by later political movements, notably the US Civil Rights movement. These methods included:

- mass rallies
- extensive use of music and songs to promote political objectives (including commissioning work from commercial songwriters)
- sit-down protests and other actions designed to obtain the maximum amount of publicity.

Not surprisingly the Wobblies were disliked intensely by the managements of American firms. More damaging to the IWW, perhaps, was its active opposition to US entry to the First World War, and particularly to conscription. This led to arrests of IWW leaders and the effective crippling of the organisation, which had fallen apart by 1920.

BLACK WORKERS AND CIVIL RIGHTS

13. Unemployment among black workers

Prior to the First World War the US black community was engaged predominantly in agriculture. Thereafter, however, there was a shift in the black population towards northern cities, and by 1970 over half of all black people lived in northern urban areas. Unfortunately this movement in population occurred at precisely the time that blue collar employment in these areas began to decline, especially for unskilled workers. Increasingly, industries were relocating in the (mainly white) suburbs, leaving decay and poverty in the inner cities. On average the black unemployment rate has been double that for whites, reaching 50 per cent for black teenagers in certain periods. More than a third of the long-term unemployed are black, and two-thirds of all jobs obtained by black people since 1980 have been at wages below the official poverty level.

Black people make up about 12 per cent of the US population but represent only 3 per cent of all US managers and business owners, 6 per cent of professional workers and 6 per cent of those possessing a craft skill. Throughout the post-Second World War period the poorest 20 per cent of all families received less than 6 per cent of total personal income. At the same time the wealthiest 20 per cent received over 40 per cent. Inequality of income and wealth, of course, is not unique to the United States. What is different in the US case is the concentration of poverty within the black community.

14. Unions and black workers

US trade unions have been generally in favour of racial integration, though with some exceptions. The AFL rejected the affiliation of 'whites-only' unions from the 1880s onwards, although a number of AFL unions in practice had no black members. From its formation, the CIO was anti-racist and endorsed by both the National Negro Congress and the National Association for the Advancement of Coloured People. Nevertheless, black workers rarely rose to high positions in the CIO hierarchy.

Officially, the segregation of blacks and whites had ended with a Supreme Court ruling in 1954. However, discrimination continued in practice, leading to the US Civil Rights movement of the late 1950s and 1960s. The catalyst for change were perhaps the events in Montgomery, Alabama, in 1956 when a black woman refused to obey a local bye-law and move from the (whites only) front of a bus to sit with other black people at the back. A boycott of the Montgomery transport system plus a series of strikes by local black workers was organised by Martin Luther King, who became the leader of the Civil Rights movement.

Role of the AFL-CIO

Although the AFL-CIO initially supported the Supreme Court decision on desegregation it failed to support the Montgomery boycott, seemingly because of the influence of a small but influential group of Southern white trade unionists. At the same time, black Southern trade unionists were among the AFL-CIO's keenest members and the Federation could not afford to lose their support. Three events exacerbated the situation:

(a) In 1961 the National Association for the Advancement of Coloured People published an attack on the AFL-CIO's failure to eliminate racial discrimination in affiliated unions.

(b) Shortly thereafter the US Federal Commission on Civil Rights accused the AFL-CIO of being generally ineffective in curbing racism within its own ranks.

(c) The AFL-CIO refused to support the (massive) 'March for Jobs' led by Martin Luther King in Washington in 1963.

A split in the AFL-CIO on the race issue was seemingly imminent. However, a number of important US union leaders participated in the March for Jobs independently, and the march itself was such a huge event that it could not be ignored by the American labour movement. Shortly thereafter the Civil Rights faction in the AFL-CIO won the day and the AFL-CIO put its full weight behind the Civil Rights movement. Indeed, the incorporation of a section in the 1964 Civil Rights Act to ban discrimination in employment was largely the result of the AFL-CIO lobbying. And throughout the late 1960s AFL-CIO affiliated unions helped finance strikes concerning black issues.

By the mid 1970s, the percentage of black workers belonging to trade unions was about the same as the percentage of black people in the nation as a whole.

The Civil Rights Act 1964

This prohibited racial and sexual discrimination in public housing and employment. Also it created a legal framework whereby **(a)** the Federal authorities could require firms to attain specific equal opportunities targets within certain periods (e.g. increase the proportion of females employed in a particular grade to 25 per cent within the next 18 months) or face the withdrawal of all federal and local government contracts, and **(b)** the US President could make Executive Orders which must then be incorporated into workers' contracts of employment.

In response to the legislation (and perhaps in pursuit of lucrative government contracts) a number of US firms adopted 'Affirmative Action' programmes which set targets and timetables for accelerating the advancement within companies of ethnic minorities and female workers. The legality of Affirmative Action schemes was challenged (on the grounds that they adversely affected the prospects of non-ethnic minority non-female employees) but was declared lawful in a 1979 Supreme Court judgement. Note, however, that Affirmative Action programmes were being introduced against a background of rapidly rising unemployment and urban decay in black communities, possibly overwhelming the positive consequences of firms' attempts to further black interests.

15. Women workers

Although the 1964 Civil Rights Act provided a legal framework for the promotion of the rights and prospects of working women, its practical medium-term impact was not particularly significant. Prior to the legislation American women on average earned about 60 per cent of the wages of male workers. This figure was around the same level 15 years later, due mainly to occupational segregation. (By the early 1990s, females earned approximately 70 per cent of the average male wage.)

Women constitute about 42 per cent of the total labour force and nearly 70 per cent of part-time workers. More than 80 per cent of all clerical workers, 65 per cent of service workers and 95 per cent of all domestic workers are female. Conversely, women make up just 5 per cent of the country's managerial workforce. A majority of US women aged 16 or over have been in employment since 1978, and the trend towards women working (albeit in relatively low-paid jobs) is currently on the increase due to:

- rising numbers of single-parent families headed by women
- more single women (including the divorced and separated) in the country
- greater need for two incomes in order to support a family in certain regions.

Non-gender discrimination

Many US states have extensive laws prohibiting non-gender discrimination. Notable examples are:

- Michigan, which outlaws discrimination on the grounds of an individual's height or weight.
- The District of Columbia and Wisconsin which prohibit discrimination related to sexual orientation. The former state also bans discrimination in respect of 'personal appearance'.
- Alaska, which forbids discrimination relating to parenthood or changes in marital status.
- Pennsylvania, which makes it unlawful to discriminate against employees or prospective employees because they have educational qualifications other than a high school diploma.
- California and New Mexico, which ban discrimination on the grounds of health impairment associated with cancer.

Numerous states prohibit discrimination against persons (i) diagnosed as HIV positive or having full-blown AIDS, or (ii) who have been questioned or charged by the police. The Commonwealth of Puerto Rico bans employers from discriminating on the grounds of social 'position' or origin.

16. The Great Society Programme

Increased militancy among minority groups was a major factor, some have argued, that led to the 'Great Society' scheme of the 1960s – a poverty relief programme unparalleled since the New Deal of the 1930s. The Great Society scheme involved a mixture of direct financial assistance to the poor and federal aid to states to fund various relief and medical care programmes. It folded in consequence of its high cost (in direct competition with the resources needed to finance the Vietnam War) and the change of government from a Democrat to a Republican Administration. The latter situation was subsequently reversed, but no attempt was made to revive the Great Society Programme.

Progress test 17

1. How can a US trade union gain recognition from an employing firm that does not wish to deal with a union?

2. What is the level of union density in the US?

3. What is the AFL-CIO and what does it do?

4. Outline the origins of the Wagner Act.

5. List the main provisions of the Taft-Hartley Act.

6. Who were the Wobblies?

7. What were the main provisions of the US Civil Rights Act of 1964?

18

JAPANESE APPROACHES TO EMPLOYEE RELATIONS

EMPLOYEE RELATIONS IN JAPAN

Japanese approaches to employee relations have attracted much attention in recent years because of the formidable successes achieved by Japanese industry and the contrasts offered by Japanese management styles relative to those applied in western countries. Japanese firms, moreover, seem to have obtained the co-operation of foreign workforces, even in countries where industrial strife is commonplace.

1. Origins of Japanese approaches

Today, Japanese managements have impressive records of good industrial relations. But this was not always the case, certainly not on the Japanese mainland. The 1950s saw many great and bitter industrial disputes with strikes, lock-outs and mass dismissals. As in other countries in the early stages of the process of industrialisation, Japanese industry in the 1920s and 1930s drew much of its labour from rural occupations, and the lifestyles of these workers created all the problems of transition from agricultural to industrial working habits (adherence to strict timetables, regular attendance at work, proper timekeeping and so on) that have occurred in other cultures. Another early problem was that of low quality of output. Initially at least Japan had a bad reputation for producing shoddy goods. However, both the quality problem and currently the labour relations problem seem to have been overcome, the former through a conscious institutionalisation of the pursuit of quality, the latter by new and different approaches to job security and management relations with employees.

Following Japan's surrender at the end of the Second World War, there was a systematic, comprehensive and thorough democratisation of all the country's social institutions. The society retained its great respect for status and authority, yet became intensely egalitarian in many respects, including business and management. There is meritocratic recruitment, careful organisation, and clearly defined company rules.

2. Nature of the system

Progress within the firm is slow but assured and thus enables certain types of people who might otherwise be discriminated against (say because of their social background) to rise to the top. Note, however, that there exist virtually no opportunities for those of non-Japanese ethnic origin to benefit from the system, and women are discriminated against (they are often required to leave their jobs on marriage). There is great emphasis on conformity and obedience to authority, although the rewards to those who survive the (very severe) initial screening process for entry to major Japanese firms can be extremely large.

While the Japanese style of management is generally modest and unassuming in its approach there is much supervision in Japanese factories. Timekeeping is strict, and workers are expected to work throughout the working day. The fact that managers are so closely involved in day-to-day, indeed hour-to-hour, operations creates a disciplined, perhaps authoritarian, atmosphere on the factory floor. Various aspects of the system are considered in the remainder of this chapter.

3. Theory Z

William Ouchi, a westerner who studied Japanese management closely, labelled the Japanese approach to management as theory Z (*see* Ouchi, W. (1981), *Theory Z: How American Business Can Meet the Japanese Challenge*, Addison-Wesley). This, he suggests, consists of three strategies and six associated techniques. The strategies are:

(a) Commitment to life-long employment.

(b) Projection of the philosophy and objectives of the organisation to the individual worker, making workers feel they belong in a clearly defined corporate entity.

(c) Careful selection of new entrants and intensive socialisation of recruits into the existing value system.

These strategies are implemented through six techniques:

(a) *Seniority-based promotion systems*. Recruits expect to spend their entire careers with a single firm. They acquire experience of various aspects of the business through job rotation and steady (but slow) progression through the management hierarchy. Since there is but limited opportunity for promotion, most transfers are lateral. This develops generalist rather than specialist management skills, and well-rounded management personalities.

(b) *Continuous training and appraisal* which, combined with guaranteed job security, enables managers to construct long-term career plans. Managers might experience less stress than their western counterparts.

(c) *Group-centred activities*. Tasks are assigned to groups rather than individuals.

(d) *Open communications* both within the work groups and between management and labour. Managers and workers dress alike and eat in the same works canteen.

(e) *Worker participation in decision-making,* based on consultation with all who will be affected by a proposed change.

(f) *A production-centred approach* with, nonetheless, great concern for the welfare of the employee. There is no great social divide between management and workers.

In Japan, payments systems are seniority based. The longer an employee has been with the firm the more he or she is paid.

4. Trade unions

Another important feature of the Japanese corporation is that it will usually have just one trade union representing all its employees.

Nine union members in ten belong to enterprise unions in which **(a)** membership is restricted to the employees of a particular enterprise, **(b)** blue collar and white collar workers belong to the same union, and **(c)** union officers are employees of the firm. Since company unions embrace *all* company employees, the fates of the union and the business are intertwined. Many company executives will previously have held senior positions in the union. Employees promoted to high level management positions cease to be union members. Japanese companies do not normally have worker directors. Note that because company unions recruit from every category of skill and occupation they do not impose barriers to the redeployment of workers to different types of job.

Trade union density is about 25 per cent of the workforce. In Japan, however, unions operate mainly in large firms: less than 10 per cent of employees of businesses with fewer than 100 workers belong to a trade union. Japanese unions are self-managed and self-supporting. There is a national organisation to which most unions belong, but this has no effective power over member unions.

Typically, a union's offices are provided by the company. Experience of union work is frequently regarded as a good qualification for management jobs.

Union financing and organisation

Union dues are among the highest in the world and, uniquely for this country, involve special *ad hoc* payments whenever the company distributes a bonus. Dues increase automatically following wage rises. Most of the money raised goes towards paying the salaries and expenses of union officers (who remain, nevertheless, employees of the company). Japanese enterprise unions employ far more full-time union officials and administrative staff than do unions in any other country. There are hardly any lay workplace representatives. To become a union officer an individual must be selected by fellow workers. If thereafter the official is voted out of office then he or she (usually a he) returns to his or her old job without loss of status or salary. By law the union must convene a meeting of all its members at least once a year.

5. Origins of enterprise unionism

Many observers of the Japanese scene conclude that the prevalence of company unionism is largely the outcome of the bitter conflicts that occurred in the late 1940s and 1950s between the managements of large corporations and independent trade unions (e.g. the 100-day Nissan strike of 1953). These strikes culminated in the introduction of company unions in many large firms, and the demise of the independent Japanese trade union. Otherwise, a number of theories of why enterprise unionism arose in Japan during the post-Second World War period have been put forward, as follows:

(a) Officials of the occupying American forces instructed the Japanese government to encourage a free trade union movement as quickly as possible. The easiest and fastest way to form unions was at the enterprise level.

(b) Radical left-wing political activists were highly influential in some sectors of the early postwar Japanese union movement, and these activists favoured single-enterprise unions as the precursor to workers' control and the overthrow of the Japanese capitalist system.

(c) Enterprise unions had been encouraged by Japan's wartime government as a means for increasing workers' patriotism and dedication to the war effort.

(d) Japanese employers generally favoured enterprise unions, perceiving them as 'insiders' to the system.

(e) The Japanese union movement wished to abolish (or at least minimise) differences in the terms and conditions of white and blue collar workers (which were quite severe in the prewar years). Enterprise unions that recruited all grades of employee were eminently suitable for attaining this objective.

6. Advantages and disadvantages of enterprise unions

Japanese enterprise unions are able to negotiate with managements on a much wider range of issues than is common in the West, and have immediate access to management. They have the flexibility to adjust to changing circumstances and seem to command greater loyalty from their members than most western multi-enterprise unions. Further *advantages* are that they:

- are well-equipped to deal quickly and efficiently with local problems
- have been highly successful in organising white collar workers
- have fast and effective communications between union officers and the rank and file.

Disadvantages include their having prevented the development of a genuinely national trade union movement, their weak bargaining power in many enterprises, and their vulnerability to interference by the employing company. Also they might lack financial resources, and have been criticised for failing to support labour issues not strictly related to the company and for their lack of concern for general social welfare.

7. Industry-wide and regional negotiations

Although Japanese unions are mainly enterprise based, industry-wide and regional collective bargaining does occur in certain industry sectors, notably coal-mining and other extractive industries, textiles and seafaring. Normally an industry union negotiates directly with each major company in the industry or region, concluding a separate agreement on each occasion. In a few cases a panel of employers will bargain with the industry union. Once a broad consensus is reached, negotiations shift to the enterprise level.

The spring offensive

A characteristic of industry-wide collective bargaining in Japan is the co-ordination of activity by the industry union so as to present each employer with a demand for the same wage increase on a single day, with mediation and/or conciliation procedures being invoked and threats of strike action delivered in the same period.

Unions and politics

In the 1930s and 1940s the Japanese union movement was highly political and committed to left-wing political ideology. Today, the Japanese unions have close links with the Socialist Party and Democratic Socialist Party, both of which rely heavily on the unions for finance and manpower during national and local government elections. Also the unions often sponsor candidates belonging to these parties.

8. The legal framework

Japanese labour law is embodied predominantly in the Labour Standards Law 1947 and the Trade Union Law 1949, both of which were designed to 'secure the equality of workers and employers in bargaining situations'. The main provisions of these statutes are:

(a) Workers within a privately owned firm have the right to form a union, and management must recognise the union for the purpose of collective bargaining. If several unions exist within a firm then management must deal with each of them (though this is extremely rare in practice). Management is legally obliged to negotiate with a union in relation to the determination of works rules, but only with the union that represents most employees. The specific rules that must be discussed include shift-work management, starting and finishing times, holiday entitlements and wage payment systems. If a company refuses to negotiate with a union then the latter may sue for financial damages caused by the refusal. Note the differences involved in assessing the value of such damages.

(b) Any management decision likely to affect working conditions is subject to discussion with the union.

(c) If an agreement is concluded between management and workers in one establishment of a business, the management can apply for a court order to have the terms of the agreement compulsorily imposed on workers employed in other establishments of the same firm.

(d) Under the Trade Union Law, unions must include in their constitutions a provision that strikes may only be called following a majority vote by secret ballot of union members or their elected representatives. However, strikes occurring without a secret ballot or majority vote by a company's workers are *not* illegal *per se*.

Article 28 of the Japanese Constitution (introduced in 1946) guarantees Japanese workers the right to organise. This goes considerably further than the right to 'freedom of association' embodied in the constitution of many western countries. Article 28 has been interpreted to mean:

- that the interests of employees can take precedence over the interests of other citizens
- union members can lawfully pressurise other workers to join a union
- officials of a bona fide trade union have the right to office space on a company's premises
- picketing (including mass picketing) is generally lawful.

Managements are at liberty to require that all employees be union members as part of their contracts of employment. However, it is illegal for firms to apply contractual terms which forbid workers from joining trade unions.

9. Japanese employee relations methods

Work is organised around teams which exercise some discretion over how they complete tasks, and which assume responsibility for the quality of their outputs. Each team receives clearly defined inputs from other working units and is given a range of productivity and quality targets. Five to ten minute team meetings between supervisors and workers might occur twice a day, usually at the beginning and end of each shift. Some Japanese companies have abandoned the use of the term 'worker' or 'operative', or even 'employee' when referring to their people, preferring instead to call them 'associates' or 'partners'. This supposedly helps break the attitude that lower grade workers are somehow less important for the firm's survival than is management, but can lead to charges of managerial hypocrisy: employees in Japanese enterprises do *not* share power or profits on equal terms with the owners and managers of the company.

It is important to note that despite the large amount of consensus decision-making that occurs at the workplace level, Japanese firms are in many respects highly authoritarian. They demand strict conformity with company rules and unquestioning compliance with cultural norms. However, the exercise of authority is limited to matters necessary for the organisation's survival and success.

10. Wage determination

Japanese approaches to wage determination recognise that labour and management represent disparate interests when a company's profits are being distributed, but seek to utilise differences in outlook to achieve constructive rather than destructive ends. The essential principles underlying Japanese wage bargaining are:

(a) Employees should be paid a 'basic wage' sufficient for them to maintain a reasonable standard of living. This basic wage should not depend on special incentive payments, overtime, bonuses, fringe benefits, etc.

(b) Workers' incomes need to be stable and secure.

(c) Increases to the basic wage must be objectively justifiable in terms of (*i*) the demands and contents of particular jobs, or (*ii*) the provision of genuine incentives to additional effort. The latter could relate to enhanced productivity or to the improvement of individual skills.

(d) Trade unions should be *actively* involved in the technical aspects of wage determination (e.g. statistical analysis of recent changes in company performance and forecasting the consequences of proposed wage increases for the well-being of the firm).

Wages, therefore, ought to be agreed through consensus between management and labour and not result from debilitating conflicts which the strong side wins but only to the long-term detriment of the business. In the last resort, pendulum arbitration (*see* 9: **21**) is commonly used to resolve disagreements.

The success of Japanese industry in the 1960s and 1970s led to continuing increases in living standards for Japanese workers. By the early 1980s (if not before) the average after-tax take-home pay of male full-time Japanese employees was higher (according to the OECD) than that of the typical full-time male worker in the US, France, Germany and the United Kingdom. Note, however, that Japanese workers put in longer hours (some of which are paid at high overtime rates) than their western counterparts (particularly in smaller enterprises) and that in Japan women and temporary/part-time workers receive relatively low pay.

Japanese employees at the bottom end of the pay scale do comparatively well in comparison to western workers, because many Japanese companies distribute perquisites (housing allowances, travel expenses, help towards the education of children, vacation allowances, etc.) to *all* their workers and not just to managers. The majority of large Japanese firms make extensive use of annual or biannual bonus payments to workers, based on the overall performance of the company. These payments are in addition to the basic wage (*see* above) but can represent as much as one third of workers' total remuneration in successful businesses. Wage negotiations normally take place in late March and April each year. Nowadays, strikes in Japanese companies are extremely rare; grievances are resolved quickly, and the Japanese worker has a reputation for high productivity and commitment to quality that is the envy of the world.

11. Security of employment

Although most large Japanese companies publicly espouse life-long employment, in fact less than 30 per cent of Japanese workers are employed under a contract that actually guarantees life-long employment, and there is compulsory retirement (normally) at age 55 for employees with such contracts.

Nevertheless, Japanese managements generally *feel* the obligation to provide career-long employment to full-time permanent (but not part-time or casual) workers. It is still the case that career-long employment contracts are predominantly given to men. Career-long employment and seniority-based pay and promotion systems seemingly began in the early years of the present century in certain large Japanese businesses which provided these employment conditions as a direct extension of craft apprenticeships completed within an enterprise. However, they did not become commonplace until the 1950s, partly to encourage workers to join company rather than independent trade unions.

Those selected for career-long employment are recruited direct from college, and are hired for their overall characteristics and abilities rather than for their possession of a specific skill. Japan's educational system creates great numbers of highly qualified personnel. Great importance is attached to obtaining qualifications and to life-long training. This results in large part from government education and training policies going back over many decades (arguably to the last century).

Seniority-based pay and promotion is by no means unique to Japan: many western companies apply this model to at least a limited extent. Its main problem, perhaps, is that since the younger the average age of the workforce the lower the average wage, then fast-growing companies hiring predominantly young employees automatically possess a wage bill advantage over mature rivals that hire few new people. An ageing Japanese workforce means escalating wage costs for Japanese companies, which might not be able to finance these given the rise in competition from lower wage cost Asian countries (Taiwan, Korea and Singapore for example). Further problems with the career-long employment system include:

(a) The most able young people normally wish to work for large companies that offer lifetime employment, creating recruitment difficulties for small firms unable to guarantee career-long job security.

(b) Workforces cannot easily be reduced in response to downturns in demand.

(c) Lifetime contracts are given to some workers while others are employed on a temporary basis and have no employment rights. Temporary employees are subject to instant dismissal and, in the long term, their resentments might lead to serious challenges to the system.

(d) Incompetent workers continue in employment.

(e) Company mergers and acquisitions can become difficult because Japanese law prohibits mergers or acquisitions not unanimously approved by a company's board of directors who, very often, are themselves employed under career-long contracts.

12. Employee communication

Management–labour communication within large Japanese firms typically occurs via the circulation of statements of intention prior to the implementation of plans. Top management reserves the right to take all major decisions, but all levels of employee (including work teams on assembly lines) have the opportunity to express views and exert influence. This should help overcome resistance to change and encourage commitment to new projects There is much face-to-face communication between all levels in the organisation. Managers spend much time on the factory floor dealing with operational matters. Even the most senior managers frequently work in open-plan offices.

Japanese firms demand far more than the mere *compliance* of workers with new working methods – they require employees willingly and actively to participate in their implementation. The approach to workplace management decision-making is consensual, but with a heavy emphasis on the role of the first-line supervisor as the main controller and motivator of employees. Employee involvement with decision-making is facilitated by the provision of **(a)** training *throughout* an individual's career, and **(b)** numerous welfare benefits including company housing, health services, holiday schemes, help with the education of children, etc.

13. Advantages of the Japanese approach

Japanese firms have long-term relationships with their workers. Many people are involved in decision-making processes and there is shared responsibility for decisions. This means that decision-making takes a long time, but that once made a decision is speedily and wholeheartedly implemented. Also, the fact that employees invest so much of their life energy in a single employing organisation results in their becoming totally committed to its long-term survival. There is much training, job rotation and employee participation in operational decision-making, and hence an improvement in the general quality of operations at the grass-roots level.

Note, moreover, that the need to protect employees' jobs regardless of economic circumstances forces management to adopt a long-term view of the organisation's strategies: in particular to seek a constantly expanding market share in preference to immediate short-term profits, thus creating the ability to provide long-run security of employment. This drive for market share arguably leads to:

- rapid and frequent adaptation of existing products rather than new product innovation in order to avoid high-risk activities that threaten jobs
- aggressive marketing, low-price policies, numerous dealer incentives and high expenditures on advertising.

Further advantages claimed for the Japanese approach are:

(a) Emphasis on group work rather than individual discretion encourages harmony within the workforce, consensus between management and labour, and a high degree of employee co-operation.

(b) Because Japanese managers experience many internal transfers within their employing companies during their careers they obtain a wide-ranging appreciation of all aspects of the company's operations.

(c) Single status for all employees (Japanese managers and other workers dress alike and eat in the same canteens) can significantly improve loyalty to the organisation, morale and team spirit.

(d) The Japanese have a first-class track record for improving productivity and performance at both the individual and corporate levels. Although the Japanese system relies heavily on the contributions of casual workers, the latter should themselves benefit through higher company profitability which can then generate better wages and conditions.

(e) Workers are able to develop their skills and are given the opportunity to be creative and to assume responsibility for output. Individuals are offered the chance to be recognised and rewarded for their efforts, to learn a wide variety of competencies, and to receive constant feedback on their performance.

14. Problems and disadvantages of Japanese approaches

Arguably, the success of Japanese business is attributable more to effective government than particular management practices. The Japanese government was highly interventionist in the post-Second World War period, encouraging the introduction of new technologies, facilitating the availability of finance to companies, planning the overall development of the economy, establishing an education system designed to support high-tech businesses, imposing external tariffs (thus guaranteeing home markets to Japanese firms), and so on.

Specific criticisms of the Japanese approach include:

(a) It represents 'Taylorism (*see* 8: **2**) by the back door'. The Japanese approach involves *very* close supervision of workers' activities. Orthodox human relations theory (*see* 8: **11**) has always advocated giving workers maximum discretion over how they perform their tasks and the speed of working.

(b) Not only is trade union organisation and capacity to take industrial action undermined, the trade union movement is *itself* used as an instrument to help exploit labour.

(c) The Japanese approach is nothing more than a managerial confidence trick intended to brainwash workers into subservient obedience to management's wishes.

(d) There is much discrimination against women in Japanese industry.

(e) The emphasis on conformity and obedience to authority might itself eventually become a barrier to the introduction of new methods and the acceptance of change.

(f) The new generation of younger Japanese managers may resent restrictions on the speed at which they can progress through an organisation and thus might themselves eventually become the agents of change who will disrupt the system.

Japanese approaches to employee relations result from the fusion of traditional Japanese perspectives with the special circumstances prevailing in that country in the 1950s. The system has proven to be durable, surviving deep recessions (as in 1974, for example, when the Japanese growth rate plunged from 9 per cent to −1 per cent, inflation rose to 30 per cent, and yet there were no significant lay-offs of permanent employees). As Japanese society becomes more prosperous, however, increasing numbers of young Japanese people may prefer risk and opportunity to the security of employment the present situation provides.

(g) Workers become highly dependent on working procedures imposed by management.

(h) Job satisfaction among the employees of Japanese firms need not be greater than in other enterprises. The pace of work is intensive and workers are expected to give their all to the company; Japanese production operatives are subject to large amounts of stress. There is a high suicide rate among Japanese workers.

Note how within Japan itself a significant variety of production and management techniques are actually practised. What has come to be known as the 'Japanese approach' is in fact that adopted by the country's leading corporations.

15. Japanisation of western working practices

The term 'Japanisation' is sometimes used to describe the alteration of group working arrangements and social relationships following the introduction of Japanese production methods (cell structures, just-in-time assembly lines, etc.). Note, however, that to some extent it is incorrect to say that just-in-time, total quality management, etc., are 'Japanese' techniques, as they are known to have been practised in the West (albeit under different names) quite independently of Japanese influences.

It is wrong, moreover, to refer to employment practices associated with anti-union managerial activity, attacks on collectivism and collective bargaining, and so on, as the 'Japanisation' of work, because individualist and/or anti-union orientations generally have little to do with Japanese management. Rather, the Japanese approach since the 1960s has been to overcome the boredom and alienation typically associated with automated production lines. This is (hopefully) achieved through single status (*see* 9: **17**), the removal of as many restrictions as possible on how workers do their jobs, and employee involvement in management decisions (via quality circles for example).

Attempts at translating Japanese production *techniques* without simultaneously adopting new approaches to employee relations and human resources management frequently run into difficulties, and it is hardly surprising that many western manufacturing businesses have sought to copy some of the human resources management practices of their Japanese rivals. Examples of the types of employee relations methods needed to implement Japanese-style production systems include:

- single-status terms and conditions of employment
- provision of welfare benefits
- extensive in-company communications
- objective setting and appraisal

- recruitment only of those individuals whose attitudes fit in with the culture of the company.

16. Barriers to the transfer of Japanese methods

Although the Japanese approach is precise and unambiguous, Japanese companies have in fact been extremely cautious when transplanting their management methods to subsidiaries in other countries. In Britain, for example, Japanese firms have recognised the need to reach agreement with trade unions at all stages in the development of new investments, and to modify working practices to suit local cultures. Nevertheless, a number of transplantation problems have arisen, including:

(a) Language and cultural barriers between Japanese managers and their (locally recruited) immediate subordinates. Some Japanese companies have attempted to overcome this by sending local managerial recruits to live and be trained for several months in the firm's Japanese head office.

(b) Western workers' typical dislike of what they perceive as their employing firms' interference with their private lives.

(c) The possibility that western supervisors and middle management might resent the Japanese practice of having engineers, designers and other high ranking technologists approach shopfloor workers directly to canvass their opinions on design and engineering matters. Arguably, basic grade workers welcome Japanese methods with greater enthusiasm than their immediate superiors, seeing its egalitarian nature (regular consultation, team briefings, etc.) as a welcome change from traditional hierarchical management attitudes.

(d) Hostility towards the imposition of the Japanese work ethic, with its emphasis on long hours, unquestioning loyalty and obedience to the company, intensive working, conformism, and so on.

(e) The Japanese practice of only recruiting young people to work in their foreign operations, generating much resentment in the local workforces around subsidiaries. Recruitment of young workers is justified by Japanese employers on the grounds that youngsters have no inhibitions about flexible working practices, are more receptive to discipline, and are physically fit and energetic. They have hopes for the future and will willingly accept overtime and greater responsibility.

(f) Foreign subsidiaries of Japanese firms pay local wage rates, without investing enormously in fringe benefits. Wages are usually a little better than the regional average, but not excessively so. Often Japanese companies locate in areas of extreme high unemployment, relying on excess supply in local labour markets to keep wages at comparatively low levels. This has led to accusations that the Japanese are exploiting the economic misfortunes of local residents.

(g) Lifetime employment is not compatible with a system in which skilled and professionally qualified employees regularly change their employer in order to advance their careers. The availability of state and private employment agencies, headhunting firms and a well-developed market for job hunting (evidenced, for example, by the Appointments pages of the quality press) discourage employees from spending their entire careers in a single firm.

(h) Single-union deals are still regarded with great suspicion by many people in the union movement.

(i) Provision of welfare benefits by employers may be viewed as disagreeable paternalism.

(j) Unless employee fringe benefits are given by *all* the firms operating within an industry, the companies which make them available will face a cost disadvantage with regard to rival firms.

(k) In some countries trade unions have fought long and hard to extend collective bargaining to cover work allocation at the shopfloor level, the procedures whereby new technologies are introduced, and the organisation of work in general. This contrasts sharply with Japanese approaches to total labour flexibility and the close supervision of work.

In the UK in particular, it has proven difficult to establish workplace cultures wherein operatives are attuned to the idea that they should be personally responsible for the quality of their output (as is standard practice in Japan). Rigorous inspection by independent quality control personnel has always been the norm in this country. Single status is rare in British industry. Management is predominantly hierarchical, with numerous status symbols attached to each level. Often, moreover, Japanese approaches are only partially applied. For example, management may expect enthusiastic employee participation in, say, a quality improvement programme while totally rejecting the idea that workers should participate in any other aspect of the firm's operations.

OTHER COUNTRIES IN THE PACIFIC RIM

By way of contrast to the Japanese approach it is instructive to examine the basic elements of the employee relations systems of some other Pacific Rim nations. Countries such as Singapore, South Korea and Hong Kong have high rates of economic growth, rising living standards, and manufacturing labour forces for which effective employee relations policies are increasingly important. A basic cause of economic growth in the Pacific Rim is the increase in the area's population. Contrast this with minimal population growth for Western Europe as a whole, and population declines in certain European states. The average age of Pacific Rim residents is about 25 years, compared to an average of 37 years for the United States and the European Community. This has to be borne in mind when considering employee relations issues in these countries. Key aspects of the employee relations situations of Hong Kong, Singapore and South Korea are outlined below.

17. Singapore

A system of compulsory arbitration of industrial disputes has operated since 1960. This is administered by an Industrial Arbitration Court (IAC) with which all collective agreements must be filed. The Court interprets the provisions of agreements and refers disputes to referees. There is no appeal from the Court's decision. Strikes relating to a dispute are unlawful once the dispute has been referred to the IAC. In any event, strikes require a two-thirds majority of workers in the enterprise before they become lawful, and are automatically illegal in essential services. A law of 1968 prohibits matters such as promotions, transfers or dismissals being determined by collective bargaining.

Each year a tripartite body, the National Wage Council, sets guidelines for wage increases. Managements and unions are expected to follow these guidelines.

18. Hong Kong

At the time of writing, industrial relations in Hong Kong are based on a legally regulated conciliation procedure, albeit dependent on voluntary participation. Hong Kong's Labour Department has a statutory duty to approach the parties to a dispute, suggest compromises, explain the law, and generally facilitate agreement. Otherwise, the Hong Kong government has a policy of non-intervention in industrial relations affairs. This means there are no legal requirements to compel employers to recognise or negotiate with trade unions.

Hong Kong has around 400 trade unions and 30 employers' associations. All unions must register with the authorities, and only registered unions may lawfully operate within the territory. Registered unions enjoy civil immunity in relation to industrial disputes. The basic source of employment law in Hong Kong is the Employment Ordinance, introduced in 1968 and periodically amended. Under the Ordinance, employees with certain periods of continuous employment with the same employer become entitled to specified amounts of paid holiday, sickness and maternity leave, notice period and severance payment.

Any attempt to prevent workers from joining or maintaining their membership of a union is illegal, as is:

- refusing to employ workers whose names are on blacklists of union activists
- victimisation of or discrimination against union members.

The Hong Kong government is legally entitled to order a 'cooling-off period' prior to any strike likely to (a) damage the economy, (b) affect the livelihoods of a large number of people, (c) jeopardise security, or (d) pose a threat to public health and safety.

Employers are well organised, with three main employers' associations representing specific groupings of industry sectors. The union movement is fragmented and split between communist, anti-communist, and politically neutral unions. Additionally there are union splits between occupations and between blue and white collar workers. Union density is about 15 per cent of the

Territory's workforce. Membership of unions is highest in small firms in traditional industries and lowest in the high-tech export sector. The great majority of Hong Kong firms refuse to recognise trade unions so that in practice collective bargaining plays little part in wage determination. Wages are set by the forces of supply and demand. Hence unions focus on providing members with benefits outside the workplace, rather than on collective bargaining *per se*. Also, unions **(a)** help individuals to negotiate with their employers on a one-to-one basis, **(b)** 'suggest' the levels of wages that workers should demand and co-ordinate the presentation of demands, and **(c)** frequently initiate public demonstrations.

An interesting feature of Hong Kong unions has been their lack of involvement in political activity directed against the state, compared to other colonial territories where labour movements invariably become closely connected with the drive for political independence. Hong Kong has not had a significant independence movement and hence the Territory's unions were not influenced in this way. Unions have never held any sway over the Hong Kong government, in sharp contrast to the managements of businesses operating in the Territory.

19. South Korea

South Korea has a population of about 45 million, 40 per cent of which live in the country's four main industrial cities. This is due in part to land reforms which forced large numbers of workers from agriculture to cities, thus creating a large pool of low wage labour. Korea's drive for industrialisation has made it one of the strongest newly industrialised countries in the Pacific Rim, with an average growth rate exceeding 6 per cent per annum since 1965. Unemployment is and has been low, at around 4 per cent on average.

Korea's labour movement began in the 1920s, but was suppressed by the occupying Japanese. Following the defeat of Japan in 1945 an 'All Korea Council of Labour Unions' was established, but was disbanded following the division of the country in 1948 and the subsequent civil war. The provisional American military government set up the 'Korean Independent Labour League', which was dominated by the (pro-American) Liberal Party. Other union organisations were declared illegal and suppressed, and there was in reality very little free collective bargaining. All union activity was outlawed following a political coup in 1961, but restored to legality in 1962. Current labour law in Korea has its origins in the 1962 legislation, which formally recognised the right to strike but numerous constraints were imposed on workers' abilities to organise and bargain collectively, as follows:

(a) Employers were not allowed to provide facilities to union officers (office space, time off for union duties, etc.).

(b) Unions had to supply regular and extensive information on their activities to the country's authorities, including membership lists and minutes of all meetings.

(c) Major union decisions were to be taken at meetings (conventions) with a majority of members present.

(d) Union political activity was forbidden.

(e) The government was empowered to cancel or amend any union decision deemed to be 'contrary to public interest', and could order the election of new union officers.

(f) Five days prior to a strike the union was to notify the local government authorities, which ruled whether it was legal. If the dispute was deemed legal a compulsory 30-day cooling-off period ensued during which the union had to ballot its members and the state arbitration service attempted to settle the conflict. Most strikes in 'vital' industries or foreign-owned firms were declared illegal.

(g) It was illegal for 'third parties' to be involved in an industrial dispute.

(h) Strikes by local government workers and employees of state-owned or defence-related firms were automatically illegal.

The legislation (introduced to accompany the country's first five-year economic plan) provided for industry-based unions, which in practice were company based. Another coup in 1970 led to the banning of strikes in foreign-owned companies. All strikes were illegal from 1973 to 1980. Note, however, that during the 1970s government restrictions on union activity were increasingly ignored and many workers obtained significant gains through (technically illegal) industrial action. A further *coup d'état* led to fresh legislation on industrial action in the early 1980s, as follows:

- All companies employing more than 100 workers had to establish works councils comprising equal numbers of employee and management representatives. These councils could determine wages within the enterprise (thus undermining the role of trade unions).
- Strikes became legal provided the workers concerned had first taken their case to a tribunal for independent arbitration.
- The government assumed the right to ban any trade union and/or remove its leader if the government deemed this to be in the public interest.

These measures caused large reductions in union membership but failed to stem the tide of industrial unrest, particularly in the late 1980s. National minimum wages were introduced in eight industrial sectors in 1988. In law, collective agreements are legally binding, although in practice there have been no successful court actions over employers' breaches of contract.

Clearly it is not easy to be a trade unionist in South Korea. Specific problems facing the Korean union movement include:

- long working hours for Korean workers (averaging about 54 hours per week)
- low wages – females receive around half the average wage of men
- poor health and safety standards – industrial accidents are said to cost the country about 1 per cent of its annual GNP
- lack of opportunities for union representatives to develop bargaining skills.

The Korean Trade Union Congress (KTUC) was formed in 1989 and comprises 14 regional union councils plus two industrial unions. Its objectives are:

- a 44 hour maximum working week
- equal pay for men and women
- total freedom of association, expression and collective bargaining
- reform of the country's tax system (with the introduction of more progressive taxes)
- removal of foreign cultural influence
- full democratic rights for the population as a whole.

Progress test 18

1. What is theory Z?

2. List the disadvantages of enterprise unionism.

3. Which major statutes determine Japanese labour law?

4. What are the disadvantages associated with seniority-based pay and promotion systems?

5. How do large Japanese companies communicate with employees?

6. List six barriers to the transfer of Japanese methods to Western countries.

INDEX